'A funny, irresistibly offbeat tale about the risks and rewards of living, and loving, with an open heart.'   **Kirkus Reviews**

'The story of how DeRoche overcame her fears, her self-deprecating humour and her way with words would have been enough to make this a great story. The fact her Argentinian boyfriend combines the passion of a Latin lover with the grit and spirit of a Scandinavian seafarer makes this book a Hollywood dream come true.'   **Sydney Morning Herald**

'By turns gripping, laugh-out-loud funny, moving and uplifting... Almost any reader with a sense of adventure or a desire to confront their fears should love it.'   **Australian Bookseller & Publisher**

'Wow, what a book. Exciting. Dramatic. Honest.'
Australian Associated Press

'DeRoche has penned such a beautiful, thrilling story you'll have to remind yourself it's not fiction. Her language is effortless.'
Courier Mail

'I was hooked from page one! Love with a Chance of Drowning is an epic tale of love and fortitude that will thrill its readers. Torre is a natural storyteller with a knack for extracting the dramatic, comedic and romantic from every incident. An incredible journey, both literal and metaphorical – it will sweep you away ... fresh, funny and exhilarating.'

Veronica Henry, author of *The Long Weekend*

'Torre's book is more than just a love story. It's a story about conquering the fears that keep you from living your dreams.'
Matthew Kepnes, author of *How to Travel the World on $50 a Day* and blogger at nomadicmatt.com

'An armchair voyage [with] all the perfect ingredients for a sweet love story, above and beyond the adventure of it all.'
Tania Aebi, author of *Maiden Voyage*

'A story of finding courage when your gut clenches and all you want to do is go home.'
Normandie Ward Fischer, author of *Becalmed*

'You'll get a lot of things out of this book, I promise you. You will ask questions about your own life, your fears, your ambitions and your spirit. But at its heart this is a love story that will keep you turning the pages and leave you feeling bereft as you finish the last line.'
The Modern Woman's Survival Guide online magazine

'wonderfully written... a tale of an amazing journey that will sweep you away.' **bookdout.wordpress.com**

'Luminous, sparkling... Those words describe the spectacular waters she visits and sails, but they also describe Torre herself as she lets us in to her inner world.' **bukinan.blogspot.com.au**

'The best travel memoir I have ever read, hands down.'
theartofslowtravel.com

'If it's not the best travel book I've read this year, I don't know what is.' **whatsdavedoing.com**

AMAZON REVIEWS

'a little work of magic'

'Her memoir will be one of the best books you read in your life. It is truly unforgettable and her message of living fearlessly to experience life and love is something we all need to be reminded of.'

'Whether you are a fellow traveler, need a swift push to tackle a dream or just in need of a good old fashioned adventure story, Love with a Chance of Drowning *is the book you need to read this summer!'*

'Could. Not. Stop. Reading.'

'I think we've all got a fearful adventure inside of us and reading this book might just inspire you to start yours.'

'Be warned, this book may stir up a yearning for adventure somewhere deep in your soul; your desk might not look the same tomorrow.'

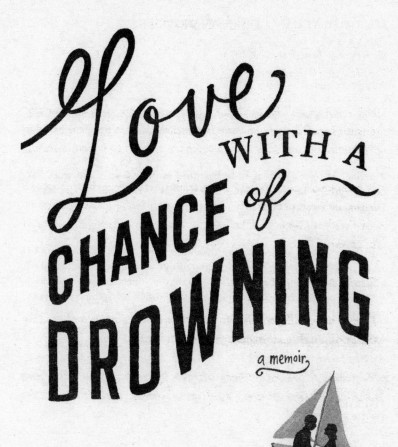

Love

WITH A

of

CHANCE

DROWNING

a memoir

TORRE DeROCHE

summersdale

LOVE WITH A CHANCE OF DROWNING

Copyright © Torre DeRoche, 2013

Summersdale Publishers Ltd
46 West Street
Chichester
West Sussex
PO19 1RP
UK

www.summersdale.com

Printed and bound by CPI Group (UK) Ltd, Croydon, CR0 4YY

ISBN: 978-1-84953-418-5

'Now it is the story between Joshua and me, between me and the sky; a story just for us, a great love story that does not concern the others any more.'
Bernard Moitessier, *The Long Way*

AUTHOR'S NOTE

This is a true story. All of the events and embarrassing mishaps recounted in this book are authentic. In some cases, names were changed to protect the identities of certain oddballs encountered en route, and in order to spare the reader from unnecessary backstory, one minor character has been composed from two people. In an effort to pull the reader into the experience, much of the story is told through dialogue and, while it's not verbatim, conversations have been reconstructed to remain true to either actual discussions, or to articulate the actions and motivations of each person represented. Some sequences of events were shifted for pacing, and a few voyage destinations were omitted in order to capture a three-year experience into a concise read.

CONTENTS

PART ONE
FIRE

'Love is a fire.
But whether it is going to warm
your hearth or burn down your house,
you can never tell.'
Joan Crawford

ONE

A BEAM OF MORNING sun pierces my closed eyelids and draws me from the dark depths of a hangover. Memories race in from last night. 'I'll have a dirty Martini.' What was I thinking? I scorn myself as the bass amp is turned up in my head, reverberating through the soft tissue of my brain. But I have worse things to worry about right now than a hangover. Like the fact that I've just woken up in a stranger's bed. Naked.

I hear a shower going in the bathroom. Good – there's time to work out how I got here. Memories flash: stormy green eyes, dusty blond hair, an overall appearance too stylish and clean to be straight. I thought he was gay. This is San Francisco, after all.

'So are you going to tell me your name?' he asked.

'I'm Torre.'

'Nice to meet you, my name is—'

I snap upright in bed. *Oh my God, I don't remember his name!* Important information has been drowned in gin and vermouth. I'm not the kind of girl who forgets the name of the guy she's just gone home with... in fact, I'm not the kind of girl who goes home with a man she's just met.

The name 'Ivan' rings from a neglected corner in my brain, scattered with dust bunnies and useless trivia. I frantically scan the bedroom for clues – an electricity bill, a degree hanging on the wall, a dusty old sports trophy – anything to save me from certain awkwardness.

Bingo. A wallet on the bedside table. Would that be wrong?

I hear the shower stop. John Doe will need to towel off and dress, which leaves at least sixty seconds to find out who, exactly, I just slept with. I nudge the wallet with the tip of my index finger, hoping to 'accidentally' flip it open and spy his name through the licence window, but, poking with sharp jabs, I'm only inching it farther away. My opportunity is ticking by, so in one clean swoop, I snatch up the wallet and locate his licence.

I remembered right, he *is* Ivan. Ivan Alexis Nepomnaschy. It seems he was named by a cat walking across a keyboard. When I try to pronounce 'Nepomnaschy' out loud, my mouth sounds like it's full of peanut butter. Six feet tall, blond, green eyes, thirty-one – seven years older than me. His headshot is handsome, just as I remember thinking before I guzzled that damn Martini like a cold beer on a hot day.

A cupboard door slams in the bathroom, and I flinch, guilty and nervous. I work fast to slip the licence back in the wallet, fumbling as I imagine what I'd say if caught. *'Yes, good morning, Ivan… What's that? Oh, you mean this wallet? Ha ha, no, I wasn't stealing anything, I just couldn't remember your name, so I… Oh, no, please don't call the cops!'*

I don't even know myself right now.

The licence slides back in and I toss the evidence away. But he doesn't come out of the bathroom, so I collect my clothes from beside the bed and throw them on – a pencil skirt, a turquoise silk blouse, a black sateen blazer – feeling odd to be wearing yesterday's work attire at 8:30 a.m. on this Sunday morning.

Head pounding, I collapse back into bed and try to work out when my memory became fragmented.

It all began with a phone call. I was leaving a job interview when I heard an annoying ringtone following close behind me. Just before I spun around to see who was there, I noticed the ringing was coming from my handbag. The annoying ringtone was mine.

It was my housemate calling – the only friend I had made since moving to San Francisco on my own from Australia a month before. A few weeks earlier, while staying in a hotel, I'd come across an ad for a shared house in the Western Addition. A seedy neighbourhood, as it turned out, but after meeting the three down-to-earth housemates (plus a fourth four-legged roomie named Disco Dog), I decided to take it. Anna, a psychology student my age, won me over immediately with her odd ability to combine crass candidness with compassion.

I flipped my phone open, silencing the annoying ringtone.

'Torre!' Anna hollered down the line. 'What are you doing right now?'

'I just had a job interview,' I told her.

'On a Saturday? I thought you had a job already.'

'I do, but this was for a position with *The Onion*. I couldn't resist applying.'

'Oh, dude, I totally want to make babies with that newspaper. So you nailed it, right? I bet they swooned over your Aussie accent. Americans dig that shit.'

'Yeah, it went well, but it occurred to me mid-interview that I can't spend my days designing black-and-white graphics. I'll go stir-crazy without colour.'

'Well, lady, you're in the right city, then. Now listen up! I want to introduce you to San Francisco. Come to Oysterfest and meet some of my friends. They'll adopt you immediately if you just shake their hands and say, "Throw uh-nu-tha shrimp on tha bah-bee." Got it?'

She gave me directions and I hung up the call, smiling.

At Oysterfest, the sun was shining, and apart from the gritty, oversized D-grade shellfish, my day was going superbly. The fun continued when Anna proposed a guided tour of the city's bars and restaurants, so we sipped our way across town, sampling everything from hot coffee mixed with vodka to sangria floating with fruit.

After the last six months of stressing over whether or not I'd be able to land a job, find a home, make connections and survive in a foreign city with only two suitcases and my entire life savings of $3,000, my anxieties were being silenced with clanking glasses and the laughter of new friends. Life was clicking into place.

We had dinner in a Haight-Ashbury restaurant and, when the time came to go home, I congratulated myself for remaining clear-headed despite a day full of drinking. But that was about to change.

As we were trying to hail taxis home on Haight Street, we passed a Persian-style cocktail bar, spilling light onto the footpath, where hippies sprawled playing guitars, burning sage sticks and hawking crafts for dope money. I was tired from a long day, yet a spontaneous impulse urged me into the bar.

'One last drink?' I asked Anna.

She checked her watch and returned an uninspired frown.

'Just one,' I said, darting inside before Anna or her boyfriend could say no.

Inside, candlelit lanterns cast patterns across the walls. Persian-style archways led to nooks for mingling in the dimmed light. It was cheesy and charming at the same time.

'What are you having, Torre?' Anna asked, putting her order in with the bartender.

'I'll have a dirty Martini,' I said, quoting *Sex and the City*. Freshly arrived from my almost exclusively beer-drinking homeland of

Australia, the only cocktails I was familiar with were the ones I'd seen Carrie Bradshaw drinking.

I sipped from my stemmed glass, feeling elegant in my sleek outfit with a Martini in hand, until the olive toothpick stabbed my lip. While rubbing my injury, I noticed a guy on his own across the bar, leaning over his cocktail as though he were wearing an invisible backpack loaded with the weight of all the world's sorrows. *Why is he so sad?*

I reminded myself to steer clear. I hadn't travelled to San Francisco to hook up. In my US arrival documentation, I could've written 'Finding myself' as the reason for my visit, but not only would I have baffled the Department of Homeland Security, I would have overwhelmed myself with sheer pressure. So, taking a less existentialist approach, I kept my plan simple: leave my comfort zone, work in a foreign city, enjoy some uninhibited fun and return home in one year. My mum, dad and five sisters sent me off with two requests: (1) Please do not fall in love with an American man and never come home, and (2) Please come home in one year.

Having five sisters is like having five best friends who also moonlight as your surrogate mothers, and when they – along with my parents – spoke up with what must have been the only request ever made of me over the course of my liberal upbringing, I listened.

'*One year, no American men*,' I'd promised them. And it was a promise that I had no desire to break. But how could I forgive myself if I stood by and watched a handsome young man wallow miserably on his own? Plus, in his neat leather jacket and tidy shirt, I'd have sworn he was gay.

Feeling tipsy and daring, I separated from Anna and her circle and made a beeline toward the sad stranger, sat down on the empty bar stool to his left and leaned over to him. 'Why are you sad?' I asked, skipping the small talk, or even a polite greeting. I sipped my Martini, carefully navigating around the sharp toothpick.

He looked up and I took in his appearance: light complexion, defined nose, full lips, chiselled jaw, the exaggerated chin of a superhero, undeniably handsome. His serious, stormy green eyes softened as they met mine. 'I look sad?' he said.

'Well, maybe not now but you did a second ago. You were staring into your drink, all sombre and serious.'

'That's strange. I don't feel sad.'

'You're sad,' I said with an insistent nod.

'Okay, well… Um, let me see. I suppose maybe it's because I just broke up with someone. I've moved to San Francisco and I don't really, like, know anyone yet.'

I noticed he spoke with an Antonio Banderas accent, peppered with iconic Californian Valleyspeak.

'You're not American!' I declared. I'm sure he already knew this, but his accent took me by surprise, and I felt the need to broadcast this news aloud.

'Right. I'm Argentinean.'

Excellent, I thought to myself, *he's not an American man. Technically, I'm not breaking any promises, then.*

'Why are you in California?' I asked.

'I immigrated here with my family when I was seventeen. You're not American either. Hmm… let me guess. Dark hair and light green eyes, exotic, but too fair-skinned to be Latin. You remind me of Monica Bellucci, so—'

'Who?'

'Italian model-turned-actress.'

'Ha! I think you may have lost a contact lens in your cocktail.'

'I'm going to guess you're British.'

'Australian, actually. I'm only staying one year, though,' I said, reciting my family-imposed terms and conditions upfront. 'I'm going home in December.'

'Are you working or travelling?' he asked.

'Both. I've been travelling around the US since late December, but I've been living in San Francisco for four weeks now, since the start of March. I have a design job with a start-up and I'm settled here until the end of the year.'

'So then you're an artist?'

'Kind of. Graphic design and illustration, which generally involves selling my soul to the corporate devil.'

'You and me both,' he said. 'You travelled to San Francisco alone?'

I nodded.

'Awesome. So you're an artist on a solo adventure in a new city. I'm very impressed.' He raised the rim of his cocktail to clink with mine. '*Salud.*'

He shifted on his bar stool to face me and we began chatting away, waltzing from families to music tastes to ex-relationships. I mentioned that I'd just ended a long-term relationship in Melbourne and we began to connect on the topic of our failed relationships. With the help of some liquid courage, our conversation quickly turned intimate and reflective.

'My ex lacked motivation,' Ivan confessed. 'She showed an interest in studying film and I thought, *Great! Ambition!* She couldn't afford school, so I paid for her college tuition with the money I was earning from my first IT job. Turns out she wasn't into it, and when I started doing her homework just so she'd pass, I realised: you can't force traits on to someone else. Things had basically fallen apart between us and I needed to get away.'

'I know exactly what you mean,' I said. 'My ex wanted to be a Disney animator and he had the talent to be a shoo-in. But instead of following the dream, he perfected the art of avoiding it – courses, menial jobs, phantom ailments. Walt Disney himself said, "If you can dream it, you can do it," but that means nothing if you don't have courage. He was afraid to try new things and he'd let that dictate his life. I once chased him around the house with a spoonful of homemade pumpkin soup because he wouldn't taste it – not even once – and for some reason that infuriated me. It was really delicious! And I guess I knew that if he wouldn't try something as minor as soup, then our life together was going to be extremely limited. Rather than acknowledge that red flag, I chased him with the spoon, yelling and cursing like some sort of demonic incarnation of Nigella Lawson. "TASTE IT!" That was *not* one of my most shining moments.'

Ivan laughed. Even though I knew I was oversharing with this man from the bar, verbalising my relationship breakdown for the first time felt good, and since this almost-anonymous stranger was listening and nodding and replying with comments like 'That would bother me too,' I kept going.

'The soup was just the beginning,' I said. 'It only got worse. Moving in together was a problem. Travel was a problem. Doing anything impulsive was a problem. Every step forward was an uphill battle. After five years, I gave up. I told him: "I can't be with someone who won't go after his dream." He immediately applied for a job at Disney and got it, but unfortunately it was too late for us by that stage. I'd spent years ignoring the fact that we were a bad fit. So when he moved to Sydney for the job, I decided to follow my own dream. Since I was little, I've wanted to live a year in the States because my parents are American. So, yeah... here I am.'

Meanwhile, in between the divulging, I guzzled distracted sips of Martini, losing track of just how many sips, exactly. Which explains why, after exchanging tales of love and woe, my memories of the night become a series of tungsten flashes.

'Your English is perfect,' I told him.

'*Gracias.*'

'Speak Spanish for me.'

'*Tenés ojos hermosos.*'

'Which means…?'

'You have beautiful eyes.'

He asked me to speak in Australian English and I said, 'You're a *spunk*,' which I translated into American by telling him it means he's hot.

He put his hand on mine and electric sparks shot up to my already-dizzy head. It was then that I reminded him again of my plans to return to Australia. 'I'm not kidding,' I told him. 'I'm going home in December. I can't meet anyone, not even you.'

'Okay,' he said, before leaning in to kiss me.

MY PHONE RINGS, bringing me back to the present. I lean over the side of Ivan's bed and dig through my handbag for the phone. It's Anna calling.

'Torre! Oh, thank God, you're okay. I was totally worried you'd gone home with some nutjob last night, like the dude from *American Psycho*. Where are you?'

'I just had my first one-night stand,' I whisper.

'Get! Out! With Patrick Bateman?'

'With a man called Ivan Alexis Something-Something.'

'You're still at his house?'

'Yep, in his bed.'

'Um, Torre… hello? You're doing it wrong. When you have one-night stands, you're supposed to bail out right about now, not hang around and wait for him to offer you a breakfast buffet. Come home. I'll take you for dim sum if you tell me all about your Mr Something-Something.'

I hang up the call and muffle my grin with a fistful of bedsheets.

Ivan is still in the bathroom and I feel silly lying in bed wearing yesterday's wrinkled outfit, so I get up and wander around his small apartment. One thing is immediately evident about this Ivan fellow – he's an extreme minimalist. Apart from the bed and two white armchairs facing a TV, the apartment is crisp, white and empty. His personal effects consist of a world globe, a model ship sitting on the mantel and a big book of world maps with the dust cover missing. This kind of freakishly stark minimalism can mean one of only two things: (1) Ivan moved in here yesterday, or (2) I just slept with Patrick Bateman.

The bathroom door opens and Ivan walks out, interrupting my paranoid conjectures. He smells of a divine lavender aftershave. Dressed in jeans, a white T-shirt and stylish brown boots, he looks even more attractive than his licence photo. I almost tell him this, but I catch myself right before blurting out that I went through his wallet.

'Good morning,' he says. 'Can I make you some eggs? A smoothie? I make an awesome smoothie with frozen strawberries. Coffee?'

'No, thank you,' I say, entranced by his eclectic accent. The words 'frozen strawberries' comes out in a staccato *fro-zin stra-be-riz* while 'awesome' is elongated and entirely Southern Californian.

'So,' I say, 'I guess you just moved into this place?'

'Yeah, I did.'

Phew. He's normal.

'Well, actually,' he continues, 'that was, like, six months ago now.'

'Six… months?'

He nods.

Where the hell is his furniture? I stare at him, waiting for more information as to why his apartment is psycho-killer minimalist. He doesn't expand, so I don't probe, I just grow insanely curious. Perhaps his rage-filled ex-lover cleaned him out? He did say he'd just ended a relationship…

'I'm really sorry, but I have to go,' he says. 'I'm going to DC and I've got a flight to catch. I have a meeting there first thing Monday morning. Can I drive you home on my way to the airport?'

In his car, I catch a glimpse of myself in the sun-visor mirror. Yesterday's slick ponytail is now a mane of dark, wavy locks. The collar of my blazer is wrinkled from being tossed aside in the heat of the moment. My cheeks are flushed and my lips – rubbed crimson from so much kissing – are fixed in a delighted expression from last night's impulsive escapade. One groomed eyebrow arches up mischievously and I try to poke it down but it refuses to cooperate. The last time I looked, I was a lanky, downhearted twenty-four-year-old girl, but the woman in the mirror looks daring, sensual and alive. I hardly recognise her.

I direct Ivan to my terrace house in the Western Addition. He pulls over by a car with a smashed window that sits outside of the public housing building adjacent to my home. This car's alarm woke me late one night and, from my bedroom window, I watched two thieves clean out the subwoofers. You don't need a TV when you have *CSI: Western Addition* live outside of your house.

Ivan taps my number into his phone and gives me a quick peck just as I'm stepping out of the car. 'I'll call you,' he yells from his window as he speeds away.

Standing on the street, I touch my lips as I surrender the devilish grin I've been holding back all morning. My Latin lover may never call, but either way I'm thrilled with myself. What's the harm in having some fun? That's precisely why I travelled here, after all, to live a little.

WHEN I FIND myself at work a few days later google-stalking Ivan, I can't deny the truth: he's on my mind. His lavender aftershave has permeated the collar of my jacket and I've been unable to control my foolish grin for days.

Normally, I'd feel bad for doing this at work, but I've been hired into a design role that doesn't yet exist. In a revamped warehouse downtown, the design team waits on standby for an anticipated flood of work, hoping it'll put an end to the tedium of staring at sand-blasted brick walls and exposed plumbing. My colleagues are a team of talented people, but only the account managers are busy, as they generate leads. Meanwhile, in order to appear somewhat deserving of my paycheck, I sit behind my Mac – legs crossed, back straight, skirt smoothed, brow furrowed, fingers on keyboard – and get busy looking up the guy I slept with last weekend.

Since I have no chance of remembering his last name, I decide the best alternative is to read up on Argentina, hoping that if we meet again, I can charm him with mind-blowing grenades of knowledge, or – more specifically – conceal the fact that I know nothing whatsoever about his home country.

I discover that Argentina is a beef-steak-shaped landmass on the southern tip of South America – a fitting form since Argentineans eat the most steaks per capita of any region in the world. Their national beverage is a herbal tea called *maté*, which is sipped through a straw from a piece of apparatus that looks illegal. I wonder if Ivan drinks maté. I'll ask if I see him again.

Only, it's now Wednesday, and I've given up on the idea of hearing from him ever again. According to the non-existent (but widely referenced) *Complete Compendium to Dating*, Wednesday is the final deadline for receiving a phone call after a weekend hookup. The same guide also claims you can't meet a man in a bar and that all the good ones are gay or taken. To make it worse, the rules state that guys only pursue women who play hard to get.

I've breached every rule.

Having had only one boyfriend in my life, and being single for the first time since I was nineteen, my inexperience with The Dating Game is showing.

I e-mail my mother with a chatty update just as I've done every day since I left Australia, and then shut down my 'work' for the day before walking to Market Street to wait for my bus.

The city is alive with office workers, aimless tourists and shoppers carrying handfuls of bags. My eyes wander in the direction of Union Square and I contemplate an expedition to Macy's for a new set of lacy underwear. I've never owned nice lingerie, but I'm feeling the urge to shop for some now.

My handbag buzzes.

It must be Ivan!

I fumble through my oversized bag. Novel, purse, umbrella, tissues, lip gloss. Fourth ring... fifth ring, I'm going to miss the call! Sketchbook, pen, one earring, AH! Side pocket? Yes!

Flip. 'Hello?'

'Good. Afternoon. Ma'am. How. Are. You. Today. I'm calling today to let you know that you have won our sweepstakes and we would like to give you a pair of...'

'No thanks.' *Flip.*

It rings again.

Flip. 'Hello?'

'Latin lover hasn't called yet, has he?' It's Anna.

'How'd you know?'

'You answered your phone in, like, one nanosecond. Give it a few rings before you pick up or you'll come off as totally *desperado*.'

'He's not going to call anyway,' I sigh. 'It's Wednesday.'

'Right. He missed the deadline. But don't worry, I have the perfect fix. Tonight, I'm going to introduce you to Godzilla. Best sushi ever.'

I hang up the phone and throw it into my bag.

Give it up, Torre, I tell myself. You let yourself get giddy over some guy from a bar. Yes, he was interesting, gorgeous and smelled lovely, but you don't want to get into a relationship right now anyway, remember? The last thing you need is some guy complicating life when it's time to return to Australia, back to your friends and sisters and your mother, who you e-mail every day with a thousand words just because you miss her so much already. Remember? Stick to the plan. A year in San Francisco, an experiment in independence, a taste of a different life, then home. Remember the rules: *Do not fall in love and never come home.* I make a pact with myself: if Ivan calls, I'll turn him down.

My handbag buzzes again.

Rummage, grab, flip – 'Hello?'

'Torre? Hi. It's Ivan. I'm sorry – I meant to call earlier. I missed my flight to Washington after I drove you home the other day.'

'Because of me?'

'What was I going to do? Make you catch the bus home? I had a really nice night with you, by the way.'

My cheeks flush. 'Me too.'

'So then I almost missed my flight today too! I was waiting to board at Washington airport and I finally had a spare moment to call you. I reached into my pocket and realised my phone was missing because I'd left it at security. My flight started to board, but I had to get the phone because I couldn't lose your number, so I took off running, caught a train across the airport, ran some more, found the phone at security, then sprinted back to my boarding gate and scraped past the doors just as they were closing. So anyway, I wanted to call you earlier, but I had to wait to land in San Francisco.'

'Wow,' I say, visualising the whole story, starring Ivan dressed as Indiana Jones.

'Can I take you out to dinner tomorrow night?' he says.

'Absolutely.' I clap my phone shut and spin on my heel in the direction of Macy's.

MY DOORBELL RINGS. I check my outfit in the mirror for the tenth time: tailored pants, a scoop-neck knit top and my favorite boots. I smooth down my glossy, freshly straightened hair, smack my rosy lips and nod once for courage at my reflection.

Ivan stands outside, clean-shaven and dressed – once again – as a stylish gay man. 'Hi,' he says. 'You look beautiful.'

'So do you. Uh, I mean you look handsome.' Blood rushes to my cheeks. I'm confused about the protocol – are we lovers? Or strangers? We've already slept together, so do we kiss and hold hands, or do we act first-date awkward? I'm bad at this.

'Hey,' he says as we walk toward his car. 'Do you mind if we go to the Golden Gate Bridge before dinner?'

'Sure. I'm easy,' I say, turning densely red at my poor choice of words. This is awkward: *we're strangers*.

We drive through a roller coaster of streets and come to a beach that overlooks the bridge. I've never been to this part of the city and I haven't seen the Golden Gate this close.

Ivan parks the car and I open my door to blustery wind. As we start to walk, he wraps his arm around my shoulders, pulling me close. We don't speak, we just walk in comfortable silence, humbled by the red bridge, which is partially lost in fog. The view is stunning.

I notice that, in my heeled boots, I'm just a little shorter than his six feet – a nice fit under the crook of his arm. I breathe in his aftershave, a smell that is both foreign and familiar. *We're lovers*, I realise with a smile.

'So what made you decide to move to San Francisco?' he asks, breaking the silence.

'This city has always appealed to me. It's full of culture and creativity – similar in many ways to Melbourne. I love Melbourne too, but I just felt like my life there was getting a bit, I dunno, dull.'

He nods. 'I cut through corporate red tape for a living. I know what dull looks like.'

'I'm kind of embarrassed that I haven't asked this yet, but what do you do for a living?'

'Project management. IT stuff. I won't bore you with all the geek speak. I work an hour away in Silicon Valley. Actually, I usually don't get out of work this early, so I never get to see the bridge in sunlight. By the time I get home, another day has disappeared into darkness.'

'That's sad,' I say. 'Don't you think it's weird how, when you're young, people always tell you, "The world is your oyster, *blah, blah, blah*." But then you go into the world and you find that the "oyster" is actually just politics, an angry alarm clock, bumper-to-bumper traffic—'

'And a dreary office with no fresh air,' he adds. 'Surprise! Here's your grand prize for sixteen years of education.'

'Would you like a mortgage with that?'

Our laughter is whipped away on a strong wind, which drags along the steely blue water under the bridge, churning it up into a mass of white crests.

'It kind of makes you wonder, doesn't it?' I say. 'Like, what is the point of life? But when I say that out loud, it makes me sound depressed, doesn't it?'

He turns and fixes his eyes on mine and I feel like I'm oversharing again, but this time without the help of liquid courage. Instead of shutting up like I probably should, I begin babbling self-consciously. 'Maybe I *was* depressed in Melbourne, or just chronically disappointed, or… I don't know. Shouldn't there be something more than working to live, living to work? Why do so many people settle down in shitty relationships and never leave the town they grew up in even though they hate it? That isn't enough for me. There's a whole world out there. Just look at this bridge! Bloody hell, I'm really sorry. I don't know why I'm complaining about all of this in your ear, it's just... What were we talking about again?'

'Chronic disappointment.'

'Right. Anyway, I guess that's why I came to San Francisco: to see if that's all there is to life. Work. Sleep. Work. Sleep. Sorry. Please stop me if I'm rambling.'

'Actually,' he says, 'you're making perfect sense.'

We get back in Ivan's car and drive to a tapas restaurant in the Mission District. Flamenco guitar noodling and warm lighting set the scene. I open the menu and panic internally to discover the menu is in Spanish and there isn't a single food item I recognise.

'I can order if you like?' Ivan says, intuiting my dilemma.

A leader. I like that.

He calls the waitress over with a flick of his hand and speaks to her in fast-paced Spanish. He points to the menu: *uno, dos, tres.* He oozes a certain kind of chutzpah that I find irresistible, and if he is trying to impress me with his Spanish, it's working.

The waitress brings a jug of sangria and Ivan pours two glasses. '*Salud,*' he says, clanking my glass. 'That's how we say "Cheers" in Argentina.' He takes a sip and then bashes the base of his glass into his plate, momentarily silencing the restaurant. He's clumsy – how adorable.

'So, that tea you drink in Argentina,' I say, 'how do you pronounce it? Is it *mate*? As in "G'day, mate"?'

His eyes light up. 'Maté? How do you know about maté?'

'I... just do. So you say *mah-tay*? Like that?'

'That's right. You've tried it?'

'No, but I'd like to.'

'Oh, I'll make it for you.'

I smile at his offer.

'Americans don't often know what maté is,' he says. 'I once had a cop pull me over at nine in the morning. I had my maté in the cup holder and the cop looked at it and he was, like, "Would you please step out of the car, sir?" I got the full sobriety test – "Please walk in a straight line, sir. Please touch the tip of your nose, sir" – all that crap at nine a.m. just because I was drinking green tea from an unusual cup.'

I'm giggling as the waitress delivers our first dish.

'This is called "ceviche",' Ivan says. 'Raw fish marinated in lemon with a little onion and coriander. Oh, I forgot to ask if you like raw fish.'

'I love it,' I say.

'Awesome. Do you like sailing?'

I pause, confused by his non sequitur. Sailing? Why is he asking this? Sailing is about as appealing to me as tap dancing in steaming piles of cow crap with brand-new shoes on.

'No. I don't particularly enjoy sailing,' I confess.

'Oh, so you've tried it?' he asks.

'Once as a teenager. It wasn't my thing. I get seasick and the ocean scares me because of, you know, sharks and stuff.'

'You're scared of sharks? Why?'

'Um... have you seen their teeth?'

He returns a perplexed stare.

'I don't know why I'm afraid of the ocean,' I continue, 'but I don't think there's anything in the world that I'm more scared of. It's so dark and creepy. Everything that hangs out in seawater is horrible: claws, urchins, stinging barbs, poison darts, teeth, tentacles, suction cups, giant squid, jellyfish, those deep-sea creatures with fangs and lightbulb thingies on their heads...' I pause to shiver. '... Tentacles, creepy crawly *wet* things. It's safe to assume I'm scared of pretty much anything that would fall out if you turned the ocean upside down and shook it. That's why

I won't swim at the beach, not past knee-level, anyway.' I fork some raw fish into my mouth and bite down. 'It tastes delicious, though.'

'Wow, that's… a lot of fears to have.'

'Great start to a date, huh? "Hello, I'm Torre, I'm extremely neurotic. Let me brief you on all my fears."'

'Well, everyone is scared of something,' he says with a laugh.

'So then what are you scared of, Ivan?'

His eyes drift off as he thinks. 'Housing estates and shopping malls. Umm… theme parks, crowded places,' he says with a firm nod. 'Oh, and dictatorships.'

'Wow, you're quite the neurotic yourself,' I tease.

He laughs. 'But I love sailing. Actually, I have my own sailboat in LA. Whenever I have time, I go see her.'

Her? He owns a boat and talks to *her* with affectionate language?

The waitress interrupts to serve more plates, leaving me a moment to reflect on how this date is going so far. The stylish outfit, the romantic stroll, the alluring Spanish – something has to be wrong. A yacht owner, at his age? I know the type: On weekends he wears deck shoes, anchor-patterned shirts, white slacks and pastel sweaters tied at his neck. He hangs out at the marina and talks in nautical jargon to anyone who'll listen, but he never leaves the dock in case his sweetie gets scratched. A bored IT yuppie who's married to a fancy boat. Not my type.

The waitress leaves and Ivan walks me through the tapas. '*Albóndigas a la española, y pulpo a la plancha.* Meatballs in tomato sauce and barbecued octopus.'

I pause my critical judgement to hear his Spanish, the lisps and silent letters merged together in long, silken ribbons. His full lips move differently when he speaks his native language.

'My boat is called *Amazing Grace.* Well, that was the name she had when I bought her, but I like to call her Gracie.'

'Gracie'? Yep, 'she' is his sweetie all right. I take an extra large gulp of sangria and snatch a covert glance at my watch, wondering how long this guy is going to talk about yachting.

'I've thought about moving Gracie to San Francisco, but the weather is warm and mostly calm in LA, which is better for sailing. And my parents live close by to the boat, so I can visit them too when I go down there. I sail to Catalina sometimes.'

'Sounds like fun,' I lie.

'You should come sometime. You'll love it.'

'I dunno, maybe,' I say, feeling slightly irked. 'As I said, I'm not really an ocean person.'

'I'll take you to Catalina Island,' he says, running away with my 'maybe.' 'It's six hours from LA and incredibly beautiful. If you sail there during the week when there are no crowds, it feels like you're arriving in a secluded paradise.' He sips his drink and clanks it back down onto the table, full of enthusiastic energy. 'Actually, I'm planning to sail Gracie around the world next year.'

I pause, a forked meatball in front of my mouth. 'Sorry... what did you just say?'

'I'm going to sail around the world. My boat's pretty much ready to go. I just have to finish up the project I'm managing and then I can start getting my boat ready for a solo circumnavigation.'

'Wait,' I say, putting down my fork and leaning in close. 'A circumnavigation? You're planning to sail around the world? *Alone?*'

'Uh-huh. Mostly I want to sail through the islands of the South Pacific. They're supposed to be really beautiful. But I'll have to, like, sail all the way around to get home again.' He chuckles, dismissing two-thirds of planet Earth as a minor commute.

'So, you're sailing around *the world*?'

'Well, yeah. I want to travel and a sailboat is a great vehicle for seeing the world. I'm leaving early next year when the weather is best.'

I stop myself from asking the same question again. I'm having trouble digesting this. I sit with my mouth in a dazzled 'O' while Ivan explains the details of his plan.

He tells me that seven years ago while he was a student living in LA, he noticed the sailboats off Santa Monica Beach while rollerblading and then he looked out at the horizon and began to ponder the places he could take a boat. He booked sailing lessons and, not long after, bought his first boat. For five years, he's been saving, planning, researching, studying, route-mapping, and, now, his dream is ripe and ready for plucking. Three years ago, he crossed the Atlantic Ocean, crewing with two others on a yacht delivery from Spain to Florida to gain experience and see if he liked ocean sailing.

'What was it like?' I ask, enthralled.

'I forgot my sleeping bag, so I had to sleep under garbage bags the whole way. I froze my arse off and got sick with the flu, but the trip was incredible. When we spotted land for the first time in twenty-four days, I didn't want to come back.'

A crevasse of difference cracks open between us and all I can do is stare with wide eyes. Twenty-four days on the open ocean with a garbage bag blanket and he calls it 'incredible'? I had him all wrong. He's not a bored yuppie. He's a man with wild ambitions. I've never met a real-life adventurer before; I've only ever seen them on the breaking news report, generally being dragged from catastrophes.

'So that explains why your apartment is empty!' I say.

He lets out an embarrassed laugh. 'Yeah. When I moved here from LA six months ago, I gave everything to my brother. Figured I wouldn't need it on the ocean. Actually, Mum offered to buy me Italian leather couches. I told her thanks but no thanks.'

'You refused free couches to live in an empty apartment?'

He shrugs. 'I think she was trying to keep me from taking off sailing. I guess she thinks it's harder for me to leave if I own quality Italian furniture. She drives me crazy. She's Jewish.'

'Oh, your family's Jewish?'

'No, no, we're atheist.'

I consider this for a moment, confused. 'So then, your "Jewish" mother wanted to buy you the couches as an anchor to stop you from sailing the world?'

'Yes, exactly – an anchor. My family doesn't really say much about my trip, but when they offer to buy me large furniture goods instead of stuff I can actually use on a boat, I figure they don't support what I'm doing.'

'Maybe they're just afraid for you? It's pretty dangerous. I'd be scared if I was your mother.'

'Yeah, well, it annoys me. But let's not talk about my family dramas. Would you like to come back to my place for tea?'

I really like this guy, I think to myself. He's so interesting – a sailor, a dreamer, a leader, a visionary, a unique soul. And the best part is, since he's leaving, it's a commitment-free relationship. We can date, have fun, and then go our separate ways at the end of the year.

'Can we drink maté at your house?' I ask.

'Sure, if you like.'

But, back at Ivan's apartment, we find far more interesting things to do than sip tea.

TWO

I SMELL LAVENDER AFTERSHAVE. My eyes open to Ivan's face inches from mine, just visible in the dawn light. For the last two months, I've woken in his apartment more often than I have in my own. Anna sends regular texts, asking where I am, and I explain that once again, I'm with 'The Man from the Bar.'

'Invite him over,' she keeps insisting. 'We'll have a dinner party. Then we'll do what all good friends do for each other: we'll size him up.'

But I'm trying to keep a safe distance between my friends and Ivan. I don't want to overcomplicate the situation by taking him to parties because The Man from the Bar is supposed to be a casual, commitment-free fling. Only, Ivan is making that difficult...

'Good morning, baby.' Ivan drums my face with a thousand quick kisses. This man is a woodpecker of affection.

On the bedside table sits the first sign that things between us are threatening to become serious. It was Ivan's gift for my twenty-fifth birthday last week. He told me he'd take me anywhere, so I chose the artists' open studios in Sausalito, where we watched ceramicists and painters working on their crafts. There, from a gifted ceramicist, Ivan bought me a sculpture of a mermaid. This generous gift tells me that, if we're still seeing each other in seven months when Ivan moves onto his boat – just as I'm due to leave San Francisco and head home – our fling won't be ending with a quick squeeze and an *adios*. Ivan's enchanting mermaid is seducing me toward a rocky shore.

'Hey, I have an idea,' he says between kisses.

I pull the covers over my head and speak through muffled layers of sheets and blankets. 'An idea? Now? It's so early. Let's go back to sleep.'

'I was thinking, if you want, we can call in sick and go on a road trip to LA for the weekend. I'd love to show you my boat.'

'Don't you think it's a bit soon to be introducing me to your other woman?'

He laughs. 'Don't be nervous. She'll love you.'

I check the time: 6 a.m. I have another hour until I have to get ready for work and catch a short bus ride downtown. Ivan is usually showered, dressed and gone by the time I wake up because he has an eighty-minute peak-hour commute to Silicon Valley, the IT capital of the world. There, he wrangles subordinates in line by waving a stern finger and threatening overtime to the chimps on keyboards, while he paces the aisles, whipping the slackers with obsolete cables. 'That's supposed to be C, colon, slash, slash! Not C, slash, slash, colon!' At least, that is the vision I drift into when he goes on about project management, software implementations, telecommunications and other jargon that sifts through my Swiss-cheese artist's brain.

'Monkeys,' I say, dazed in sleepy thoughts.

'What?'

'I said okay.'

I cough down the phone line to my boss, then I shower, slip into a summery cotton dress and pack a weekend bag. I toss it in the back of Ivan's car and open the passenger door to find a travel pillow and a fleece blanket carefully folded on my seat.

'It's a seven-hour drive,' Ivan says. 'So I want you to be comfortable. I've packed sandwiches, drinks and snacks. There's a cappuccino for you in the cup holder.'

'Thanks.' My heart beats a little faster.

He jumps in the car with his maté gear. Before he starts the ignition, he pours hot water from a Thermos into a carved wooden cup half filled with green tea leaves. We've spent all this time together and I still haven't had the chance to taste maté.

'Can I try?' I ask.

He hands me the cup and I suck tea up the straw. I recoil, first at the boiling water in my mouth, then at the bitter taste. It's disgusting.

'Well?' Ivan says. 'What do you think?'

'Can I be honest?'

'Of course.'

'It tastes like ashtray.' I take another small sip to be sure. 'Yep, ashtray mixed with soil. Sorry.'

'That's okay. It'll grow on you in time.'

We leave the city behind us as we speed down the 101 South. San Francisco merges into green rolling hills, then into farmland. I pull the blanket around my shoulders and snuggle into the pillow, brimful with happiness to be swept away on a whim.

I BECOME AWARE of a dampness on my right cheek. Damn, I've been drooling on my travel pillow. I wipe my face and turn to see if Ivan has noticed.

'Welcome back,' he says, looking right at me. 'You've been sleeping since Santa Barbara. You're so cute when you sleep.'

I go pink in the cheeks. I don't know what he saw, exactly, but I bet it involved a spreading of knees, an open mouth, gurgling noises and lots of misplaced saliva. Who looks like Monica Bellucci now, huh?

I notice we're almost there when we turn off the Santa Monica Freeway exit. Los Angeles is everything I imagined: grey buildings, air pollution, traffic congestion and thin palms reaching up vertically as though they're trying to breathe fresh air above the smog cloud.

We emerge onto a road that trails the ocean and the concrete claustrophobia diminishes. Masts tell me we've reached the marina.

Walking along the dock, I notice all types of boats, from waterlogged skiffs to pimp-daddy mega-yachts. Marina del Rey is a place where A-list celebrities' yachts are forced to mingle with the commoners': there's no Bel Air to separate the grotesquely rich from the floating vagabonds.

My eyes dart around, excited and nervous like I'm meeting a member of Ivan's family for the first time. He's told me all about his boat, how he searched for a year before he found his perfect match in San Francisco, how he sailed it down the coast, even though the forecast predicted a gale and advised all small crafts to stay off the ocean. I asked him what it was like being in bad weather and he said he felt alive and happy, despite his seasickness.

'There she is,' he says. 'Gracie.'

Amazing Grace is twenty-six years old, one year my senior, but much older in boat years, and it shows through her greying hull and worn teak that's flecking varnish like it's seen too many dry summers. Despite her years, she looks strong and capable, and there's something in her canoe-like shape that reminds me of a majestic Viking ship. She doesn't look old, she looks wise, and if she could speak, I'm sure she'd have many stories to tell.

'Come up,' Ivan says, boarding the boat with a gazelle leap.

I cling to the railings and haul myself aboard, eyeing the black-green water below like it may jump up and swallow me.

I'm treated to the grand tour of the boat and Ivan rattles off jargon that goes over my head: *roller furling jib, double line reefing that leads back to the cockpit, lazy jacks, wind vane.* I tell him I'm very impressed, but I have no idea what he's talking about.

'Basically, she's all rigged up for solo sailing,' he says. 'I can set the sails from the cockpit. Most boats need two or more people to make sail changes – Gracie can be sailed by one.'

He leads me down the stairs and into the homey nest of her cabin. She smells of diesel and kerosene and the papery pages of old books. The late 1970s design shows in the brown, tan and orange decor. Teak lines the walls, aged to a deep shade of fine-wine red. It's warm and cozy inside the belly of this ship.

The kitchen is tiny and basic, and adjacent to it is a navigation station for plotting maps, controlling switches and all that boat business. A switchboard of mixed breakers is labeled with functions: *Bilge Pump, Aft Lights, Engine, Water Pump.* Wires are visible in the back as though someone overstuffed the cupboard with electronics and quickly closed the door.

The middle part of the boat is the living area – the salon. Two sofas run up either side, both upholstered in an awesome hue of orange vinyl that begs to be accessorised with a lava lamp.

Farther toward the front of the boat, Ivan points out a potbelly fireplace, which strikes me as both darling and deadly. 'For cold regions,' he says. 'This boat is so strong, you could take her to Antarctica.'

I inspect Ivan's library on the small bookshelf. *Sailing Alone Around the World* by Joshua Slocum, *The Long Way* by Bernard Moitessier, *Taking on the World* by Ellen MacArthur, *The Incredible Voyage* by Tristan Jones – there isn't a single novel among all the sailing nonfictions.

'Got a bit of tunnel vision, do you?' I tease.

'You could say that. I haven't read anything except sailing books for the last five years. I've read some of those books twice. Those people have all done what I want to do.'

'They're your heroes?' I say, sliding a book out to flick through.

'Sort of, but I don't believe in having heroes, I believe in accomplishing your own things in life rather than envying someone else's life from your armchair. I suppose you'd call them my inspiration.'

'Fair enough. You must like this Moitessier guy; you have four of his books.'

'Yeah, I've read him so many times, I feel like I know him, like…' Ivan lets out an embarrassed laugh. 'This may sound strange, but sometimes I feel like he's my best friend. He's my greatest inspiration. Have you heard of him?'

I shake my head.

'He probably would've been the first guy to ever solo sail the world nonstop – in 1969 – but he abandoned the race in the last stretch. After he circled the globe, all he had to do to get the record and prize money was return to his starting point to finish the loop. He got close, but he decided not to return to land. Couldn't hack going back to civilisation. His wife and children were waiting for him and everything, but he turned his boat around and just kept going. He ended up doing another half circumnavigation to get to Tahiti. Meanwhile, another dude got the world record and the five-thousand-pound reward.'

I get a chill thinking of the sailor's wife onshore, scanning the empty horizon for a boat that would never come. 'He just left his family at the dock? Why?'

Ivan shrugs. 'That's just the way Moitessier was. He'd sailed the world with his wife before, for their honeymoon. But she had kids from another marriage and when she left them in boarding school to set sail, she missed them the whole time. She wanted to get home, but Moitessier wanted to keep going. When he went to sea again, he went alone. And he never came back for her.'

'He didn't love her any more?'

'I think he adored her, but I guess he just felt like he couldn't have both of his loves. He once said: "It's always the case of having to sacrifice one thing for the other. You have to choose between your life and a woman, and it's got to be your own life, hasn't it?" The sea was more important to him. He wanted to be free.'

'From what?'

'The instability of land, probably. He grew up in Indochina and he went through a brutal invasion by the Japanese after the French lost the war. I guess he found his ultimate asylum at sea. He called the ocean: "A nation whose laws are harsh yet simple, a nation that never cheats, which is immense and without borders, where life is lived in the present."'

'Sad,' I say. 'I like solitude too, but to live a life in utter isolation because you can't trust land any more? That's really tragic.'

Ivan shrugs. 'Land is tragic too, though. War, robberies, corruption, genocide, kids getting taken from their parents. Happens all the time. Moitessier has a point: the ocean's laws are harsh, but fair.'

I get chills down my spine thinking about Moitessier's self-induced loneliness. I grew up in a boisterous household filled with siblings, pets and eccentrics, and isolation was impossible, even when I craved it. It was chaotic at all times. My parents emigrated from California when they were young and carefree, and, bringing their late-sixties liberalism with them, they forged a life in Australia with values as eclectic as the house they built from cedarwood, bluestone and stained-glass windows. Under that roof, we kids were not judged on our academic abilities; instead, we were measured by our humour, self-expression and soul.

'Mum, Dad – I got a C in mathematics, but look at my sculpture. It has a fish's head and a woman's legs instead of a tail. I know it's really ugly, but that's because it's a reverse mermaid. It's twelve feet long, so I needed help dragging it home from school.'

'Oh, honey, that's fantastic! It'll look great in the living room by the piece your sister made of a broken-hearted man spurting his blood and arteries down the canvas.'

By day, my mum was a busy housewife and my dad was a successful scriptwriter, but by night, they were unruly bohemian musicians. Friends would pour in, beers would open, instruments would manifest and bluegrass jam sessions would go until late. It was not uncommon for me to wander from my room in the morning to find a stranger sleeping off a night of indulgence on the couch. I'd tiptoe around him, careful not to trigger that inevitable moment of panic that always comes when people wake up under a beam of midmorning sun to find an irked ten-year-old looking down at them, saying, 'Um… hello? Was that *you* who vomited in our bathroom?'

Seeking refuge from the noise and the party animals, I found my happy place within the solitude of my bedroom. Hours would slip by as I'd draw, paint and write to explore the far reaches of my inner world. The arts gave me a sense of control that I couldn't find within a mob of siblings and strangers. Inside my imagination, I had the power to reverse mermaids and obliterate party animals.

My older sisters would join the parties, but I would opt instead to be alone with my imagination. 'She should relax and enjoy life a little more,' my family would say, usually behind my back when they thought I couldn't hear them. 'They should learn to be grown-ups,' I'd complain to my friends at school. I envied their straitlaced parents who enforced rules and curfews, who lived in quiet brick homes that didn't waft plumes of smoke until dawn.

When I moved out at age twenty after landing my first professional job in Melbourne, I found all the solitude I'd ever craved living with two housemates who were never home. There was no clang of dishes, no sibling rivalry, no dueling banjos, no family friend at the kitchen table lamenting after four bourbons, no phone ringing off the hook, no cat running across the piano, no '80s pop songs blasting from bedrooms, no *tssst* sound of beers cracking, no father plucking a riff on the bass, no mother strumming wistful country tunes on her Martin guitar.

My haven was blissfully quiet! Then it was profoundly silent. Then it became outright depressing. The cacophony of my bizarre family had embedded itself deep into my bloodstream.

And while I, like Moitessier, tend to slip away from the crowds to recollect from time to time, I can't imagine a trauma that would turn me off the warmth of human connections forever. One would have to feel deeply betrayed by humanity to feel comforted by the cold embrace of the open ocean.

I slip the book back into place, rubbing away the goosebumps on my arms.

Ivan continues the tour through the boat, leading me toward the narrow end, the bow.

'Here's the bathroom,' Ivan says, opening a folding door to reveal a toilet, a sink, a small mirror and a shower all crushed into a broom-cupboard-sized space.

We reach a triangular nook built within the pointiest end of the boat. 'Here's the main bed, the V-berth,' he says. 'It's got freshwater tanks below, that's why it's so high up.'

The small V-shaped bed is raised three feet off the floor and with just over two feet of space between the mattress and the ceiling, you wouldn't want to sit up abruptly after a bad dream.

As we move back through the boat, Ivan lifts wooden lids and opens doors, showing me all the nooks and cupboards for storage. It's a floating Armageddon bunker with room to house a year's worth of supplies.

'If you don't mind me asking,' I say, running my hands along the old teak, 'what does a boat like this cost?'

'Usually a 1979 blue water boat like this would cost at least ninety to a hundred thousand dollars or so, but I bought Gracie for half price. The Valiant boat designers experimented with a fire-retardant fibreglass in 1979 that turned out to be susceptible to blistering. She already has a few blisters and a lot more will pop up once she reaches the tropics, but it won't affect the integrity of the boat. Professional advice confirmed what I already knew from researching these boats: it's an aesthetic issue only. This is one of the best blue water boats out there.'

'Smart purchase,' I say.

He smiles and continues. 'I spent every last cent in my name to pay for her a year ago. Since then, all of my earnings have gone into my sailing kitty, including the money from selling my first boat, *Mahalo*. A lot of people would spend the same money on a home deposit, but I'd rather have an experience than own one-third of an apartment in San Francisco or LA.'

'Well, this is kind of like owning an apartment anyway, except it floats!'

'And it can take you anywhere in the world,' he adds. 'So do you like her?'

'I love her.'

He smiles wide. 'Really? You're being serious?'

'Yes, I am,' I say, surprising myself. 'I really do.' I don't have to fake my enthusiasm. She really *is* beautiful, not ostentatious with refrigerator-white fibreglass and forty-inch plasmas in every room, but rustic and warm like my childhood home. Her interior is welcoming and snug with earthy charm.

'I'm so glad you like her,' he says. 'It's not a luxury boat, but I wanted a really simple, sturdy boat, like Moitessier always had. Simple means less maintenance and it means she can run off a few solar panels. If the electronics were fancy, I'd be less self-sufficient. With Gracie, I can travel to remote places and stay for a long time, plus if I had anything bigger, I'd need to save for much longer. This way, I can take off next year.'

'You're really keen to escape, aren't you?' I say.

He doesn't answer; instead he opens a bottle of wine and invites me outside into the cockpit. He makes a couch on the fibreglass seats with a spread of cushions and lights some tea candles and places them around the semicircle cockpit. We watch the sky turn a flaming yellow and all is quiet except for the delicate sound of water lapping at the boat.

'This is the only place in this city that I like,' Ivan says. 'When I lived in LA, I'd come to my boat every weekend and drink maté and read sailing books and just escape the traffic and crowds. It was the only place I wanted to be.'

'What an incredible retreat,' I say.

We sip our wine in silence and watch the sky turn purple.

'Have you ever been to France?' Ivan says, inspecting the bottle of French wine.

'No,' I say. 'But it's on my list of places to see. One day I want to eat my way through Europe, so I'll have to tour by bike to pay off my daily carb debt.'

He laughs. 'Sounds like an awesome plan.'

'Why do you ask?'

'I was just thinking… I'd like to take you there one day.'

'You want to take me to Europe?'

'Of course. I want to see the whole world with you.'

My skin is charged with a thousand electrical pulses. He takes my hand and, wordlessly, he draws me down into the boat. We climb into the small bed, tangling ourselves into a mess of limbs before we figure out the space. Intimate is the only way to be in this small boat.

His warm whisper in my ear sends my skin into goosebumps. 'Thank you so much for coming here with me. *Te quiero.*'

My skin softens under his lips as he undresses me. I see the moon through the square hatch above the bed. It's a tiny, delicate crescent that looks like a curve, a waist, a hip, a cupped hand, a breast, a satisfied smile. Nothing appears ordinary with Ivan.

Gratified, we lie with our toes touching in the narrowest part of the boat and I drift off to the dance of *Amazing Grace* moving in rhythm with the wind, the soft percussion of hardware, the groaning of ropes and the kisses of water on the hull.

In the morning, we walk around the marina to Ivan's favorite breakfast spot and take a table outside in the warm Los Angeles sun. The café is busy with stylish couples wearing oversized sunglasses as they sip on lattes, cappuccinos and macchiatos.

'So did you experience culture shock when you moved to LA from Argentina?' I ask.

'Yeah. I started learning English when I was twelve – five years before I arrived – but I got here and I was, like, "What the hell are people saying?" I had to watch children's TV for the first few months; it was the only thing I could understand. It was hard for sure. At first, my parents, my brother and I all crunched into a two-bedroom apartment. We worked odd jobs and pooled every cent to pay bills and between the four of us, we only earned eighteen thousand dollars the first year. Then twenty-five thousand in the second year, and thirty-six thousand in the third.'

I shake my head, trying to visualise what it would feel like to live for a year on just $4,500 per person in a city where Hummers, Aston Martins and stretch limos congest the freeways. 'That must have been tough.'

'It was,' he says. 'But we got by. When I was in college, I moved into my own apartment. I worked full-time at Starbucks and with seven hundred dollars a month, I paid for living expenses and school fees and I still managed to save up to buy my first boat.

I took a can of creamed corn to school with a spoon – that was lunch.'

Breakfast arrives: a platter of antipasto with a whole smoked trout, cheeses, dips, cold cuts and crusty bread. Fancy food for the guy who used to live off canned corn.

'Why did you leave Argentina?' I ask, forking meat off the smoked trout.

'Uh...' Ivan looks down at his plate and a heavy sadness comes over him. 'Argentina was unstable. When I was born, the country was in a dictatorship that was very oppressive. It ended when I was nine and, even though we had a democracy after 1983, there were several coup attempts to overthrow the government and I was always scared it'd happen again and we'd go back to living in fear. I wanted to be free. I wanted to make something of myself too and there were no opportunities there, so when I was seventeen, I told my parents I wanted to leave Argentina and they decided to leave too. You always hear about the "American Dream." Well, I guess it's true. My boat, the money I've saved to go sailing – there's no way I could have done that in Argentina. And I don't have to watch over my shoulder here like I did there, you know?'

I don't know. I have no idea of what he's lived through. Ivan's Third World childhood is far removed from my upbringing in Australia, where everything was safe and reliably mundane in the suburbs. The only political instability Australia has faced was when we accidentally misplaced our prime minister in 1967, Harold Holt, when he went swimming at the beach and was never seen again.

'So, yeah, I had culture shock, but life here is much better,' Ivan continues. 'My mum and dad have done well for themselves in LA. They own several properties and they have good jobs. Mum teaches yoga to senior Angelinos and Dad works in a car yard.

My bro, Eric, is a chiropractor, so he's done well too. We wouldn't have that if we'd stayed in Argentina.'

I kick myself for assuming Ivan to be a rich, yachty type when we first met. The boat, the plan to sail the world – this dream is so much more than a rich boy's fantasy.

'Ivan,' I say, 'my friends are having a dinner party next weekend, and I was wondering if you'd like to come with me?'

He smiles. 'Of course.'

FIFTEEN OF US sit around the table dipping crusty bread into bowls of home-cooked *bœuf à la bourguignon* prepared from scratch by Anna, who is dating a Frenchman.

I snatch up the first available silent moment to brag about the man at my side. 'So, Ivan is planning to set off sailing around the world in April next year,' I say, getting a thrill out of the impressed nods that circle the table, as though I, somehow, am bold and adventurous simply for dating the guy.

Questions start firing and Ivan becomes a mini-celebrity.

'What kind of boat do you have?'

'A Valiant,' he replies.

'How big?'

'Thirty-two feet.'

'Are you scared of storms?'

'No, I was in bad weather coming down the coast once. I got a chance to test my boat out; she handled it beautifully.'

'Are you going alone?' Anna asks, eyeing him suspiciously.

'No. Torre will come with me.'

The room turns silent. Somebody coughs and a spoon falls loudly onto a plate – mine. The entire dinner party looks at me, silent and excited as they await my response.

Anna shoots me an accusing look: *You didn't tell me!*

I shrug at her: *There's nothing to tell!*

I turn to Ivan, confused: *You can't be serious?*

The look on his face is deadpan: serious.

My smile drops. I feel my cheeks burn with a blend of embarrassment and anger. What the hell is with this guy? He's taken it upon himself to decide that I'm going with him on a tiny boat into the dark depths of the Pacific Ocean? Wasn't he listening when I explicitly told him that I'm scared of the ocean?

I stare him in the eyes. 'Ivan. That. Will. *Never*. Happen.'

IN THE CAR on the way home, I'm livid. 'Make whatever public broadcasts you want, but there's no way I'd do something like that with you, Ivan.' The nerve of this guy, declaring I will go with him as a statement of fact: the Earth is round; birds lay eggs; Torre will sail oceans with me.

We're driving over the Golden Gate on our way back into the city. I look down at the black mass of water beneath the bridge and it fuels my fire. 'I mean, why did you say that?'

'I don't know, the idea just came, and I—'

'Let me guess, you're going into the lonely ocean and you'll take the first piece of arse that comes along for company, huh?'

'That's unfair. I've been planning to solo sail this whole time. Don't forget that you approached me in the bar and—'

'I wasn't kidding about being afraid of the ocean, Ivan. It *terrifies* me! And I already told you I'm going home in December. I can't do this with you.'

'I understand, but... maybe one day soon you'll let me take you to Catalina. It's an incredible spot and I promise I'll keep you safe.'

'Ivan! I won't even swim at the beach! We talked about this on our second date! I've never misled you on that.'

'Yes,' he says, rubbing his warm palm on my knee. 'I just... I want to take you to beautiful places, that's all. I'm sorry, I didn't mean to make you feel embarrassed in front of your friends, or pressured or anything, okay? I really like you, Torre. I don't even know what I was thinking. Sorry. Please forgive me.'

His apology softens my temper, but fails to soothe my panic over where this relationship is headed. I don't know what to do, but continuing with him seems reckless. What was intended to be a casual romance has somehow turned into something much more. I'm losing control here.

'What's the point of this?' I ask.

'Of what?'

'Of us seeing each other?'

I see his face lose colour, even in the dark car. 'I don't understand,' he says.

'You're leaving soon. Why are we doing this?'

'Why? Are you kidding me? So what if I'm leaving? Don't make decisions for the future like that. You never know what will happen.'

'I *know* what will happen. You'll leave for the ocean and I'll go home to Australia. We should get real about this. It's dangerous to keep this going.'

He scoffs. 'Dangerous? Why is it dangerous?'

'Think about it. It'll only get harder the more time we spend together. Can we just… make this easy? Let's just—'

'Why can't we live for now?' he interrupts. 'I bought my boat intending to do a solo voyage because I'd already resigned myself to being alone. In the South Pacific, I can't be any lonelier than I am here, but at least the view will be better, right? Then, all of a sudden, there's a girl sitting next to me at the bar asking me why I'm sad. And I look up and we start talking, and I realise this gorgeous woman is also intelligent. She's courageous. She's independent. Funny. Warm. Tender. Ambitious. She's talented enough to support herself by creating art, and I'm completely blown away. I'm sitting there at the bar thinking: *Holy shit! This wouldn't be happening if I didn't impulsively decide to have a cocktail tonight.*

'Who was *that* girl?' I joke, mopping the tears gathering in the corners of my eyes. 'Is she a nice piece of arse?'

'She has the best arse I've ever seen in my life.'

We laugh and the tension disappears.

'You're incredible, Torre. And I can't tell you what will happen in December and where it will leave us, but that's seven months away. Please. I don't want to end this because it may be impractical. The best things in life are never practical. As long as we're having fun, that's all that matters, isn't it?'

The promise I made to my family feels like it's in grave danger and I'm flooded with terrible guilt. A painful lump forms in my throat when I remember my going-away party. I hugged my sisters, my parents and all eight of my nephews and nieces, but my closest nephew, Harper, the seven-year-old, clung tight and wouldn't let go. His tears wet my shoulder as he told me not to leave.

'Ivan,' I say, swallowing the pain in my throat. 'I *have* to go home at the end of the year. I promised.'

'Do what you have to do, Torre. Just don't forget to live in the moment. Life is about making *yourself* happy in this moment, right now.'

I unfold my arms and stare out the window, struck mute by his words. He has a point. At home, I wasn't making myself happy. I became consumed with trying to make someone else happy, and it was exhausting. There's only one thing I know for sure: when I'm with Ivan I'm both terrified and exhilarated to the core of my being.

'So,' he says, breaking the silence, 'am I dropping you off at your place? Or… or will you come home with me?'

This is it, Torre. Be sensible. Plan for the future. Sever the relationship now. Sleep in your own bed. Make it easy on everyone.

'Your place,' I hear myself say.

THREE

'IVAN'S PLACE' IS NOW my apartment too – we've been officially living together for three of the six months since we met, and, while my conservative shoulder-angel is accusing me of behaving recklessly, the daredevil is screaming in my left ear: *Live in the moment!* Those powerful words keep hushing my voice of reason.

Which is why I'm now shivering with fear in the small cockpit of *Amazing Grace*. I've agreed to let Ivan take me on a six-hour sail to Catalina Island. It's an easy journey, Ivan assures me, but the stretch of Pacific between here and there is deep and no doubt sharky. The thought alone makes me feel nauseated.

Ivan senses my nerves and sits beside me. 'It'll be okay,' he says. 'It's a super easy trip. The weather is really calm. I promise, it'll be fine.'

I try to let him know with a smile that I'm okay, but I'm unable to relax the crease of worry between my eyebrows. It's already October, which means I have only two and a half months left before I'm due to head home. Only now, I'm so deeply entrenched in this 'fling' that going home feels unimaginably complicated.

'We'll see dolphins,' he says, trying to cheer me up. 'I guarantee you.'

For some reason, this is calming to hear, perhaps because I've heard that where there are dolphins, there are no sharks.

'Did you get enough to eat?' he asks. 'Eating helps to prevent sickness.'

'Yes, I think so.'

'Well, if you get hungry, tell me. I've made sandwiches. There are apples and oranges and plenty of other snacks from Trader Joe's. Have you had a seasickness tablet?'

'Yes. And I have these on,' I say, waving my arms to show off my acupressure wristbands, which seem to be nothing more than fuzzy grey sweatbands that push beads into the ligaments of my wrists. It's possible that the wristbands are a placebo, but I'd suit up in a gorilla costume if there was a chance it'd cure seasickness.

Ivan presses the ignition and a huge waft of grey smoke puffs out from the back of the boat. Diesel fumes linger and my stomach somersaults.

After a taxi through the marina, we round the bird-covered breakwater and get our first sight of the Pacific. It's deep blue and perfectly calm. The surface is mirrorlike, but the ocean is not flat. Waves surge below us, thrusting us upward before pushing on resolutely toward distant lands – as far as my Aussie home. There's monumental power in the sheer volume of water moving around us, and this power doesn't notice or care that we're here.

'We won't be sailing,' Ivan says. 'There's no wind.'

Without wind, we're on a seascape of rolling, glassy hills. I try to imagine what those rolling hills would look like *with* wind and the thought brings on a flurry of panic. I swallow it down.

Ivan fiddles with some instruments and sets the boat to steer on course all by herself. 'Come to the bow with me,' he says, taking my hand. 'There's an uninterrupted view and no fumes.'

I take his hand and follow him along the side of the boat, carefully stepping over snaking ropes, wooden handrails and metal instruments, wondering how anyone manages this during rough seas. To steady myself against the swell, I let go of Ivan's hand and grip the lifelines with my right hand and the teak handrails with my left. I edge forward, trying hard to ignore all the sloshing blue in my peripheral. A swim in the deep end is only one clumsy error away.

Ivan lays out pillows and I sit in the bow with my back leaning against a sail bag, staring out into the silent ocean. He puts his arm around me and I begin to relax.

The quiet is pierced by the sound of planes zipping overhead, transporting a stream of people in and out of LA. I look back toward the city and notice it's disappearing into a yellow orb of smog. It's so disconnected out here, so private, so far from the crowds and the traffic.

'See that island there?' Ivan says, pointing to a barely visible landform on the horizon. 'You see how there's a dip between two high ridges? That's called the isthmus. That's where we're headed.'

I nod and fix my eyes on our destination, which seems impossibly far at the speed we're drifting. A slight breeze picks up and turns the ocean's surface into a kaleidoscope of dancing blue shards. The sound of sloshing liquid lulls me into a daze.

MY WATCH TELLS ME we've been travelling four hours already. I've been staring contently into the water, captivated in the same way that one is by the dancing flames of a campfire. Meanwhile, the isthmus has grown larger ahead.

'There's only two hours left and we haven't seen dolphins, Ivan,' I tease. 'You've only got two more hours to come through with the promised goods.'

'Don't worry,' he says, coolly. 'They'll come.'

Ivan has asked me to teach him to sing, after he learned that I grew up in a musical house. Through years of being subjected to my parents' late-night bluegrass jam sessions, I've learned a thing or two about music.

Ivan claims that he's not only tone-deaf, he's rhythm-challenged too.

Turns out, he's not wrong.

'*Dohhhh,*' I say, resonating my best middle-C. 'Your turn.'

'*Dd-Oo-hoO,*' he says, sounding like a choirboy turning the awkward corner into puberty.

'Okay, try again. More like this: *Dohhhh.*'

'*Ddd* – hey, look!' Ivan says, pointing.

A pod of dolphins in the distance weaves toward us, bouncing across the surface like skipping stones. They join the boat and swim ahead of *Amazing Grace*. I lean over the rail and watch their glistening bodies. They move in a choreographed shuffle, taking turns to break the surface and peer up with curious eyes and friendly grins. I can't help but return the smile.

'They must like your singing,' I say.

'Or maybe they thought someone was dying and came over to help.'

I laugh hard. I adore that he doesn't take himself too seriously, even though he's a stoic explorer with a ship and a special ability to summon dolphins.

I hang my legs over the bow, trying to get near them. I wriggle my toes as close to the water's surface as the boat allows, hoping one will jump up and nuzzle me. I'm suddenly aware that I'm unafraid.

'Thank you,' I say, kissing Ivan's cheek. 'For showing this to me.'

The land has been taking form for hours and now we've arrived at an island all for us. If the Australian outback and sunny California made a love child, it might look like this: arid hills, gum trees and rows of skinny palms reach up to a blue sky. Hillsides encase us in a protected nook. Long locks of seaweed grow from the sandy floor below. It's so pretty and wild that I have to remind myself we're just off the mainland.

Ivan coils loose ropes and covers the sails to transform his sailboat back into a home. He turns on the radio and acoustic music plays throughout the boat. The sky is dimming, so he lights candles and arranges them around the cockpit. The boat has electric lights but Ivan says we can't run them for long or they'll eat up the battery power. I like the candles better anyway.

I stretch out on a cushion in the cockpit, covering myself with a blanket. I watch the mountains and palm trees turn to silhouettes against an indigo sky. Ivan bangs some cupboards in the kitchen and comes back up the companionway stairs with glasses of wine. 'To your first sailing trip.' He clinks his glass with mine.

Fog is rolling in over the mountains, bringing with it a chill that I feel against my cheeks. Ivan kneels beside me and brings his face close. I feel his warm breath against my skin. 'Congratulations, baby.' He kisses my forehead.

'Thank you.'

'You did it,' he whispers and plants another soft kiss on my cold nose.

'I did.'

'You've sailed the Pacific Ocean.' A kiss for each cheek.

'I have.'

A soft kiss on my lips. 'It wasn't hard, was it?'

'I'm not sure yet,' I say as I pull him under my blanket.

PREPARING PANCAKES for breakfast in the boat's kitchen requires negotiating the tiny area with a great deal of awkwardness. There's a two-burner stove and an empty space below it where an oven might go if there was one. A few wooden drawers and a small cupboard provide space for kitchenware, while another sliding door behind the burner reveals a row of condiments. A small fridge cools food when the boat is plugged into the dock, but away from land it's just a cold box full of melting ice.

I flip a pancake and then stand on the bottom step of the companionway so that my legs are in the galley, but my head is outside, watching Ivan in the cockpit.

He lies shirtless, eyes closed, absorbing the morning sun.

'So, what about pirates?' I ask. 'Will there be pirates?'

He cracks his eyes open. 'Yeah, maybe. But I'll only have to worry about pirates once I'm past the South Pacific, towards Indonesia.'

'Are you going to Indonesia?'

'Not sure. I'm just concentrating on the South Pacific for now – I'm looking forward to that the most. It's warm, easy and I can island-hop the whole way across to Australia.'

I tuck my head into the boat to check the cooking pancake, knocking my skull against the hatch in the process. Even though I'm careful, I'm specked in bumps and bruises from walking into steps, levers and equipment, unfamiliar with the small space and how to negotiate my limbs within it.

'How long will that take you? To get to Australia?'

'You don't sail it all in one shot. You cross from country to country, island to island. The first part is the hardest. From the US coast to French Polynesia, it's twenty to thirty days.'

'A month without land?'

'Yep. But after about ten days at sea, you reach the trade winds. The trades make perfect sailing weather. They blow from the east, which is the ideal direction for sailing west, and they're warm and predictable, making for easy sailing. The chances of a big storm are low in the trades, as long as you leave around March or April, early May at the latest.'

I duck back into the boat to tend to the pancakes. 'So once you get to French Polynesia, how many days does it take to get between islands?'

'It depends where you're going, but usually a few days, maybe a week at the most.'

That's not so bad, I think. Getting to Catalina was six hours and that was easy. A few days couldn't be that much harder. 'So where will you go first?'

'An island called Hiva Oa in the Marquesas Islands. It's supposed to be incredibly beautiful. Then the Tuamotu Archipelago. They're rings of coral with blue lagoons inside them. It's very remote there – I could find an atoll to myself. After that: Tahiti and the islands around Tahiti, like Bora Bora, Huahine, Raiatea, Moorea. Then the Cook Islands, Tonga or Samoa, New Zealand… anywhere I want. That's the beauty of sailing.'

'Wow,' I say, awestruck. 'That would be amazing! I've never been to any of those places.' My enthusiasm gives away more than I care to reveal.

'Once you're below the equator, the sailing is easy. It's tropical and the weather is steady.'

'So, you just have to get through that first bit? The twenty or thirty days?'

'Yeah, that's the hardest part.'

In the kitchen, I squeeze oranges for juice and drift off for a moment, wondering what Tahiti and Moorea are like. Aqua water, green palms, skies that are always blue. I've only ever seen such places on my screensaver at work when I sit too long without clicking my mouse, which happens a lot in my San Francisco job.

'What about money?' I say from the kitchen. 'Are you worried that you'll run out?'

'No, I should be fine for a while. The boat's all paid for, which means it's rent-free and bill-free from now on. I have enough savings to cover several years that way. For the two of us,' he adds. 'If… you know… if you decide to come.'

His offer makes my knees ~~~ken – at first with rapture, and then with fear. 'What happens if you hit a storm?'

'In a storm, I'd set the boat to point into the wind. It's called "heave-to". It means waves can't knock the boat on its side or roll it over. Then you just wait it out, go down below, watch a movie, read a book, whatever.'

He has a way of making an ocean storm sound like a rainy Sunday spent curled up on the couch with a novel. He's not letting me flush out that seed of apprehension that I'm looking to find within him, the one that will confirm that his adventure is a bad idea.

I pause, straining for a more challenging question to throw at him. He's so confident, surely he must be nervous about something. I pull out the big guns. 'What if you're sailing along one day and you hit... I dunno, a floating tree or something, and it rips a hole in the boat and you start sinking?'

'I'd press the button on my emergency rescue beacon, called an EPIRB. It sends a satellite distress signal to the coast guard with the boat's GPS position. I'd get in the life raft and wait for rescue, generally by another ship in the area.'

Incredible – he's unshaken. Nothing frightens him.

'So one month of sailing, then it's just hopping island to island? To places like Catalina?'

'Exactly. Except it'll be so much better. It'll be supremely awesome.'

After finishing off his pancakes, Ivan stands tall in his board shorts, ready to jump off the side of the boat. 'Do you want to come in?' he asks. 'I can kick all the sharks away for you.'

I scan the surface, searching for a dark, lurking shape below, a fin or the telltale theme song – *Duh Duh... Duh Duh...* – that signals an approaching shark. 'Nah, I'll just watch you.' I lounge in the cockpit with a book, eating my breakfast and absorbing the sunrays.

Ivan jumps in and I contemplate doing a spectacular dive off the side of the boat to prove I'm not a complete chicken. But I'm too much of a complete chicken to go through with it.

I pick up my book to resume reading but I can't concentrate on the words. I'm mulling over memories, trying to recall why being in seawater deeper than my waist makes my skin crawl. It's been that way as for as long as I can remember. But why?

I strain for clues and get flashes of a horrifying vision: *I was swimming freestyle along the surface of the ocean, all alone and oblivious to the fact that beneath me, in the dark depths, a mouth of razor-sharp daggers was barreling up, a shark the size of a boat heading straight for...* me? No. That didn't happen to me. It's the poster for the movie *Jaws*.

I must have been four the first time I saw that film. My dad is a horror-movie writer by profession, so gory films were as much a part of my youth as Barbie dolls and Warner Bros. cartoons. Dad liked to use his six children as guinea pigs, studying the intensity of our horror recoil: the louder we screamed, the more his eyes sparkled with fatherly joy. We loved it. Having the shit scared out of me was as exciting as getting a new bike.

Since movie ratings weren't acknowledged in our household, at the video store I'd head straight for the covers that featured the most blood per square inch. I always paid for it later, though, after the lights went out.

'That won't be me,' I'd say, both horrified and delighted by the blood spray. 'I will *never* let that happen to me.' I developed a list of survival skills, vowing never to be like the morons who ended up killed in horror movies. My manual was simple: lock your doors, hide, be quiet, play dead, don't walk in the woods at night, don't do anything at night for that matter, and – above all else – *don't go in the water. Ever.*

As I watch the water off the side of the boat, too afraid to jump in, I acknowledge a sad fact: I'm phobic of deep water because of a famous animatronic shark.

'Now!' Ivan says, cuing me to untie the mooring and release it back into the water. It splashes down and we float free.

Catalina grows small behind us and already I miss our island escape. I walk to the bow, not nearly as anxious as I was the first time, and plant myself in the 'V' near the anchor to watch the water and reflect on the trip. I think about the people sitting in traffic on the mainland, commuting to boring jobs, and a curiosity expands around me – imagine living this life for a whole year. No alarm clocks. No crowded peak-hour buses. Just the peaceful sounds of the sea and all the time in the world.

As the yellow orb of civilisation grows larger, I surprise myself with a thought: *I don't want to go back to Australia yet.*

'Torre, are you crazy?' Anna says, slamming down her cup, sending her cappuccino foam into a slosh. As a psychology major, when Anna uses the word 'crazy', it bites. 'You've known each other for... what? Seven months? And now you're suddenly thinking of sailing around the world with him?'

'Seven and a half,' I say, shrieking above the clamor of the café. 'And no, I'm not going. I'm just saying that maybe I should, I dunno, consider it. Besides, it's not the whole world, it's just the Pacific Ocean.'

'*Just* the Pacific Ocean? Dude, that's only, like, the biggest ocean on the planet. What's wrong with you? Have you sucked down too many of those love bubbles floating around your head right now?' She pulls her light brown hair into a tight ponytail – something she does when she's tense.

'I know. It's crazy. And that's why I'm probably not going to go.' I roll pieces of tomato, buffalo mozzarella, rocket and basil around in a pool of oil and balsamic, before stabbing it all with my fork. 'It just seems as through this amazing opportunity has landed in my lap. The tropics, the chance to go anywhere in the world, the adventure of a lifetime with a man who—'

'Might strangle you to death! Don't you remember Billy Zane in *Dead Calm*?'

'Ivan's not into murder, as far as I know.' I bite into my salad and balsamic drips down my lip. I quickly mop it up with my napkin, staining it brown-red.

'*As far as you know*. Exactly. The middle of nowhere isn't an ideal place to discover your Latin lover has a fondness for kitchen knives... and not because he loves to cook, you know what I'm saying?'

'You're disturbed,' I say. 'And you should know that I conclusively ruled out "psycho killer" when Ivan captured a cockroach from his apartment and let it out in the backyard. But thanks for your concern.'

Anna pushes a fork around in the last few bites of her goat cheese and caramelised onion tart, stalling for a moment while she works up a new angle. 'You'll be stuck on a boat together day and night,' she says. 'You'll get cabin fever. That's what happens when people are locked up in small, confined spaces. They go nuts and stab each other.'

'I love small, cozy spaces. All that time to read, draw and daydream is my idea of heaven. And with Ivan there too, I won't get lonely.'

Anna pushes her plate away, looking appalled. 'Ugh! Torre! Listen to me. I totally sound like a mum. Did you tell your parents you're considering this?'

'Yes. Dad's already telling people the story of how I might be sailing home on a yacht. He's beside himself. I know he'd be really proud of me if I did something like this.'

'I'm sure he's already super proud of you, Little Miss Intrepid.'

I shrug. 'I think he hoped I'd do something really impressive with my life. He wanted me to be like Scully from *The X-Files* –

you know, an FBI agent who goes around kicking paranormal arse for a living. It's kind of hard to be a kick-arse graphic designer.'

'Not true!' she rebuffs. 'Somebody needs to save the world from bad fonts and colour violations. You kick Bad Taste in the arse every day. Don't you *ever* underestimate that.'

'Yeah, well, thanks,' I say with a grin. 'But you have to understand, my dad writes for film and television. He mixes with stars. He's lunched with Tarantino. It's impossible not to feel stunted in his shadow.'

Anna gives me a sympathetic glance. 'And your mum? What does she say? Surely she's on my side?'

'Mum's nervous, but supportive. I sense that she doesn't want me to go, but her last e-mail said, "It's a great opportunity, and if you decide to go, I'll miss you, but I've always preferred to stick feathers on your wings rather than clip them off."'

'Aw, wow, that's terrific. *And totally fucking insane!* What the hell is wrong with your parents?'

'They're hippies. I was raised free-range style.'

'Clearly! If you were *my* duckling, I'd be shamelessly clipping your flap-happy wings right now.' Anna snips the air with scissor hands to punctuate her point. 'No kid of mine will be crossing oceans with strange men.'

I arch an eyebrow at her. 'You think Ivan is strange?'

'No,' she says, softening her tone. 'It's just… you spend all of your time with him and we never hang out. But jealousy aside, Ivan's lovely and he totally adores the pants off you. Any douche bag can see that.'

'I adore him too,' I say, my grin spreading to idiotic proportions.

'But, Torre, that doesn't mean that you won't end up strangling each other!' Anna gathers her hair back into an even tighter ponytail. 'Do I love my boyfriend? Yes. Do I daydream of running away on some grand adventure with him? Yes, I do. Would it be super fun to get hot and steamy together on a luxury cruise liner? Sure! Would I attempt to cross thousands of miles of stormy ocean with him on a thirty-two-foot floating coffin? *Fuck no!*' She sips her cappuccino, slams down the cup and looks away.

'Anna,' I say gently. 'You do remember that I'm leaving in a month anyway, right?'

She gives me a sad nod. 'Can't you stay another year with me? It seems like you just got here.'

'It *feels* like I just got here.'

She sighs. 'Torre, I don't want to lose you, but I can already tell by the foolish look on your face that you're going to be sailing home and to be honest, I'm worried. It's a dreamy idea, but you have to admit that it's a tiny little bit *batshit crazy*. And since you have nobody else here to advise you, I feel it's my job to tell you this.' She looks into my eyes with her intense psychologist's gaze. 'Torre. Don't do it.'

A COLOURFUL GUIDEBOOK on South Pacific sailing has appeared on Ivan's coffee table, most likely planted as a part of his scheme to win me over one picturesque image at a time. I'm not falling for it – I won't yield to such obvious measures. At least, not while he's watching.

Home from work an hour before Ivan, I sit with a steaming cup of tea and turn the pages slowly, taking in the images with wide eyes.

We've haven't yet discussed what will happen to our relationship if I decide not to go. Ivan's upcoming voyage is rarely addressed out loud. It's a sticky topic, so we sidestep it completely. Not once has he attempted to persuade me with words, but for months now, he's been planting sailing books around the house that feature images of impossibly beautiful destinations.

Plunging into the pages of these books, I study maps and distances to get a sense of timing. As I read up on practical advice, like what to pack and how many cans of food to take, the concept transforms from quixotic to feasible. Other people do this, I realise. It's possible.

I become deeply engrossed in descriptions from experienced sailors: *The cruising life will lead you to destinations where you won't be alone – whales and dolphins will keep you company. Paradise will be found in the tropical fruits and the abundant fish. Imagine the stories you can tell your grandchildren...*

I snap the book shut and push it away like it's infectious. Then I start imagining a conversation with my grown nephews and nieces. 'Aunty Torre was a graphic designer when she was younger,' I'd tell them, 'and I used to make brochures, websites and logos for corporate companies. And guess what? Aunty Torre *almost* sailed to paradise with a gorgeous Argentinean. Almost...' At that point, I'd no doubt drift into one of 'Crazy Aunt Torre's Spells' and wouldn't emerge from my vacant gaze until the late evening.

Damn you, nieces and nephews. Damn you, inspiring book. Damn you, Ivan and your little mousetraps left all over the house. I'm getting snapped in every one of them.

When he leaves on a business trip for a few days, I find a new book has appeared on the coffee table – a memoir. One page in, I'm hooked.

The book, *Maiden Voyage*, is about an eighteen-year-old girl named Tania Aebi who set off to circumnavigate the world. She departed from New York on a troublesome sailboat with no GPS and very little modern technology. She used celestial navigation to find her way, the tricky old-school system of taking measurements from the stars. Along the way, she endured almost every imaginable hardship, and despite luck not being on her side, she made it back to New York, completing a full solo circumnavigation – 27,000 miles in total.

I beam with vicarious happiness at the part where she gets back to New York and her dad says, 'You did it! You really did it! I'm so proud of you.'

I imagine my own dad saying those words, and the thought brings tears to my eyes.

IVAN WALKS IN the door wearing his suit. He puts down his travel bag and wraps his arms around me. He smells of plane upholstery. Over the last few months, as he's been finalising a complicated IT project, late nights have become the norm. Sometimes he's up until 3 a.m., resolving critical glitches over the phone. Though he's always energetic when we're together, he can't conceal his exhaustion – his eyes are underscored with dark circles, his skin is pale and waxy, and he drifts off into dazes for minutes at a time.

'How was your trip?' I ask.

'Work,' he says with a dismal shrug. 'How are you?'

'Does your boat have a full keel?' I say.

'Um... what?'

'I read that a full keel is best for ocean conditions. Does your boat have one?'

'She has a three-quarter keel, which means she's a little lighter but still strong and... wait... how—'

'Do you have a sextant? For celestial navigation, in case the GPS fails?'

'No, I'll have backup GPSs. I can get one, though. Why are you—'

'What about a wind vane? Does your boat have one? And what about the engine? What horsepower is it?'

'Okay, wait, where did you learn about all this stuff?'

I stop short in my frenzy of questions. 'I read Tania Aebi's book.'

'You read the whole book already?'

I nod.

'Wow! So you liked it, then?'

'Loved it. It was so inspiring. I can't believe she did that in her crappy little boat with an engine that kept breaking. And she didn't even have a GPS.'

'I know,' he says, smiling wide. 'I know, I know.' His tired expression has been replaced by elation.

'And when she arrived in the islands after so many days at sea... I loved that part. And the part about all the whales and dolphins and sea life she spotted along the way.'

'Exactly. Now you know why I'm doing this trip.'

'I get it. I totally get it. And... it got me thinking,' I say.

Ivan freezes on the spot and waits for me to continue.

'If eighteen-year-old Tania could do it, well, maybe...' I pause, unsure of where I'm going with this stream of thought. 'I don't know... I'm not saying... it's just, well, Tania Aebi didn't really know how to sail a boat. She didn't know how to navigate. She was scared and seasick. But she did it anyway. She was just an average girl like me and then she sailed the whole world on her own. Even though she had it hard, she still loved it.'

'Exactly.'

'Her experiences sound so incredible: arriving in new countries, the friendships with other sailors, the love affair with the boat and the ocean. I never even knew that world existed, the life of a cruiser, a sea nomad, an island drifter. It would be life-changing.'

'Yes. Yes!'

'And we'd get to be close to nature and make our own power. It's environmental. I like that. I'd get home to Australia one year later than I planned, which isn't too bad. So it made me think that maybe I'm just being a big wimp and really, if I push myself outside my comfort zone, maybe – and I mean *maybe* – I can go with you.'

'Baby,' he says, swooping me into his arms. 'That is totally awesome. *Te quiero*. I love you so much.'

'But wait,' I say, pulling away, 'I have to learn to sail first and see if I like it. I want to learn as much as possible: theory, mechanics, safety – all the ins and outs of sailboats. I want to feel prepared.'

'Of course. There's a sailing school in the marina. We can book you in there. They have small, basic sailboats that are perfect for learning on.'

'Okay. So I can come and live on the boat with you and help you prepare, and if it doesn't work out, well…'

'No problem,' he says, lacing his fingers into mine.

'One year on the ocean?'

'Well, more like eight months at sea. We'll prepare the boat at the start of next year, get going by early April and be in Australia by October or November.'

'You'll move to Australia with me?'

'Of course.' He pulls me into a deep kiss and I want to surrender and give in to him, but my head is charged with anxiety. Maybe this is an ill-conceived fantasy? Maybe Anna was right? A young girl gets whisked away by a romantic Latin man into tropical island bliss? That isn't how real-life stories unfold. I pull back from him and turn serious. 'Ivan? What if the boat sinks?'

'I told you, we'd push the button on the EPIRB and get in the life raft and—'

'No, what if something happens and what if we… die?'

He looks directly at me and, without pause, he says, 'Some people die of old age without ever having lived their dreams. Some people die without ever having loved. That's tragic. We'll both die someday, that's a guarantee. If something happens on the ocean, we'll die as two people in love who are living a remarkable adventure. That's a good way to die.'

With that, I nod, fall quiet, and surrender.

I PULL THE APARTMENT DOOR shut and we pause for a quiet goodbye to San Francisco, my incredible home for the last eleven months. After quitting our jobs and selling all the furniture, we're bound for our new home with no postal address: a floating vessel in Marina del Rey. For the next three months, we'll be living on the boat in Los Angeles as we ready ourselves for the big journey ahead. If all goes according to plan, we'll throw the docklines and sail away a month before my twenty-sixth birthday in May.

The car is stuffed with all of our possessions and there's only just enough room left for a coffee in the cup holder. Even with my seat so far forward that my knees are mashed up against the glove box, the car's cargo space is too small to accommodate everything. I carry two cartons to the street corner and reassure myself that the abandoned clothes and shoes will offer a nice surprise to the next passerby with a fondness for boho-glam vintage fashion. *I won't be needing all that stuff in the islands anyway,* I remind myself.

My life of friends, career, dinner parties, shopping, cafés, hairdressers and twice-daily skin-care regimens has been abandoned to accompany a man I met in a bar nine months ago to a world of salt water, storms, seasickness and sunburn. Leaving my job was easy, since the work had never gained momentum, and getting paid to google random topics on a full-time basis was no longer cute. But saying goodbye to Anna was hard, if inevitable. She still thinks I'm completely crazy, and maybe she's right.

To soothe my worry, I remember my chat with Grandma.

Just before I met Ivan, I was visiting my eighty-three-year-old grandma at her home in Oceanside, California. We sat at her dining table and I opened up about life's disappointments. 'Is this what life is, Grandma?' I asked. 'I've been focused on my career since I was sixteen. High school, university, job after job. Isn't there something more?'

'Now listen, honey,' she said. 'Here's what I'd suggest.' She lowered her voice and became serious, like she was about to hand down the secret to life, and I leaned in close, a listening ear turned toward her.

'Honey, you should be with a Latin man, at least once.'

I snapped my head back in shock.

'They make incredible lovers, Torre,' she said, with her head nodding in agreement with herself. 'They're very passionate – not just in sex, but also in life.'

That's it, Grandma? That's your great secret to life?

I don't know why I was surprised to hear this from Grandma. She's always had a thing for Mexican men. From the time we were little, Grandma has sent me and my sisters punctual birthday cards that feature Mexican men lying naked on tropical beaches. *'Happy eighth birthday, my darling Granddaughter. Here's a picture of a dark-skinned, mustached man and his cute butt!'* Even though I knew what to expect, I always got a jolt of surprise each birthday when I pulled her greeting cards out of their envelopes. The funniest part was, Grandma's cards were home-crafted, which meant she'd taken the time to carefully scissor the pictures from magazines before découpaging them onto folded white cards.

Her fixation started over thirty years ago when she began a hot affair while on a vacation in Mazatlán with a Mexican man twenty years her junior. For nine years, she kept up the affair, flying from San Diego to Mazatlán to rendezvous with her Latino lover. She eventually followed her heart and leapt without a parachute, moving south of the border for a full-time love affair, leaving behind her country, her culture and her four grown children.

After five more years of good times south of the border, the relationship ended, but Grandma didn't return to the States; she stayed in Mazatlán for another twenty years and had relationships into her seventies with men less than half her age. Her last lover was thirty-five and 'A real looker!' she insists.

All these years later, back in the US, I sometimes catch Grandma flirting with her boyish Mexican gardener, batting her eyelashes and flattering the young man in flawless Spanish. The funny thing is, he eats it up in great spoonfuls. Eighty-three and she's still got it.

Her daughter, my mother, took a blind leap of her own. Mum flew across the Pacific at eighteen to follow her heart to a new world. My parents met playing in a band together in California and, at age twenty, Dad dreamed of a faraway place where he could get his writing career started, a place with wide-open spaces, good surfing, beer and – most importantly – a vast body of water between himself and his controlling mother. Forty years and six kids later, they still play music together in Australia.

Which is probably why my parents were so supportive when I told them about my plans to sail across the Pacific with a man they haven't even met. They know all about reckless pursuits for love. After all, it runs in the family. To my parents, life is about only one thing: the stories.

As Ivan and I get in the car, it starts to rain lightly. We drive out of the city and the windscreen wipers keep beat with the sensual voice of Norah Jones singing 'Come Away with Me' on the radio.

Yes, I think, as I leave San Francisco behind. *Yes, this is the right decision.*

FOUR

'BLOODY HELL, IVAN,' I say. 'Why can't we just agree on this?' I close the slats on the boat's companionway, which has been our front door for the last two weeks. I want to spare the resident seals and seagulls of Marina del Rey from our domestic dispute.

'Look,' he says. 'You're being unreasonable. I don't want to fight, but we're *not* going to sink in the middle of nowhere and end up in the life raft, so let's just drop it.'

The vinyl sofa squeaks as I sit down and it sticks uncomfortably to my sweaty skin. Ivan sits across from me, arms folded over his chest. I stare at him and begin to rip my nails off with my teeth. I can't believe that I'm discovering *now*, just over two months before our planned departure in early April, that Ivan's idea of 'safety insurance' for a year on the Pacific Ocean is food, water, a bilge full of beer and 365 condoms.

'Ivan, I don't understand why you're not factoring in the possibility that we might sink. Why not get a ditch kit just in case we *do* sink?'

'We won't sink,' he repeats.

'Argh! Ivan, *please* stop making that claim.'

I give my fingernails a break while I shuffle through a pile of research books and printouts scattered over the foldout table. I retrieve a book – a guide to sailboat cruising – and start flicking pages, looking for information to validate my argument.

Before we began getting *Amazing Grace* ready for her big trip, I thought preparing the boat was a matter of stocking supplies and breaking a bottle of celebratory champagne over the bow. That was before – much to Ivan's disgust – I began to gather every piece of ocean safety information I could get my clammy hands on.

I hold the open book in front of him and stab the page with my index finger. 'Look. It says here if the boat sinks, we'll need a kit for the life raft with water, food, an extra EPIRB, a watermaker, a handheld radio with batteries, dry clothes, fishing gear, flares and medical supplies. You know, stuff to help us *survive* if something happens and we end up in the life raft.'

I want him to make this easy and say, *Oh, I see, that sounds reasonable*. Instead, he glances down at the book for a microsecond and gives me a look as though I've just asked if I can take a pet elephant along for the ride.

Maybe I *am* being unreasonable? I've been researching a lot since we moved onto the boat. Advice comes in many forms and there is no shortage of it going around. Finding a voice of reason between the kamikaze-brave and those too afraid to leave the dock is the challenge. Conflicting opinions have me agonising around the clock, trying to decipher which items are essential and what's a superfluous safety measure, equivalent to, say, wearing kneepads and a helmet while riding public transportation.

'We have a life raft, right?' I say. 'So what good is a life raft if we don't have survival gear while we wait for rescue? Have a look at this book.' I fumble through my pile. 'This guy sank his boat and spent *seventy-six days* in his life raft before he was rescued. He had a full ditch kit with—'

'Think about the odds, though,' Ivan interrupts. 'We're not going to end up in the life raft and, if we do, we have an EPIRB.

We'll just push the distress button and it'll send a signal to the coast guard with our GPS position.'

'But what if they can't rescue us straightaway? Look at this book, *Rescue in the Pacific*. A convoy of boats got stuck in a force twelve weather bomb between New Zealand and Fiji and the rescuers couldn't get to everyone because limited resources meant—'

'I know the story. You found it on *my* bookshelf, remember? Do you think maybe you're reading too many ocean tragedy books?'

Probably, I think. But I'm feeling far too defensive to agree. 'No. Reading about tragedies is helpful. I'm learning what to do if things go wrong.'

'But things won't go wrong.'

I slide up into third gear, irritated by his lack of acknowledgement that bad things happen sometimes, like it or not. 'Ivan. There are a number of things that could go wrong. We could run into something. We could take on water from a broken seacock. Orcas could attack the boat and—'

'Orcas!' He throws his arms up and shakes his head at the ceiling.

'What? It happened to that family who were attacked in the Pacific. Whales sank their boat and they spent thirty-eight days in their life raft. I read it in this book.' I start turning pages rapidly, trying to find the evidence to show that I'm not being irrational.

'That was a freak occurrence,' he says. 'That won't happen to us.'

I slide into fourth gear and address him with slits for eyes. '*Ivan.* People who end up in life rafts do not, in fact, set that as a goal for themselves. They don't decide: "Oh, hey, great idea: Let's sink our boat. It will give us a chance to test the new life raft." They sink by mistake and then they survive because – and only because – they're prepared for the worst. Nobody *plans* to sink their boat. But guess what? Some do!' I fold my arms and rest my case, gloating at my flawless logic. That will convince the jury.

'Yeah, but we won't sink.'

'Bah! Ivan! That's your only argument? You have no more points to make? Only a psychic premonition?'

'We won't sink. I guarantee you.'

'Guarantee? Oh no, you did not. You can't guarantee that.'

'We won't sink – guaranteed.'

I'm in top gear now, pedal to metal. 'Well, what if we do, huh? Then you'll be like, "Oh, gee, you were right, baby, we should have packed warm clothes and a radio and survival food." But guess what? It will be too late because we'll be stranded and freezing and starving and then *we'll be bloody dead.*'

'Stop freaking out. I don't want to fight, okay? You're convinced that our boat will sink. Gracie's strong and I'll play it safe. We'll be okay. All these people you're reading about – they didn't have the modern gear we have. The guy in *Adrift*, for example, his EPIRB was inferior to ours. Our EPIRB signals to the coast guard, but the old EPIRBs would only send a signal to planes that happened to be flying overhead or ships in the area. That's why a ditch kit was necessary back then.'

'I know, it's just...' I take a breath and calm myself. 'I want to prepare for the worst, you know? Insurance.'

'But the thing about insurance is, where does it stop? We could get a second life raft, immersion suits in case the life rafts fail. We could paint the decks fluorescent orange to aid air rescue, spend a thousand dollars on another EPIRB, twenty thousand on a brand-new engine, hell... while we're at it, five hundred thousand on a steel boat. But we'll never leave.'

'So how do we know what we should get, then?'

'Probability management. Weighing up odds and making decisions based on that. We can take fifteen years to get the boat ready, spending more and more money. But I don't want to wait until retirement age. The odds of getting injured or dying before sixty – car crash, cancer, Armageddon, whatever – and never going: those odds scare me. That's why few people do this trip. They put off going to make their boat safer, better, newer, and time gets the best of them. You're right – shit *can* happen out there, but chances are that nothing will, and no matter what we do, we can't make a trip like this danger-free.'

'I know,' I say, 'I'm just…'

'I get it, you're scared. You don't need to be, though. We have a life raft, an EPIRB, an SSB radio and three GPSs. I have two sets of charts: one digital, one paper. We have a boat built to handle all oceans. Rather than prepare ourselves for sinking, we should prepare ourselves for floating. We can use that money for other things, like learning to scuba dive or renting cars to tour islands or going to restaurants or stocking up on art materials for you to paint. If we keep waiting until we feel safe, we'll never leave. We have to just go.'

'I know, but this book says that a ditch kit is "essential", which makes me think that—'

'You shouldn't worry. We're not going to sink. It's not going to happen.'

'Why do you keep saying that? You don't know that for sure.'

'We just won't.'

'But how do you know that?'

'*We just won't!*'

'You don't know that!'

After a long standoff, Ivan releases a tired breath. 'Okay. We'll get a ditch kit, if it makes you feel comfortable.'

He comes and sits beside me and pulls me into a make-up hug. I smile weakly and hug back, while I fix my eyes on the long checklist of tasks sitting before me on the table. Suddenly the ten weeks we have left before departure – to learn to sail, prepare for a major ocean voyage and iron out relationship differences – seems hopelessly insufficient.

MY INSTRUCTOR introduces himself as Gavin.

I tell Gavin that I'm setting off across the Pacific in eight weeks, and not only do I have no sailing experience, but if someone were to ask me which direction the wind was coming from, I would lick my finger, point it into the air and then declare I have no idea whatsoever.

'Let's see what we can do about that,' says Gavin, as he clips the buckle of an undersized flotation vest around his swollen midriff. A fold of belly peeps out from beneath his salmon-pink polo shirt to offer a hairy hello. He pulls a canvas sun hat over his last remaining tufts of hair, then fumbles through pockets on his cargo shorts to retrieve a fat stick of zinc, which he smudges over his nose, lips and capillary-covered cheeks. His face is already protected from the sun by an impressive awning of overgrown eyebrows.

He thrusts the zinc toward me and asks if I want some. I decline.

Gavin's accent is English, although I suspect it's put on. LA, after all, is a place where everyone and their dog is a superstar practicing for a role, even if only on a stage in their own minds. Gavin told me that, when he's not teaching, he dabbles in a little acting and scriptwriting, but he's yet to land his big break.

Floating on our small sailboat in the safety of the marina, I observe that today's conditions are ideal for learning: blue sky, light breeze and very little boating traffic on this weekday. I'm excited – this is going to be good. After three days of lessons with Gavin, I should be armed with a foundation of nautical knowledge to prepare me for crossing oceans.

'Okay. Ready about?' Gavin asks.

'Ready for what?' I say, but there's no time for him to reply. Gavin releases a rope, tugs another and pulls on a wooden stick. The sails swing to catch the breeze and we shoot off through the marina.

'Okay, your turn, Torre,' he says. 'Go ahead, take the tiller.'

'I'm sorry – what did you want me to do?' I say.

'The tiller. Take the tiller.'

'Um… what's a tiller?'

'The tiller, Torre! The thing that moves the rudder!'

'Rudder?' I hardly know the boat's elbows from its arsehole.

'Torre…' Gavin tries to rub out the etched lines on his forehead. Two minutes in and he's already skirting the edge of a nervous breakdown. His frustrated breath reveals all: Gavin wants to be in Hollywood delivering Oscar-winning dialogue alongside Meryl Streep. But Gavin is shit out of luck, stuck on a tiny wooden sailboat, teaching a beginner how to sail. This is going to be challenging for reasons other than those I had anticipated.

'The tiller, Torre, is the stick that controls the rudder. The rudder is a fin that controls the direction of the boat. Therefore, *the tiller* steers the boat, much like *the steering wheel* in your car. I assume you use that to help you drive without crashing? Or do you not know how to use a steering wheel either, Torre?' He sniggers through his nostrils, proud that he cracked a funny.

'Yes,' I reply, deadpan. I just located the boat's arsehole.

'Right-e-o, then. Now, take hold of it and do not let go, Torre. Rule number one: never let go of the tiller when you're captaining a boat. What is rule number one, Torre?'

'Never let go of the tiller when you're captaining a boat.'

He applauds. 'Excellent, Torre. Bravo. Good girl. Now, are you ready to take the tiller?'

Why yes. I'm ready to take it and shove it up the boat's arsehole. I swallow my frustration, grip the tiller and politely await instruction.

'Now, Torre, steer towards that buoy there with the seagull.'

I pull the tiller toward the buoy, working it like a steering wheel, but the boat turns the wrong way.

'Torre, what are you doing? Where are you going? I said *towards* the buoy, you silly girl! Where are you taking us? To the rocks? Torre, do you want us to hit the rocks?'

Not us. You. I want you *to hit the rocks.* I tighten my lips.

With no help from Gavin, I figure out that the tiller moves counterintuitively – opposite to a steering wheel. I fix my mistake and put us back on course.

Crisis over, Gavin.

'Okay, right,' he says. 'Torre, winch the jib sheet and secure it to the cleat.'

What part of 'I don't know anything about sailing' did you not understand, you miserable, washed-up... I bite my lips closed. Instead of back-talking, I regress to what I'm best at: feeling ashamed of myself. 'I'm sorry, I don't... really know what you're talking about. I literally know nothing about boats.'

He goes quiet for a long time, then locates his Zen and pulls himself together. 'The jib is the sail at the front of the boat. The winch is this metal thing here. You use it to help wind in the ropes by wrapping the rope around it clockwise two times and using this handle here – the winch handle – to twist the winch and draw in the rope. The cleat is here. It ties off the rope once you're done tightening it. Do-you-understand-that-Torre?'

Yes-now-that-you-are-actually-teaching-me-I-do. I clench my jaw and nod.

'Right-e-o, great, excellent, ready then?'

'Yes.'

He cups his hand to his hairy left ear. 'I said, are you ready, Torre? With a little enthusiasm, please!'

'YES.'

'Excellent. Bravo, Torre. Now, steer to starboard and bring the boat upwind. When the sails luff, make fast the sheets for beam reach, and don't forget to say "helms-alee" to communicate your intent to tack. Got that?'

DAY TWO. Gavin sits me down in the classroom for a theory lesson. He pops a video into an ancient TV setup.

'*Bonjour*, Torre,' he says, today a Frenchman. 'I'm going to play this tape on dealing with a man overboard. It is *très important*, especially if you really are planning to sail to the South Pacific like you think you are, maybe even the most important thing you need to know about sailing, so… *attention, s'il vous plaît!*'

He hits play.

Despite being in the movie-making hub of the world, the sailing school has failed to update its instructional tapes since 1972. The video stars men and women who, it seems, have been plucked off the set of a porn movie prior to shooting *Man Overboard Rescue Techniques 101*. Dense mustaches and terry cloth shorts are *à la mode* in this production. With the way this film is going, I'm expecting a Pamela-and-Tommy-style game of hide-the-sausage on the yacht to begin.

When the film ends, I realise in a panic that I've failed to absorb the steps for rescue. I hope I never have to explain this to a drowning Ivan. It just didn't make sense: large group of friends go day-sailing, man falls overboard in perfect weather, narrator suggests that one person watches the guy in the water, one releases the sails, one starts the engine and the fifth passenger steers the boat toward the victim. Then the group of muscles all pitch in as a team to lug the wet body (who is no worse off, apart from his wet mustache and soiled terry cloth shorts) back on board.

What about us? I wonder. How would this work with only two people?

'So did you like that, Torre?' Gavin says, snapping me out of worried thought. 'Do you have any questions? No? Okay. Please open your study book to page—'

'Wait, I have a question,' I say. 'What happens if there are only two people on the boat and one of them falls overboard?'

'*Je ne comprends pas.* What do you mean? You just employ steps one to eight as outlined! Were you not watching, Torre?'

'But… the video had five people aboard, each with an important role in the rescue. I'm going sailing with one other person, so if he falls, or if I fall… well, none of that advice applies to us. Plus, the video was shot on a calm day, but most likely someone would fall overboard in bad weather, and—'

'To tell you the truth,' Gavin says, dropping his voice low and into a regular American accent, 'if someone goes overboard, chances are it'll be at night or in a storm, and there's really only one thing to remember to do… wave goodbye.' He looks around to double-check that we're alone. 'Let me give it to you straight, Torre. Everything in that ancient video is bullshit. It's only relevant if you're with a large group of experienced sailors on a windless day… on a goddamn lake.'

ON DAY THREE, I feel immense pressure to absorb everything I haven't already learned in order to feel confident sailing the world's largest ocean. Which is, still, pretty much everything.

'Okay, Torre, let's begin,' Gavin says, once again English. 'Head out into the marina and we'll do some tacking. You *do* know what tacking is, don't you?'

'Yes,' I lie, trying to avoid provoking one of his mood swings.

'Excellent, Torre, excellent. Let's get to it, shall we?'

Gavin steers the boat out of the slip, along the rows of docks toward the open space of the main channel. He breaks into friendly chitchat. 'Look at you out here in the marina, learning to sail. I am impressed. I must say, I'm quite honoured to be teaching you. It's not often an older man like me gets the opportunity to teach a nice-looking young girl such as yourself.'

'Oh, thanks,' I say. I could have sworn he despised me.

'You're an attractive female, has anyone ever told you that? And you're clever too – now that is a rare combination indeed.'

He looks right at me and draws his lips back. Is that... a smile? Gavin is getting creepy. I look around for the closest place to swim, if it should come to that. I notice a luxury yacht a hundred feet or so in front of us, parked on the edge of a dock.

'I'm used to teaching men,' Gavin continues. 'It isn't often I get to teach a female, such as yourself. A fine, attractive, young female like you, Torre. This is a very special occasion for me. Very special indeed.'

I wonder how cold the water is. Could I just jump in and swim away? I know Gavin doesn't have the resources to hoist up a *female* overboard.

'Not many females learn to sail, you know, Torre. I don't get much time out here with females.'

I notice the yacht ahead has become a wall of fibreglass. We're heading straight for it. Gavin doesn't notice because his eyes are fixed lasciviously on my legs.

'Um, hey, Gavin?' I say, pointing to the wall ahead.

'You see, Torre, most females are not interested in sailing.'

'Hey – Gavin?'

'But you, Torre, you're something dif—'

'HEY, GAV!' I shout, snapping my fingers in his face. 'We're about to hit something!'

'Oh, golly,' he says, yanking the tiller, which has been sitting impotently in his hand, breaking rule number one. 'Oh dear.'

I flinch, waiting for collision with the superyacht. Gavin fumbles fast with ropes and we swing away just in time, missing the boat by a few feet.

'That was close,' Gavin says, laughing nervously.

'Sure was, Gav,' I say. 'I think you better let me out here.'

I WALK BACK through the marina with my eyes on the wooden dock. The time we have to prepare for this voyage seems to be slipping between the planks. It's mid-February already, and Ivan was hoping to set off at the beginning of April.

I climb onto the boat to find Ivan in the cockpit drinking maté and picking at a plate of salami and crackers. I flop down on a cushion and tell him about my day.

'Forget sailing school,' he says. 'I'll teach you.'

I sit upright. 'Now?'

'Sure, if you want.'

We begin to get our floating house ready for her other function: sailing. Working silently, we pull off canvas covers, prepare ropes and dress for the occasion. I strap on fingerless leather gloves and deck shoes and I pull my hair into a ponytail just as Ivan reverses the boat from the slip.

'Okay, first thing we do is get the mainsail up,' he says. 'Once we hit the breakwater, the swell will pick up and it'll become a little rough, so it's better to get it up now while we're in the marina. Now, take this rope here, wrap it clockwise around the winch and crank it in.'

I take the rope and start wrapping. At least I know what a winch is.

'Okay, great. Now turn the winch handle. It'll start to bring the mainsail up.'

I do as he says, making broad circles with the handle, pushing against strong resistance. The sail sluggishly stirs from its folded pile, so I speed up the pace. I find a rhythm and block out the pain developing in my shoulder.

After five minutes, I'm breaking out in a sweat. I crane my neck and see the mainsail is only four feet from its starting point. The top of the mast is an unfathomable fifty feet away. I lower my head and get back to work.

Thirty minutes later, as the sail nears the top, I'm ready for a nap. If I had been blindfolded, I would assume I'd just hoisted a dead horse forty-nine feet into the air. I'm prematurely victorious. 'I did it!'

'Not quite,' Ivan says. 'Almost there. The last few feet are the most challenging.'

Exhausted, I rest for a moment and then grip the handle with two palms. I position my feet and throw my full body weight into the turning. Each strained pump seems to have no effect whatsoever on the sail.

I throw my body against the winch handle. I'm grunting now. Yelling. I'm straining muscles that I didn't know existed. I push. I shove. I body slam. I give it everything I've got because I can do this. I *will* lift that mainsail. I *will* sail this old boat. I *can* cross oceans because I'm strong and brave and—

'It's jammed,' I say, throwing my arms up in defeat.

'Okay, no problem. I'll finish it off.'

Ivan positions his legs wide and arches his back and locks his arms as he begins working the handle as though he's pulling oars on a rowboat lodged in mud. He goes into a pumping frenzy, turning the handle with his entire body and his muscles protrude from calf to forehead. At the gym, Ivan lifts two or three times the weight I do, but even with his toned muscles, the sail's climb to the top of the mast is slow and painful.

'Done,' he says, brushing his hands off as though our effort was a walk in the park. 'Okay, now for the jib sail,' he says with a clap.

I'm ecstatic to find that the sail at the front of the boat, the jib, rolls out like a rug. Our two trimmed sails cup the breeze and we slip effortlessly along the calm expanse of the marina, powered by the elements.

But the tranquility doesn't last. As the boat rounds the breakwater, the wind picks up and knocks us into a steep lean. Waves thrust our little fibreglass boat to and fro, gathering us up in swollen crests before casting us aside. The boat staggers to stay upright.

I notice a nagging discomfort. Nausea? No, it's far too soon for that. I'm nervous, that's all.

'Okay,' Ivan says, raising his voice above the wind. 'Say we want to go in that direction over there. The wind is coming from the northwest. That means—'

'Wait. I'm lost already. Northwest?'

'See the wind gauge at the top of the mast? See where the arrow is pointing? Now look at the compass here. See? Northwest.'

'Got it.'

'All right, so if we want to go south, we'll be best off trimming the sails to a *broad reach*, which is...' Ivan pauses to inspect my face. 'Are you okay? You've turned grey.'

'I'm not sure.'

'It's a little rough out here today, sorry. It's only seventeen knots, but the waves are bigger than I thought they'd be. They must be travelling from a rough weather system because the troughs are long and the peaks are quite high, so—'

'*Shhh*. Don't talk about peaks. Or troughs. Can't think about... Need to... stop thinking about...' I close my eyes to shut out the dizziness.

'Watch the horizon,' he says. 'You'll feel better.'

My eyes try to grab hold of the horizon, but the damn thing keeps lurching. 'Maybe if I lie down...' I climb my way down belowdecks to relax on the sofa, but the garish orange hue of the vinyl settee makes me break into a sweat. Saliva gathers in my mouth and nausea rolls around my body with peaks and troughs, *rise, fall, rise...*

I yank open the bathroom door and lift the toilet lid just in time.

Ivan knocks on the door. 'You okay in there? I'll turn the boat around.'

'Sick' is all I can manage between gags.

I feel the waves change direction beneath us as Ivan swings back to the marina, which is less than a mile away.

We turn the corner of the breakwater and the seas flatten. I hear the squawk of gulls and the clank of boats in their slips. My nausea settles and I'm flooded with a deep affection for land.

I wipe my tears, wash out my mouth and swallow the burning taste in my throat, feeling somewhat less inspired about this whole sailing idea than I was an hour ago.

In the cockpit, Ivan manoeuvres the boat back into the slip. 'Sorry,' he says. 'We'll try again another day.'

'ANOTHER DAY' hasn't yet arrived, even though we're now well into March.

We've lived at the marina for ten weeks, working ten-hour days, seven days a week to get everything done. We get up early. We drill, hammer, sand, polish, varnish, clean and stock. We drive around LA collecting equipment, loading up carts full of nautical gear, living essentials and spares. The work is never-ending because the boat is an aged lady who needs a full-body tune-up before she can be deemed fit for the marathon of the Pacific.

When the sky gets dark and we lose our light, we head to the gym for some weight training. I pump iron to build muscles so that when we hit the open sea, I can improve my chances of lifting the dead horse. We shower, walk home and crash into bed, tired and aching.

Sometimes we muster the energy for love-making in our boxed-in bed that – with only a tiny space to work within – is like getting it on underneath a coffee table. There are many mid-passion cries of 'Ouch' and 'Could you move your elbow?' and 'You're on my hair.' Then we slip off into the kind of comatose slumber that follows a day of intense physical labour. The next morning, we wake up early and do the same thing all over again.

I love it.

After a sedentary life spent clicking a computer mouse all day, being physically active feels good. As it turns out, I have a talent for handiwork. If something needs to be drilled, hammered, puttied or varnished, I'm the gal for the job. Ivan, however, should not be left alone with a toolbox. If there's a hammer in his hand, equipment that was in fine condition before ends up irreparably mangled. He's an intelligent man, but handy he is not. That's why we hire professionals, like Graham.

Graham has been at large inside the hull of *Amazing Grace* for forty minutes. He strapped on a headlamp, opened a storage locker in the cockpit, climbed in and disappeared. I didn't know a full-sized man could fit in that space.

'Why did he go in there?' I ask Ivan. 'Our engine is inside the boat, right? Under the companionway stairs?'

Ivan nods, looking just as confused as I am.

We're outside watching the locker, waiting for Graham to emerge, when I see movement inside the boat. Graham has somehow shimmied through a crawlspace within the boat and he's now spilling out of the engine compartment like a birthing mammal, lubricated head to toe with black grease.

He bounces to his feet. 'Okay, do you want the good news or the bad news?'

I notice the logo on his breast pocket, which reads *Graham's Marine Mechanics* in a retro font. He looks more like a mad scientist than a mechanic. Wiry grey hair sticks out from his head as though it's been styled by a finger in an electrical socket.

'Good news,' Ivan sings.

The mechanic looks at his list and frowns. 'Oh, my mistake, there is no good news. Here's a list of issues with your engine.' He runs through his diagnosis, bullet-pointing each problem with a greasy fingerprint. 'You two need to spend in the vicinity of... oh, around eight thousand dollars to get this engine in shape for any kind of major ocean crossing. You could use a bilge alarm, a carbon monoxide alarm, an overheating alarm and brand-new gauges. Your exhaust hose is completely pooped. Out there, on the ocean, if your engine overheats, you know what will happen? Your engine will fail and you will die.'

I do a double take. Did he just say... 'die'?

'I sail to Mexico every year with my family,' Graham says. 'Always give the engine a major tune-up before we go. Wouldn't do it any other way. Why risk the lives of my family?'

I look over at Ivan and gulp.

'Frankly,' Graham continues, leaning in close, 'in my opinion, that engine of yours is unfit for the ocean. When did you say you were leaving?'

'About three weeks,' I say.

He throws his head back and laughs. 'I'm a sailor myself and if I was planning a trip across the Pacific, well... let me put it this way. Would I depart with an engine in this shape? No siree! I definitely would not. If you go out there with *this* engine, it'll surely fail and you will surely die.'

I shoot Ivan a pleading look: *For the love of everything holy, please pay this man money now!*

'Ah, excuse us,' Ivan says to Graham. He takes me to the bow for a time-out. 'This is absurd,' he tells me.

'I know! Our boat is screwed!'

'No, I mean the mechanic's advice is absurd. I'll replace the cracked exhaust tube, but as for eight thousand dollars in improvements? Bullshit. He's using scare tactics to get us to spend up. Even if our engine fails, so what? We're in a sailboat, not a plane. An engine failure doesn't mean instant death. We have sails. Why would we die?'

'Oh yeah, why would we die?' I reiterate.

'People sail around the world without engines all the time. He's a swindler.'

'I guess. But shouldn't we get some of these things done just in case?'

'We can't just keep making endless repairs to the boat. At some point, we just have to go.'

Ivan pays the man for his work, thanks him and sends him away with his long list of repairs trailing behind him.

'Why would we die?' I murmur to nobody in particular, but his warning has already stuck in my brain like a splinter.

'No. ABSOLUTELY NOT.' The doctor clicks her pen closed and sets it parallel to the list of medications we've requested for our voyage.

Panic hits when I realise what's going on here. We're leaving in less than two weeks and my doctor is refusing to cooperate. I glance down at my list, wondering if I'm being unreasonable: *prednisone, Adrenalin, Augmentin, Vicodin, Phenergan, lidocaine…*

'You want me to give you steroid hormones, local anesthesia and hypodermics?' she says, dumbfounded, as though I've come in here asking for some recreational morphine.

I'm doing my best to sound trustworthy, but my voice sounds pinched and distinctively crack-head-ish. 'Please. We *need* those drugs. We're going to be alone in the middle of the ocean.'

'Well, that's your choice. Travelling out of range of medical assistance is a risk you'll be choosing to take. You don't need to take that risk.'

This doctor isn't the only one to think so – it seems that everyone believes we're crazy. The belligerent old man who docks his boat next to us recently took time away from spit-shining his unused million-dollar yacht to tell Ivan he's got no idea what he's doing. 'You're going to end up in trouble out there, young man.' He pointed his bony finger in Ivan's face. 'You're putting yourself and your girlfriend in danger.'

The doctor clears her throat. 'Was there anything else today?' She adjusts her glasses and glares through them with a blank expression.

'I don't think you're understanding,' Ivan begins and I brace myself for an oncoming lecture. Born a persuasive leader, Ivan gets what he wants, when he wants it – or else. I've seen him working his job before, managing people, negotiating. His expression alone can make babies cry and dogs roll over and pee on themselves. He chomps down on 'no' and spits it out like chewing tobacco.

'I realise the request is unusual,' he continues. 'But Torre and I are planning a highly unconventional voyage, which will take us to remote destinations. It's *vital* that we have the means to be self-sufficient in the case of an emergency. We've just completed an eighty-hour Wilderness First Responder course at UCLA. All the medications we're requesting were sourced from reference books written by experienced sailors and wilderness medicine professionals.' He pulls out an earmarked book to show her.

'Look,' she says, appearing bored, 'as I already explained, I am uncomfortable prescribing these medications. It takes training to administer the drugs you're requesting and some of them can be very dangerous, like this one, for instance.' She points to an item on our list: *1 × 30 cc bottle of 1:1000 Adrenalin.* 'I would only ever prescribe this to someone who suffers from severe allergies. Do either you or Torre have a history of allergy to nuts, bee stings, dairy products, shellfish – anything?'

'No,' Ivan says.

'Right. So as I've said twice now, I'm uncomfortable prescribing you dangerous drugs you don't need.'

'Adrenalin, or epinephrine, is used to treat an anaphylactic attack,' Ivan says, reciting information we learned in our course. 'Anaphylactic shock can be brought on by asthma, food, medication or the venom from a bite or a sting. A severe reaction can cause the airway to swell, which could quickly lead to asphyxiation if not treated. A zero-point-three mil shot of Adrenalin in the thigh will open the airway back up. Is that correct?'

'Yes, but—'

'Now. I've never been stung by a jellyfish or any other ocean creature, so I don't know what kind of reaction I would have. What about you, Torre? Have you been stung by a jellyfish before?'

'No, never,' I say, my heart pounding from my own prolific supply of adrenaline.

'So we cannot say for certain if we're likely to have a reaction. Being in a remote place with no help or medicine available is *not* an ideal time to find out, wouldn't you agree?'

A small surge of panic rises in the doctor's eyes. 'Okay fine, I can prescribe the epinephrine but... I'm... I'm still uncomfortable prescribing all those other things you're asking for.'

'Well here's another *uncomfortable* situation,' Ivan says. 'We are alone in the middle of the ocean. Torre becomes injured. We're far from helicopter rescue. Helicopters travel two hundred miles from land, you see, so picture us somewhere in the twenty-four hundred unreachable miles between here and our first destination. If we put out a Mayday and summon a ship in the area, it could take a day or a week to get help. Until then, I would be her only available aid. Let's assume she's broken a bone, or has internal bleeding from a fall. Maybe she's developed appendicitis.' He turns to me. 'Have you had your appendix out, Torre?'

'Um, no,' I say, suddenly nervous.

'So,' Ivan continues, 'let's say I can reach a doctor over the satellite phone and get instructions on helping Torre or keeping her stable. It may not be ideal, but it's better than nothing, right? There are two scenarios: (A) with medication and no pain, or (B) without medication and with extreme pain. Whether she suffers or not – that is your choice.'

I swallow hard.

The doctor doesn't reply. She shifts on her seat and pushes her glasses up once. 'Fine,' she says, clicking her ballpoint pen.

As she writes our stack of prescriptions, I rub anxiously at my lower left abdomen. 'I think my appendix hurts,' I whisper to Ivan.

'Other side,' he reminds me.

IVAN KNOCKS ON the front door of his parents' apartment. Smells of barbecue make my stomach rumble. 'This will probably be our last dinner with Mum and Dad,' he says.

Ivan's parents live just fifteen minutes from the marina in Brentwood, so we stop by three times a week for a home-cooked Argentinean meal prepared by Ivan's dad – a man who cooks with such focused precision you'd think he was disarming a bomb.

The door swings open. Ivan's mother, Monica, pulls us each into violently affectionate hugs. '*Hola*, Ivan! *Hola*, Torre.' She rolls the '*rrrrrr*s' of my name in an elongated trill.

'Now, guys,' Monica says, ushering us into the apartment, her straight brown hair bouncing with excitement, 'for dinner, Jorge make for you steak and salad. Is okay? Are you hungry, *niños*?'

'Yes, very,' I say.

'*Goooooood*!' she says in singsong, peaking up to soprano with her enthusiasm. 'Very *goooooood*.'

Nothing seems to make Ivan's parents quite so happy as when we devour meat together. While sitting at their dinner table, I've tried everything from cow gland to blood sausage. I've forced down a mouthful of marinated cow tongue with an approving nod, disguising a gag at the texture of another animal's tongue stroking mine. The things you do to impress.

'*Hola, chicos,*' Jorge says, standing over a smoking grill with tongs in hand. '*¿Cómo están?* How are you?'

Monica walks into the kitchen and Jorge takes a break from his cooking to snap her in the backside with a tea towel. She squeals, '*Jor!*'

Ivan takes after his father in a lot of ways. Jorge's constant affection with Monica reminds me of Ivan and there's a distinct resemblance in their features too. Jorge has the striking looks of an actor, with his thick mane of salt-and-pepper hair and his brawny body. He has the same intense eyes as Ivan. Jorge doesn't speak a lot, but he listens carefully and chimes in when it's important. He talks the way he cooks: slowly selecting words to form precise sentences. His careful English is limiting, so most often he chooses to speak in Spanish, which Ivan translates for me. He doesn't offer the same service for his mother, though. Monica fills space with chatter, throwing the odd Spanish word in the mix. Ivan scorns her when she slips. 'Ma. It's not *"berenjena"*, it's "eggplant",' he snaps. 'Speak in English, otherwise Torre can't understand you.'

She puts her hands up defensively and says, 'Okay, okay, Ivan, don't bite my head off.'

There is a playful aggression between Ivan and his mother. They snag on almost every topic, bickering continually.

When we sit down at the table, Jorge serves up steaks that take up 85 percent of the plate, not so much cuts of steak as large portions of cow.

'Help yourself to salad,' Monica says, pointing to the bowl of lettuce, tomato and onion that looks ridiculously small alongside the steaks. 'So,' she continues. 'How is everything, guys?'

'Good,' Ivan says, short and closed like he often is with his mother.

'How is the boat?'

'Fine.'

'And what have you been doing?'

'Getting everything ready. We're really close to leaving, actually.'

Monica inhales sharply. 'My God, guys, how am I going to sleep at night? My son and my lovely Torre out there on the ocean. My God. Already my heart is going *pa-pomb pa-pomb*.' Her voice is thick with anguish.

Jorge clears his throat and speaks. His Spanish comes out stern, his expression is serious and his eyes are intense. I hear my name brought up. What is he saying?

I burn holes in the side of Ivan's face. *Translate! Translate!*

Ivan stares at his dad, his jaw clenching and unclenching. I've never seen him angry with his dad before.

'Ivan,' Jorge says, *'no tenés experiencia.'*

No experience? I've heard my name, then 'no experience.' Oh, shit, they're talking about me. It's true: I have no experience. I still don't know how to sail the boat. Ivan's parents must be confronting him about it. I slice off more steak than is comfortable to chew, anxiety-munching while I wait to understand what's going on.

Ivan takes off on a fast-paced rant in Spanish. '*¿Por qué me decís eso ahora? ¿Por qué decís eso a mí adelante de Torre?*'

I shrink down in my seat, humiliated to be the topic in an argument that I can't understand, mortified that Ivan's parents don't think I'm fit to sail. I wish they knew how hard I've been working on the boat. I want to hold up my hands for them to see the blisters and split nails and calluses. I've replaced my entire wardrobe with moisture-wicking fabrics and Gore-Tex, for crying out loud. Doesn't that show my commitment?

Monica joins in and the three of them are arguing at a million revs per minute. I watch the speedy dialogue exchange like I'm following the ball in a Chinese ping-pong match.

'*¿Qué quiere decir que no tengo experiencia? Estoy preparándome hace siete años.*' Ivan spits his words. I've never seen him this mad before.

I stay small in my chair at the dinner table, pink in the cheeks, eyes down on my plate, feeling as significant as that piece of dead cow.

After thirty minutes of tension, Ivan huffs and pushes his plate away. 'We have to go. Thanks for dinner.'

On the drive home, Ivan is fuming from the top of his head. He looks like a different person when he's mad: hollow eyes, tense lips and a stiff air around him that it seems could make plants wither.

'You guys were really intense with each other,' I say. 'What was that about?'

'Nothing.' He keeps staring out the windscreen, his jaw clenched.

'Please, tell me. Is it me? They think I'm not experienced enough, don't they? It's true, but I learn fast and—'

'That's not what they were saying. My parents adore you. It's me they have the problem with. They think…' He pauses for a long time and I wait, giving him time to open up. 'They're having doubts about our trip. They think *I'm* not experienced enough.'

I gulp quietly while I count the number of people on my fingers who have warned us of the danger we're heading into.

Ivan stews for a while and then finally erupts. 'Bullshit. Seven years of sailing experience, five years of planning, solo trips to Catalina, reading, studying routes and oceans, an Atlantic crossing and all this time spent in the marina getting the boat ready. We're a couple of days from leaving and *now* my parents are trying to tell me I'm not experienced enough? We've quit our jobs, moved aboard and spent thousands of dollars on equipment. We've got five thousand dollars' worth of food supplies in the boat and now they're all: "*No tenés experiencia, Ivan.*"'

'Don't worry,' I say, trying to play peacekeeper. 'They're probably just scared. I mean, what parent wouldn't be scared? You're taking a major risk, so—'

'But why did they have to say that in front of you? Shit, you're already worried enough as it is. So many people have given us crap about our trip, which is why I kept this a secret for five years. Do you know I didn't tell anyone about my plans – not friends, workmates, anyone – because I knew I'd get that kind of reaction? I didn't want to hear: "You're going to die" or "It's not safe" or "You're taking an unnecessary risk" or "You're not experienced enough".'

I gaze outside as Ivan releases steam. City lights zip past, glowing neon in every font, an orb of light drowning out the moon and stars.

'The only people I told were my parents and my brother,' he continues. 'All this time, they've said nothing. But now, right before we leave, right in front of you, they unload all their doubts. And you know what it makes me realise? They didn't think I would really do it. They've just been indulging it like, I don't know, like I've said I want to grow wings and fly to the moon or something. "Oh, that's wonderful, son, you fly to the moon." But now everything is ready to go and they're realising I'm dead serious about this. *Now* they're freaking out. If that is their opinion, why not tell me when I'm alone? Do you know how humiliating that was? To have my parents tell me I'm not experienced enough while you're sitting there?'

I put my hand on his knee, trying to calm him down. 'Ivan, I'm sure they're just—'

'"Why don't you get crew to go with you?" Mum said. "Somebody with more experience." Can you believe that?'

'Well, it's not an unreasonable suggestion. A crew person could help with—'

'No! I do not want crew on my boat! Our trip would be so different with a stranger aboard. Imagine: we couldn't talk, eat, kiss or make love without someone else knowing about it. No way. We don't even have a door on the bedroom.'

'Okay, okay,' I say, feeling that I've accidentally stumbled and fallen in the path of Ivan's steamroller. 'But she has a point, that the more people you have aboard, the safer it is out there.'

'No, that's not true! Here's a sickening story for you about a guy called Bison Dele who played for the Chicago Bulls. Dele and his girlfriend were sailing around French Polynesia with Dele's brother, Miles Dabord, plus a skipper. All the people aboard the boat were never seen again... except Dabord, the brother. Cops found the boat with the name painted over and patched-over bullet holes. The dude was probably jealous of his famous brother, you know? Wanted a piece of it? They got out on the ocean and the guy must've just gone psycho, killing everyone, throwing their bodies overboard, then patching up the holes and painting over the name like he could just cruise back into port and get away with it. Cops got him, though.'

I don't reply, I just listen to the rumble of the car's tyres on the road for a few quiet moments.

'I loved Bison Dele,' Ivan says, his anger softening.

I wait, feeling confused about where he's going with this.

'I followed his career. Totally related to the guy, you know? When he died, I felt like it was someone I knew, a friend who'd been killed. It really hit home, I guess. It didn't just feel like some oddball story you read in the news; it was real. And I remember thinking: *What a bullshit way to die*. If the ocean kills me, fair game. If some angry prick kills me... well, I'll never find out because I'll never get crew on my boat.'

'Okay, so just tell your parents what you told me.'

'I have. About a *billion* times. That's what irritates me so much. They don't listen. You know what else my mum said to me? "You can't go because you don't have storm experience." I mean – what? I asked her if she wanted me to chase down the next hurricane and point my boat into it. That's like telling someone they shouldn't go on a road trip until they have crash experience. *Oh yes, I ran my car into a brick wall at top speed, now I'm certified in Crashing 101.* Have you ever heard anything so insane?'

'No, I haven't,' I say, giving up my attempt at keeping peace.

'You prepare yourself by reading books, studying techniques, gearing up, getting a strong boat. You play it safe by doing what you can to avoid storms. You don't just sail your boat into mayhem just so you'll know for next time. You'll never feel a hundred percent ready. You just have to go.'

I wait until Ivan has spewed out all he has to say. I listen to the *tap tap* of the car's indicator as we wait to turn into the marina parking lot.

'Your parents love you, that's all,' I say. 'They're scared.'

Ivan doesn't reply. He parks the car and flicks the lights off.

We walk along the rows of boats and I notice the water off the dock is turbulent with fish scattering in all directions. We step up onto the starboard side of *Amazing Grace*. Ivan keys the padlock on the companionway, slides open the top hatch and removes the three planks of wood that slot together like a puzzle to keep the elements out of the boat. We climb down the stairs and into the darkness below, a space I can now navigate through freely without lights.

Ivan takes his clothes off and climbs up into our small bed and I crawl in beside him, covering us both with a blanket. I push open the square hatch above the bed and a breeze spirals in. We lie side by side in silence.

It's upsetting that Ivan is fighting with his parents now, right before we leave. Why can't they just suck it up and avoid confrontation, talk behind each other's backs like my family tends to do? Maybe it's not ideal, but it's so much easier than this.

Ivan's voice interrupts the silence. 'You're not... like... put off the whole trip, are you? By what everyone has been saying? By what my parents said?'

'Not any more than I usually am,' I say in jest, anticipating a laugh.

There is no laugh, just the sound of his quiet voice. 'It's just... of all the people, I thought, I don't know, I hoped my parents would support this trip.'

I hold him into a spoon and run my fingers down his arm until I hear his breathing turn heavy.

Once he's asleep, I roll over and enter a realm of nightmares. Gracie nosedives repeatedly into a turbulent liquid mountain range and a jagged rock juts up from nowhere, ripping a hole in our old boat. The engine has failed. We're going to die. 'Stop worrying! We'll be fine! Trust me!' Ivan snaps as the boat begins to go down.

My body jerks awake. I sit upright and bash my forehead against the hollow wood above the bed. Damn – I forgot about that. I rub my head and peer out the hatch into the bright morning sky.

Ivan is still sleeping, so I go outside to call Anna.

'I'm having nightmares,' I tell her, raising my voice above the sound of two seagulls fighting it out over a morsel of something rancid. Through the phone line, I hear the familiar sounds of traffic, hurried heels on the pavement and the hum of a big city. San Francisco is already a world away.

'I can't imagine why,' Anna says. 'I mean – it's not like you're attempting to cross a motherfucking ocean or anything.'

'Anna, I don't know how to sail. I tried to learn but my instructor was so weird, and then Ivan tried to teach me but I threw up even though the weather was only called "light winds" on the Beaufort Wind Scale. Not a storm, Anna. Not even a gale. *Light winds*. And then a mechanic said we're going to die if our engine fails and my doctor didn't want to give us medications because she thinks we're stupid. Then there was this old man with a bony finger and the mid-ocean appendicitis and Bison Dele's crazy brother and Ivan's parents, who—'

'Torre, stop!' Anna says, snapping me from my anxious rambling. 'Listen to me: you don't have to do this.'

'But then what?' I say, tearing up. 'Fly home?'

'That is an option, yes. You can ask Ivan if he'll change his plans. You shouldn't have to take this risk for love.'

I go quiet for a moment, stewing over the word *risk*. She's right – I don't have to take this risk. If I had to draw up a chart of my desires, *Stay on land* would be the largest pie slice, leaving a small, curious sliver to *Sail across the Pacific*. But ask him to sell the boat and give up his plans? I've seen what can happen to a person who doesn't pursue his dream. It broke down my last relationship in slow motion.

'Thanks, Anna,' I say, faking my tone to sound cheery. 'I'll be okay. I'm really excited, actually. I'm just nervous, that's all. I'll e-mail you later.'

ANGIE HAS BEEN HIRED to perform the final task on our to-do list. She's here to tighten the steel lines that secure the mast upright: the rigging. She hangs forty feet above our deck, acrobatically positioned as she tunes the rigging like a fine instrument. The defined muscles on her slender arms are slick with perspiration.

Angie has told us she's in her fifties, but you wouldn't know it by the way she looks – her blonde hair, her slim frame, her energy. Women of her age don't usually climb masts for a living. I watch her in awe, hoping that one day, I'll be half as courageous as she is.

She's crossed the Pacific before and she's been to the places we're going. When we tell her our plans, she lets out an enthusiastic yip, telling us how magical it will be, how many life-changing experiences we have ahead.

'I'm so jealous,' she says. 'You get to go to all my favorite places in the world. You'll have an absolutely amazing time out there.'

I'm absorbing her words, soaking up the rare positive reinforcement. Optimistic types like her are an endangered species. Not only is she an enabler, Angie has a magnetic presence that draws me in. She seems acutely conscious, as though she's wide awake while everyone else in the city of Los Angeles is half asleep. Is this what a life of daring adventure does to people?

'What date are you leaving?' she asks.

'Not sure exactly,' Ivan says, looking up the mast at her, shielding his eyes from the glare. 'Any day now. When we both feel ready, I guess.' He looks to me and a little wave of panic rolls through my gut.

Angie scales down the mast steps, jumps the last few feet and bounces with her knees. 'You'll never feel ready,' she says. 'There will always be more to do. If you wait until you feel completely ready, you'll never leave.'

I get a chill hearing Angie say the words that Ivan has been saying for months now.

She looks right at me. 'You'll never regret it. Just go.'

FIVE

I LOOK OVER MY SHOULDER to see if I can spot the distant outlines of the American continent. I can't. Everything safe and familiar is now in our wake. After months of planning, making the decision to undertake this came down to the simple task of stepping aboard and pushing off.

The serenity of the ocean calms my anxiety after waving goodbye to a small crowd of well-wishers on the dock. We've been travelling all day and the sky is fading into my first night at sea on a seven-day voyage south to Cabo San Lucas, Mexico. It's our maiden voyage to test the integrity of the boat, ourselves and each other, before we head into open ocean for a month-long passage.

Lights outline the Californian coast. Ivan guesses we're passing Oceanside, so I wave to my grandma, who is probably inside her home right now, dreaming about Latinos. The thought of Grandma being close by is comforting.

I snip the tags off my fire-engine-red Gore-Tex foul-weather overalls and slide them on over my thermals. A woolen beanie and fingerless gloves complete the fashionable fisherman's garb. I look down at my outfit, amazed at the transformation. Underneath this outfit is a body that's toned and tanned from outdoor work. Makeup is now pointless, and, since the boat struggles to power a hair dryer, my appearance is more natural than it has been in my adult life. I look fully prepared for a life at sea, but inside, nothing has changed. I'm still the same city girl, now dressed in a bizarre costume that would guarantee me a door prize at any nautical-themed party. Not that there are any of those nearby…

In his yellow overalls and woolens, with his unshaven face and dusky tan, Ivan looks like he's always lived a life at sea, pulling up nets of flapping fish, steering toward nowhere, answering to no one.

He moves confidently around the cockpit, tweaking hardware. The sails, the wind vane, the ropes and the tiller all need to balance to find a sweet spot that'll carry Gracie obediently forward through the night. The better she behaves, the more rest we both get. Once the boat is set to travel solo, I'll begin my first 'watch'. Hardly challenging, this involves staring at the horizon for three hours straight.

'Keep an eye on our course,' Ivan says, pointing to numbers on our bright GPS screen. 'Make sure our heading stays somewhere around one hundred and fifty degrees. Now, last thing, but most important…' he says as he points at the horizon, 'lights like those ones over there are cargo ships. They're our biggest hazard. If they seem like they're getting too close, wake me.'

'How close is "too close"?'

'See this here?' He points to a circular line on the radar. 'This is about eight miles away. If you see a dot move into this area here, it's in the danger zone. That's a hazard getting too close for comfort. Cargo ships travel at a speed of twenty-five knots; we move at five. Even if they see us, they can't slow down in time – they're going fast with a heavy load. You know how trucks take a long time to stop on the road? Trucks carry forty tons. Ships carry forty or fifty *thousand* tons, and stopping on water is like trying to stop a truck on black ice.'

'Don't worry, I'll wake you if I see them getting close.' *With a panicked scream, most likely!* I think.

'I'm going to switch the radar off to save power, but if you see a ship getting close, just turn it back on and check.'

'Out of curiosity,' I say, 'how would you do this if you were on your own?'

'I'd set an egg-timer to wake me up every fifteen minutes. Then I'd head way offshore as soon as possible. Ships are a huge threat when you're right off the coast, but once we're far offshore, we may not see a ship for weeks, even months. We can relax a bit more out there. We won't have to keep a rigorous watch because we'll be all alone.'

All alone, I think with a shudder.

'Just remember,' he adds as he steps down through the companionway toward bed, 'a ship as far away as the horizon can be on top of us in less than fifteen minutes. They move fast.'

I think about colliding with a big ship and envision a truck crushing an ant; not only would our guts squeeze out of our anuses, we'd also drown. I'm horrified by accounts I've read of cargo ship captains arriving at their destination port to find the mast of a sailing ship tangled up in their hardware, just as one might absently tread in dog poo and discover the mess only after walking on carpet.

'Captain, it appears we passed over another sailboat.'

'Darn it! Go and scrape the mess off!'

Keeping watch may be a little more challenging than I originally anticipated.

I stretch out in the cockpit and face the wake of our boat. I watch the sunset reflecting off the water, but my view is partially obscured by gear hanging from the steel railing: a yellow horseshoe lifesaver, a small barbecue, a thick steel pole that holds up the loaf-shaped radar antenna and a bunch of coiled ropes.

I check the horizon and then go down below to find some dinner in the fridge, which is just an icebox now that we're unplugged from shore power. Once the ice melts, we'll be living off long-life food: canned beans, pasta, noodles. I retrieve a piece of breaded, fried meat prepared for us by Ivan's dad before we left: Argentinean *milanesas*, eaten cold with a squeeze of lemon. It's a delicious, trouble-free dinner, and I'm thankful that I don't have to warm anything up on the stove right now.

Even though Ivan and his parents parted with unrest between them, it seems that these stacks of meat are an olive branch from them. Jorge would cook *milanesas* only on rare occasions. He'd invite us for dinner and keep us waiting until our stomachs were rumbling from the smell of meat marinating in garlic. He covered his *milanesas* recipe, secretly adding the herbs and spices, spying over his shoulder to make sure nobody was watching. When he finally served the dish, we'd eat until our waistbands were tight, then we'd pat our tummies and gasp, making Jorge smile in secret under his thick mustache. He always shows his love with food.

I look down in the deep space of the fridge. We must have thirty or forty individual *milanesas* in the icebox – lunch and dinner for most of our voyage south. That's a lot of love.

The sun has disappeared and the sky is a vignette of purple and black. The ocean merges into the darkness and I only know it's there because I can hear the sound of water slipping by. I wish I could flick on the high beams and survey our surroundings, instead of charging blindly into the darkness ahead.

We're so alone out here. Our only company is a menacing threat. Cruise ships are easy to identify because they're lit up like floating chandeliers but cargo ships and fishing vessels aren't quite so ostentatious, with only a few warning lights.

A star on the horizon seems to be growing brighter but I'm not sure if it's Venus or a cargo ship plowing toward us. I blink a few times, trying to figure it out, and then I remember the radar and switch it on.

'Scanning… please wait.' Dots begin to render on the screen, mapping themselves within the circles that radiate out from our position. I shine the torch on the screen to make out the shapes.

Oh no. There's a dot in our danger zone. Venus is a ship and she's less than eight miles away!

I dash inside and shake Ivan awake. 'A ship is—'

He springs from bed and flies on deck before I can finish my warning. He checks the radar and presses the ignition. The engine is a 1979 original and it makes itself known with a beastly roar of vibrations that travel throughout the boat, buzzing up my legs and into the roots of my teeth. Ivan kicks the throttle lever with his foot and we accelerate on a course to nowhere, running from the charging bull.

This doesn't seem real. Apparently, we're running away from an enormous vessel weighed down by a tonnage of shoes, cotton T-shirts or plastic bouncy balls in quantities that could flatten us. And I only know this because of little dots on a screen that look like Pac-Man food.

The chase ends with Ivan declaring we're out of danger. Our eight-mile safe zone is clear.

'Sorry for letting it get so close,' I say. 'I should've checked the radar sooner. I thought it was a star.'

He shrugs. 'Don't worry about it – it's a common mistake. When I was crossing the Atlantic, I saw a strange-looking light on the horizon. I was, like, "What the hell *is* that?" I woke the captain and he was stumped too. We finally worked it out. You know what it was? The moon rising. So, yeah, don't worry about it. Just do your best.'

Ivan goes back to bed, leaving me once again in charge of our lives by sorting the cargo ships from the celestial bodies.

It takes almost an hour for my heartbeat to slow. I listen to the waves and start to relax. Sitting in the darkness, I grow sleepy.

The gentle rocking of the boat and the white noise lapping of the water don't help my cause. I want to close my eyes and curl up but I don't want to get disemboweled by a tanker, so I begin to hum and slap my cheeks. I check the clock and note that time seems to be dragging like a sailboat caught in a cargo ship's hardware.

Something snaps me from my repose. The depth sounder is registering numbers. Weird. The depth sounder only registers up to four hundred feet. Any deeper and it displays dashes. We should be in two thousand feet out here, but right now it's reading forty-four feet. *Forty-four feet?*

My heartbeat spikes. Something's wrong. I can't see a thing. Are we heading toward a rock? An island? I think of the underwater volcanoes I've read about. They're impossible to chart on sea maps because they're always changing form. They spew lava below the depths, piling rock on rock until eventually the peak rises up above the surface.

'Ivan?' The rush of the surrounding water muffles my shaking voice.

This time there is no response. He can't hear me.

Are we floating over a sandbar? A shipping container? A log? A submarine? A pod of pissed-off orcas?

'Ivan!' I call, louder.

No reply – he's sleeping. Microseconds pass. The sounder is reading thirty-four feet... twenty-two feet... seven feet. *Six feet!* There's no time to get Ivan – *we're going to hit!*

I bring my shoulders to my ears, waiting for the crunching sound of collision. But I don't hear fibreglass splitting, I hear only splashing off the side of the boat. I turn my head toward the sound, but I can't make anything out in the dark water.

Eighty-seven feet.

A dramatic drop in depth – what's going on?

Sixteen feet.

My heart is going to burst a pipe.

I stand up on shaky knees to wake Ivan and, just then, a slick form propels out of the water behind the boat. The moonlight reveals a slippery dorsal fin, flukes, a bottlenose, a cheeky grin.

I get the joke: the depth sounder is reading off the backs of dolphins.

Wiping my clammy palms on my beanie, I watch the dolphins play, while my heart attempts to slow itself once again. I'm learning that night watch is a blend of deep meditative relaxation, punctuated by surprise defibrillator zaps.

When my three hours are up, I wake Ivan to switch shifts. I find him in bed with his eyes wide open, a schoolboy ready to start his first day. He springs up on deck and I melt into my pillow, letting the ocean's undulation rock me side to side. Through the hatch above my head, I see the moon swaying in a steady pendulum swing as *Amazing Grace* keeps her rhythm with the ocean.

SUN SHINES THROUGH the hatch, rousing me awake. Ivan was supposed to switch shifts with me at 4 a.m. but it's daylight now. I yawn into a stretch. *Oh, shit!* I think, cutting my stretch short. Where is Ivan?

I whistle as loud as I can. '*Wheee-wooooo.*'

'*Wheee-wooooo,*' I hear, confirming he's still aboard.

I don't even know how we got started with The Whistle; probably while trying to find each other in a supermarket. It became a special calling system between us, and one that I'm glad to have now on the boat.

I scoot myself from the bed and peer outside at Ivan. He doesn't see me, so I take a moment to watch him sitting in the cockpit drinking maté, scribbling into a journal. The pages of his notebook are crowded with his illegible scrawl as he etches his experience onto paper. Whatever he's writing, it must be happy because he pauses to stare out to the horizon with the contented face of a breeze-sniffing dog.

Despite a night of very little sleep, he looks like a man who has woken up from a deep rest. His blissed-out expression tells me he's in his element. Lightly tanned, he looks alive, healthy and unbelievably handsome. The suit-wearing, stressed-out project manager that I once knew is no longer with us.

'Morning,' I say, popping my head up the companionway.

He looks up from his journal and smiles. 'Good morning. You look so beautiful.'

'Thanks.' I touch my hair, which is pointing every which way but beautiful. 'I overslept. You were going to wake me at four.'

'Didn't need to. Never got sleepy.'

'You didn't sleep last night. Do you want me to keep watch now so you can rest?'

'Nope. I'm fine.'

Happy to leave him basking in his element, I go down below and climb back into my bed. When the boat is under way, our normal bed – the V-berth – becomes useless. Jammed into the bow, the V-berth runs headlong into the ocean waves, and when the boat lurches, so does everyone in the bed. When we're sailing, we sleep on the living-room sofas in two separate bunks. Canvas cloths tie to handholds on the roof, packaging us in our slim bunks to ensure we don't roll out when the boat tips. Once we're safely anchored, we remove the bedsheets, fold the canvas cloths under the settees and the bunks become sofas once again.

I lie nestled in my bunk, enjoying the dance of the boat beneath me, listening to the trickle of water against the hull. My stomach is settled and I'm beginning to wonder if living aboard in the marina slowly accustomed me to the motion. This whole sailing thing is turning out to be pretty relaxing.

The ocean's sway sedates me like an intravenous drug and when I wake, groggy from oversleeping, it's no longer a sunny morning but an overcast afternoon. I find Ivan in the cockpit, looking weary. His childlike energy has fizzled. 'You okay?' I ask.

'Just tired.'

'You do know you can wake me when you need a break?'

'Yeah, but you looked so peaceful sleeping.'

'I'll take over now, okay?'

He yawns and nods.

'Where are we?' I ask. 'Off San Diego?'

'No, Mexico.'

It's hard to believe that we've travelled out of the USA and into foreign territory without the obligatory burly federal officer with a gun on his hip and a stick up his butt. Everything looks just the same out here in the soup, where international borders are hidden somewhere among all the rolling blue. There's no land in sight, just cobalt hills from horizon to horizon. 'How far away is land?' I ask.

'Around fifty miles.'

Amazing Grace, at her fastest, travels about 100 to 120 miles a day. That means we've already travelled twelve hours away from land.

'We're pretty far offshore, aren't we?' I ask.

'Yeah, but we're safest out here. Hardly any shipping traffic and if the wind turns, we won't be blown ashore.'

'Safe' is not quite the term I would use to describe this. Ever since we lost sight of land, my muscles have been rock hard with tension. We're now one very long swim away from my grandma's house.

Ivan goes down below and leaves me in charge. I crane my neck and watch the clouds overhead. They're gathering themselves into folds of white and dark grey with wispy strands scattered high above.

Cirrus clouds. That's what our weather chart says. Below the image it reads: *A change in weather will occur within twenty-four hours.*

SIX

THERE'S NO DOUBT ABOUT IT: we're going to die. It's night and the wind is vile. The waves are reaching as high as our radar antenna, which must be twenty feet from sea level. We're staggering down each angry wave and my stomach keeps bottoming out.

Amazing Grace isn't so amazing right now, nor is she graceful. She's tumbling like she's hammered on salt water. Our life is in the hands of a drunken boat.

Boom! A wave collides with fibreglass. Who knew water could sound like a bomb explosion? These bombs are hitting every minute or two – a horrifying bang, followed by a sharp lurch sideways. My body rolls in my small bunk and I'm thankful for the canvas lip that keeps me from flying sideways.

Boom! I wait, trembling, praying for her to come back upright. The angle seems too steep. What is our tipping point, anyway? How far can we keel over before we tumble and get swallowed by the jet-black ocean?

Boom! Another wave-bomb hits – a clean uppercut to a staggering drunk. We're definitely going down. Somehow, she finds her way back upright but then overcompensates in the other direction.

Boom! A heavy crest comes down from above, washing the topsides with fire-hose pressure.

Ivan is out there.

'If someone goes over the side, there's really only one thing to remember to do... wave goodbye.'

I try to call for him, but my mouth is quivering and my whistle comes out flat and airy. I lick my lips and try again. *'Wheee-wooooo.'*

No reply. *He's been swept overboard!* My throat closes up in panic. *'Wheee-wooooo! Wheee-wooooo! Wheee-wooooo!'*

'Wheee-wooooo,' I hear faintly above the wind.

I breathe again. He's still on the boat.

My head is spinning and my innards are suspending and sloshing to the same rhythm as the ocean. I dash to the kitchen sink, knowing I won't make the toilet in time. Vomit comes out of my nose as well as my mouth this time but after hours of this rough weather, there is little left in my stomach by now, just warm, sour fluid that burns the soft tissue in my nostrils.

As the waves grow worse, so do my stomach convulsions. My inner ear cannot find balance on the shifting ground, so my brain has determined that the most probable cause is hallucination. This violent sickness is nothing but a vain attempt to flush out a phantom poison. If only I could get a memo to my inner ear: *Stop talking to my brain, you moron!*

'You okay?' Ivan yells above the scream of the wind.

I look up through our front door – the companionway – to spot Ivan in the cockpit just as he's washed over the head with a wave. He shakes it off and continues pulling at ropes. He shows no sign of fear, which strikes me as odd, since I can see an opaque black wave behind him that is twice his height. Every time the water gathers into a crest, it seems it will devour Ivan in one lick and swallow, but he doesn't look even a tiny bit nervous. *Amazing Grace* rides up to the peak, then comes tearing down the foamy side – a car without brakes.

I'm balancing myself with four limbs engaged, my hands gripping anything solid for stability. If I let go, I'll pinball around the boat. 'How much longer?' I ask.

'A long time. We're only two hundred and fifty miles away from Los Angeles. We're still five days from Cabo.'

I'm trapped in this floating coffin for *five more days*? I want to yell at him: '*THIS IS NOT "SUPREMELY AWESOME," IVAN! THIS IS NOT "A GOOD WAY TO DIE!"*' But I don't have the strength to yell and, besides, it's not his fault – I chose this.

The elevator plunges again. I grip the sink and heave so intensely I think I'm going to pee myself. I don't, though, so I have that to be thankful for at least. Thank you, O mighty powers, for sparing my underwear.

Heave.

I take that back. As if vomiting out of my nose wasn't already bad enough, the intense retching is now affecting my pelvic floor muscle control. 'Really?' I cry out to nobody. '*Really?*' I fear the next thing to squirt out of my body will be my large intestine.

I use the grab rails to climb my way through the galley toward bed, steadying my weight against the violence of the sea. I shed my underwear, find a new pair and tumble onto the bunk. My hands claw the sofa, gripping with every ounce of strength in an attempt to stabilise the boat with my muscles. It's a desperate attempt to force control on the situation – an unconscious reflex trigger – but it doesn't work.

Boom! We tip, and everything within the boat seems to suspend weightlessly for a moment, only to come crashing down as we collide with the trough. Gear explodes out of cupboards. The equipment I strapped down with careful, studied knots that I learned from books has spilled out all over the floor. My ropes are proving useless as items escape to waltz around in a psychotic dance choreographed by the sea. A cupboard door flings open and cans of food pop out to join the waltz. Three cans of food, a tube of sunscreen, an orange and a potted plant all dance to the same liquid rhythm. *Left, right, pause… back, left, smash! Left, forward, pause… right, left, smash!* Plant soil has scattered everywhere, but who cares about mess? We're going to die.

Our heavy toolbox, lashed to a corner in the salon underneath the foldout table, breaks out of its ropes to join in the fun. It slides across the floor and gains momentum on the downward slope of the waves. *Smash!* It collides with wood. It's full of metal tools and it must weigh sixty pounds, or perhaps several hundred with the momentum it's collecting on the downward slopes. I'm waiting to hear wood splinter as the toolbox charges obnoxiously into hollow teak at floor level. I can't move to tie it back down. I'm rigid with fear.

But something worse than the toolbox is on the loose. I can hear it banging above my head, up on deck. At the marina, we stashed two five-gallon jerry cans under the upturned dinghy, one full of water and one full of fuel.

Bad idea.

They're smashing around with the waves, leaking contents. I know this because I can smell fuel. Our deck is being doused with diesel. We're going to die – I know this for sure – but what I don't know is whether we'll burn or drown.

I put a pillow over my head to shut out the banging. There's so much noise. It's an orchestra of death. The wind is blasting through the rigging, resonating in the haunting pitch of a human shrill. There are voices: whispers, hums and well-rounded words. Packs of dogs are barking, but we're way offshore. Why can I hear barking dogs?

Then there's the eerie sound *inside* the boat. It's the wet, guttural moan of a man's voice. *'OH,'* he says. He seems close, as though his breathy words are being spoken right into my ear. '*HEY*,' I hear. But when I look up, nobody is there.

Wet with salt water, Ivan comes down below to check on me. He ties down the charging toolbox, the canned food and the potted plant. Kneeling beside me, he strokes my arm and asks if I'm okay. I'm surprised that Ivan hasn't lost patience with me. He not only manages the boat solo, but he also finds time to stroke my shaking body and soothe me with insistent claims that 'No, really, I promise you, we're not going to die.' He offers water and helps me drink from the bottle, lifts it high so I can suck from it like a dying animal.

'Sorry,' I say. I tremble uncontrollably as salty tears tumble down and soak my pillow.

'Why sorry?'

'I'm useless.'

'Don't be sorry. You're seasick.'

My eyes dash around, wide with terror. 'I can hear weird noises. Sounds I shouldn't be hearing.'

Ivan hesitates. 'So can I.'

'You can hear the dogs?'

'Dogs? No. I hear entire conversations in Spanish.' He speaks in a whisper as though 'they' might overhear him. We're both going crazy.

'*HEY*.'

'What?' Ivan says.

'That wasn't me,' I say.

'*YEAH*.'

'What'd you say?' I ask.

'Nothing.'

'*OH*.'

We linger in an uneasy stare at each other. At least we both heard the man this time. That means the sound is real and not in our heads. Doesn't it?

Spin! Spin! Spin! I run to the sink. I vomit water, still cold. Eight fast heaves. I go back to bed.

'Try to sleep,' Ivan says, popping a sickness pill from its foil wrapper to poke through my lips.

I chew. Berry flavouring dilutes the sour taste of bile. I close my eyes, wishing for sleep, but as another wave clocks us, the breathy voice of a ghost speaks in my ear and my eyes burst open with terror. My heart is trying to pound its way out of my chest and swim to land without me. Bastard abandoner.

Hours pass – an eternity of hell.

Smash, bang, bark, YEAH, spin, spin, spin.

THE MORNING LIGHT comes up. Ivan has spent the night in the cockpit, driving the boat and watching for ships. I feel nauseated and sore and terribly guilty for not helping out. What kind of first mate am I?

While Ivan mans the deck, I swaddle myself in sheets, fending off seasickness and fear with my best remedy: not moving. When I was a kid, afraid of the Boogieman, I would hide motionlessly under my bed covers for hours on end. Not much has changed since then. Out here, the ocean is my Boogieman and lying flat is my only defence. My inner four-year-old rationalises that if Ocean doesn't know I'm here, then Ocean can't kill me.

Ivan, however, is more alive than I've ever seen him. The ocean is his soul mate and he adores her wild, untamed beauty, her dangerous edge and the fact he has her all to himself for miles. She has managed to transform him: his skin is golden and the sun has put highlights in his blond hair. He's grown a rugged beard that accentuates his jaw and highlights the green tint of his eyes. Lean and sculpted, his muscles are defined and his shoulders have broadened from lifting the dead horse.

He comes down the companionway and kneels beside my bunk. 'Are you okay?'

'You must be so tired.'

'I'm fine. Don't worry, relax.' He strokes my soggy hair.

'I'm not a sailor. I'm a mess. I had no idea it would be like this.'

'Just rest, okay? I don't need help. I'm fine on my own.'

WHOA.

'Huh?' Ivan says.

'That wasn't me. It's Creepy Man.'

'Who?'

BAH.

'Him,' I say, pointing at thin air.

Ivan jumps up to inspect the source. He follows the noise around the boat, looking for Creepy Man.

HA.

Ivan goes to the kitchen and places his left ear into the sink. He waits.

RAH.

'It's the sinkhole,' Ivan declares.

The air in the plumbing is being forced up by waves, which pushes out wet notes that form single-syllable words.

OH, says Creepy Sink Man.

A wave bomb explodes and the boat dumps sharply. Our world tips on an angle for a few seconds. Ivan doesn't lose his serene face, even though I'm gripping his arm with my panicked claw.

'We're going to die!' I insist, once again.

He smiles softly. 'No, we're not. Everything is okay.'

'Everything is not okay. The waves are huge! The boat is going to roll!'

'No, it won't. It's just a little rough. This is normal. The waves are big, that's all. The sails are reefed and we're going slow. Don't worry. I'm playing it safe.'

'Are we in a storm?'

'No, a storm would be much worse than this.'

'It gets much worse than this?'

He shrugs helplessly. He can handle the weather but the burden of having a terrified person aboard is a heavy one. 'Is there anything you need?' he says. 'Water? Medicine? Tea? *Milanesas?*'

'Land,' I plead.

Ivan smiles. He thinks I'm kidding but how could I joke at a time like this?

'No, really. Can we head back to land?' I ask. 'Look at me.' I show him my convulsing fingers. 'Please.' My voice is a quivering whisper. *'I've never been so scared in my life.'*

'Okay,' he says, 'but we're way offshore and the closest coastal refuge is probably thirty hours away.'

'Thirty hours?'

He nods. 'Sorry.'

Outside, he pulls the boat off our course toward Cabo San Lucas and angles instead to the nearest refuge on the Mexican coastline. We're no longer running in the direction of the waves – we're now hitting them head-on and to the side. Worse, much worse.

Spin! Spin! Spin! Berry-flavoured water squirts out my nose and into the kitchen sink and I shed another pair of underpants.

Thirty more hours to go, I tell myself and then, when the vomiting eases, I break down into tears.

WE PULL INTO OUR REFUGE and the ocean's mayhem subsides. The boat levels out as she cuts through a wide stretch of protected water. I must look like a drowned rat with my mangy hair and skin that probably smells of the pheromones produced by animals who think they're about to die.

The land is a typical ochre-hued Mexican vista, with shrub-dotted hillsides in the hazy distance. A rusting factory dominates the shore and a weathered wall is painted with the words *Bienvenidos a Bahia Tortugas* – 'Welcome to Turtle Bay.' Everything is worn, peeling and sun-bleached. The only thing missing from this desolate town is tumbleweed.

The cove is empty, apart from two ill-fated ships lying sideways on the shore, decrepit, sand-buried hulls that once sought safety here but didn't find it. They left behind the carnage of their misfortune as an omen to other sailors. The sight sends chills from my scalp to my toes. Even here, we're not safe.

I scan the dusty town, wondering how I'm going to catch a bus out of here. But even if a regular bus service happens to run from this desolate place, I'm not sure it'll be wise for me to bus back to the US from here. A thought is knocking and I can't ignore it: like it or not, I'm going to have to stay aboard this thirty-two-foot death trap until we reach the nearest airport in Cabo San Lucas.

We're both weary, aching and bruised, but we can't rest yet because the boat needs to be pieced back together. Our home appears to have been overtaken by drunken teens at an open-house party.

Superstitious sailors consider plants aboard to be bad luck and, now, on my knees with a dustpan and broom, I can see why. My green pet, my landlubber mate, is scattered on the floor, his leaves wilted and brown from saltwater exposure. 'Sorry, little guy,' I tell him. 'You should've stayed on land. You and me both.'

I peel the sheets from the beds. They've been sitting balled up and wet for days, growing funky. I add them to the pile of clothes worn on passage, which are sour and in need of a heavy-duty wash – a task made challenging by our lack of modern appliances. I fill a five-gallon bucket with freshwater from a jerry can and use the old-school foot-stomping method to shift the dirt around a little, drowning everything in flower-scented fabric softeners. I notice there's one last fleck of crimson nail polish left on my big toe and I'm reminded of who I was only three months ago. As my scratched and bruised legs work the laundry in the bucket, that red bit of toenail seems absurd.

We string the wet laundry across the boat's rigging and leave it to either dry in the sun or blow off with the wind – whichever happens first. Seeing our sheets hanging from the lifelines makes me feel like a sailor, which fills me with pride. I watch my intimates fly in the breeze above my head: lacy flags of accomplishment.

Two Mexican men zip through the water in our direction on a skiff. I look left and right to confirm there are no other boats here – they're definitely heading straight for us.

'What do you think they want?' I ask Ivan.

He shrugs, looking edgy and nervous.

We are in a nowhere town, on somebody else's turf, and our only means of escape from danger is on a boat that travels slightly faster than a person walking a dachshund. I ponder our options for self-defence and come up with nothing.

'You have a gun, right?' my American Uncle Chuy asked before we set sail from Los Angeles.

'No,' I told him. 'We're not taking one. Innocent sailors sometimes get killed trying to defend themselves with a gun.'

'You'll need one in Mexico,' he said. 'Haven't you heard about them beheadings? Mexico ain't safe for you.'

I laughed him off, not sure if he was serious.

'What about all them pirates? Take one gun at least,' he insisted, as though just *one* doesn't really count as a lethal weapon. I sensed that he saw our sailing voyage as a legitimate excuse to open some boxes of ammo.

'There are no pirates in the South Pacific,' I said, repeating the answer to a question I'd once asked Ivan. 'But if someone boards our ship and threatens us, we'll give them what they want. Nothing we own is worth dying for. Pirates are robbers of the sea. They just want valuables. If we give them what they want, they'll probably leave us alone, but trying to shoot robbers with a handgun is asking for trouble, especially if the pirates have bazookas.'

He paused for a moment, considering my words. 'But what if you need to shoot a shark or something?'

Admittedly, this exact thought had occurred to me before but, either way, there was no point trying to reason with a man who has copies of *Shotgun Sports* magazine fanned on his coffee table.

Now, with two men speeding toward us, Uncle Chuy's words are echoing in my head. *Do people really get beheaded here?*

The men pull the throttle at the last second and the pointy end of their skiff turns just in time, sloshing water against *Amazing Grace* and causing a violent wake that sets us bouncing. They stand up and grab a hold of the teak rail of our boat. '*Hola*,' one of them says.

Ivan acts indifferent as he continues to do chores on deck. '*Hola. ¿Cómo está?*' he says.

The men launch into speedy Spanish. I can understand only the occasional word, but their tone is aggressive.

'*Nada, gracias*,' Ivan says, making no eye contact.

The men don't leave.

I hear the words *gasolina* and *agua* and I try to make sense of their words. Maybe they're going to douse us in gas and set us alight and then throw us in the water? That's silly. I'm being ridiculous... aren't I?

'*Nada, gracias*,' Ivan says. '*Despues, por favor.*'

The men continue and I hear the words I know again. *Gasolina, agua, taxi.* I hear Ivan say: '*Mañana.*'

Do what tomorrow? My head yanks back and forth between Ivan and the two men, as I try desperately to understand.

'*Nada, gracias*,' Ivan reiterates.

Whatever they want, they won't take no for an answer.

'*¿Gasolina, agua, lavado de ropa, taxi, servicios generales?*'

They're offering services. I relax.

'*Nada. Adios.*' Ivan turns his back on the men, and they give up and leave.

The VHF cuts in and I hear a new voice calling out to us: '*Amazing Grace, Amazing Grace, ¿gasolina, agua, taxi?*'

Now I understand their earlier aggression. With very few boats arriving in this desolate town, competition for business is fierce.

After the sun dries our laundry, we fold it and finish the housework. The boat is tidied, the washing is done and my mood is also scrubbed clean.

On freshly cleaned sheets, we collapse, finally reunited in our shared bed in the bow. Floating on calm water feels phenomenal. I guess that's the upside of living through hell.

'It's so nice here,' I say to Ivan, pointing around to our little desolate inlet, which after the debacle of the last twenty-four hours feels like the safest place on earth. 'Let's just stay forever?'

'We have to keep moving. Hurricane season starts in six weeks and we need to clear Mexico by then. Get rested. We'll leave for Cabo as soon as you're ready.'

'Can we at least stay a few days?' I ask, but there is no reply. Ivan is already comatose and snoring with such vigor, it seems he's trying to suck the universe into the back of his throat.

I lay awake, stewing over the voyage ahead. We're a four-day sail away from Cabo – our last landfall on the American continent before we begin our epic journey to French Polynesia. When we point the boat toward the South Pacific, we are going to reach the point of no return, with nothing in front of us for a month but the open sea. We'll be vulnerable to anything, from weeks without wind to hurricanes.

If this warm-up cruise is a preview of what's to come, then I'm screwed. What was supposed to be a 'quick sail down the coast' has turned into a traumatising odyssey, and we're not even halfway to Cabo yet.

I'm done with the waves, the vomiting and the masochistic sport of ocean sailing. I've seen myself in a new light and the image isn't pretty. I've been an incapacitated, twitchy ball of cowardly goo – hardly the brave, ocean-conquering sailor that I was in my fantasy. In fact, I'm as useless on the boat as a rusted-shut Swiss Army knife.

Why would I keep torturing myself with this? And where is the line between unreasonable fear and real, likely danger?

Suck it up and do this! I tell myself. *You're brave, you're strong, you can do it!*

But my attempts to cheer myself on are ridiculous. I need to face up to the truth: I can't do this. I don't *want* to do this. If we get to Cabo alive, I'm never going to make the mistake of stepping foot on a boat again.

Ever.

SEVEN

'WE MADE IT, BABY,' Ivan says, giving me a fist-pump, then a big hug as we round the spectacular rock formations of Cabo San Lucas, three weeks after departing Marina del Rey.

This eight-hundred-mile journey was supposed to take a week, but after long breaks in Turtle Bay and Magdalena Bay, where we ate fish tacos washed down with Pacifico beers and soaked in the sun to avoid the reality of our dilemma, we took *three weeks*. Now it's May and hurricane season begins in June. We have no time left for stalling, but I push this grim detail aside once again to enjoy the moment.

We made it! The realisation slams into me. I didn't think we would, but through hell and high water we're here. A feeling grows from the pit of my belly, a surge of something profound and unfamiliar: extreme pride. This is it – the mountaintop perspective, the big 'O' of my first adrenaline climax, and it feels amazing. I grin until my cheeks ache.

I devour the beauty of this crowded getaway. Jet skiers zip around in the bay. The beach is lined with luxury resorts and seaside bars bustling with drinkers. Vacationers dot the white sand, making the most of a cloudless sky. Never in my life have I been so grateful to arrive in a place packed with tourists wearing white sneakers and bum bags. What a contrast to where we've been for the last twenty-two days – I almost forgot that the world is neither an expanse of ocean nor a barren desert landscape.

Gliding through the bay, we pass two enormous cruise ships at anchor. I look up at the vertical wall of steel and get a true sense of what we've accomplished in our tiny boat.

'Look at this place. We sailed here!' I say.

I have a strong urge to get on a megaphone and shout to the crowds: *Hello, everybody, we're here! You don't need to worry about us any more! We defeated the ocean!* I want to jab the beach with a flag and declare it conquered. My erupting ego is expecting the sunbathers to throw down their John Grisham novels and break out into a round of applause. *I'd like a small celebration, please, nothing too extravagant, maybe some balloons, banners and a marching band.* Instead, the crowds continue to relax, not noticing us, despite my beaming aura of pride.

We've reached latitude 23° – the subtropics – and the weather has warmed up as if we have just passed through a door at the bay's entrance with a hanging sign reading *Subtropical Room: Kindly Close Door Behind You.*

Ivan carefully negotiates *Amazing Grace* through a peak-hour congestion of nautical traffic. Party boats overflow with bikinis and muscular bodies and only now does it occur to me that I haven't showered or brushed my hair in a long time. Do I even have pants on? I feel around to be sure that I do.

Ivan swings *Amazing Grace* into her snug slip and I leap over the lifelines to cleat the boat to shore. I stand tall and marvel at the feeling of being stationary. Ivan joins me on the dock and pulls me into a giant hug. '*Te quiero,*' he says. 'I'm so proud of you.'

I'm astonished. 'You are?'

'Of course I am. You did it.'

Despite witnessing me tucked into a cowardly ball; despite seeing me vomit up everything but my intestines; despite enduring

127

volumes of tears and snot showered over his neck and being asked more than fifty times if we're going to die, this man still loves me. But not only that, he's actually *proud of me*. He's a keeper.

We leave the boat and take off exploring. Handicraft stalls line the streets, flogging colourful wares. It's junk, but it's pretty, and it has me under a spell. I know I don't need a pair of maracas, a giant sombrero or a ukulele, but I'm drawn in like a bug to light, entranced by the sensory overload. I stop to fondle an image of the Virgin Mary in hologram mounted in a shell-collaged frame. I love the shamelessly kitschy way that Mexicans celebrate their religion.

We loiter around, listening to a soundtrack of business owners competing for our dollar. They pursue our trail, fanning handfuls of brochures, yelling, 'Honeymooners! Honeymooners! Come, come! Where you from? A fishing trip for your *hombre*, *señorita*? A romantic sunset sail on a pirate ship for you American honeymooners? Why are you leaving? Come back, honeymooners!'

Seedy salesmen approach, their eyes wide and cautious until they're close enough to whisper: 'Marijuana? Vicodin? Vicodin, ten dollars each pill.' If that's the going rate, we have a thousand dollars' worth of these opiate painkillers in our emergency medical kit aboard.

It's only midday but bars are blasting pop medleys to drunken crowds. I am alarmed to see so many porcelain-white travellers slamming back rows of shots. Tomorrow, many of them are going to wake up with hangovers and sunburns that make them look as though they've been slapped on the back of the legs by Cuban bongo players.

Carrying heavy sacks of laundry in desperate need of a good wash, we find a laundromat. A laundromat! The pleasure of a coin-operated washing machine does not go unappreciated, and I drop to my knees and thank the sweet Virgin Mary rendered in hologram for mankind's electrical miracles. There is nothing quite as unromantic as having to scrub the crotch of your partner's underwear by hand. After a machine wash, the clothes come out of the dryer as lighter, perfumed versions of their previous selves.

Back on the street, grilled food smells waft from restaurants, making my stomach rumble. We pick out a table that overlooks the marina and, to celebrate, we order gazpacho, fish tacos and two frozen margaritas served in salted glasses that could comfortably accommodate goldfish. The sun combines with the tequila, filling me up with warm joy. I slip off into a high, drunk on my surroundings – the jabbering Spanish, the smell of spices, the garish colours. The sun embraces my body and begins to melt my apprehension. Accumulated anxiety puddles at my feet, leaving behind a thawed version of myself: a happy, hopeful optimist.

I did it! It seems so hard to believe. All of the pain, discomfort and torture it took to get here is beginning to fade. I faced my greatest fears and I'm still alive. The buzz of this accomplishment brings on a deeply satisfied joy that I've never felt before. Even if I never go to sea again, I can keep this sense of empowerment for life.

ANOTHER WEEK IS LOST to tacos, margaritas, mariachis and indecision. Anchored in Cabo's wide bay, overlooking the famous rocks, we've watched the sky turn purple with sunset for seven days, as pirate ships packed with honeymooners have made their way back to port.

Hurricane season is rapidly approaching, which is why Ivan keeps trying to gently extract a decision from me – am I flying out of Cabo or sailing on with him? Every day, as the sun rises in Cabo, my dread rises too. I've been avoiding the elephant in the room (and an elephant in a boat is large indeed). I made a promise to myself that I'd quit this torturous sailing gig, so that means I have to go home.

We're sitting on the beach, surrounded by sunbathers trying to pack in as much reading, tanning and relaxing as they can on a short getaway.

'Tomorrow looks like a good day to head out,' Ivan says, pouring sand from his fist into an open palm. 'Weather report said ten knots and fine conditions for the next five days.'

I stare into the sand.

'Remember, baby... hurricane season starts soon, and—'

'I know, I'm sorry. We have to leave. I mean, *you* have to leave... Shit. I don't know what to do.'

'It's okay. I don't want to pressure you.'

'Ivan?' I pause. 'What would you do if I didn't come with you? If I just went home and waited in Australia?'

He doesn't answer. He just starts sifting sand faster.

'I'm not a sailor,' I say. 'I'm a city girl. I'm not even the outdoorsy type. I love art and culture and people and cappuccinos and craft markets and *solid ground*.'

No reply, just more sand sifting. His silence hurts my guts. I'm terrified to know what he's thinking.

'I am not adventurous,' I say. I want him to agree that I'm unsuitable for this, to let me off the hook so we can call it a day.

'But you *are* adventurous,' he says. 'You came to the US with three thousand dollars in the bank. You didn't know anyone, you had no job, no place to live. Wouldn't you call that adventurous?'

'Well, a little bit, but—'

'I saw it the moment I met you. I love how, on our date at the tapas bar, you were willing to taste everything on the menu with me. You're impulsive. You're not afraid to try things. You're an explorer of the world. Maybe you don't see it, but I do.'

'But I'm not brave. I had this dumb fantasy that I'd get out there on the ocean and become someone new, cured of a lifelong fear. But it didn't happen that way. I'm a waste of space on the boat.'

'But, baby, listen to me. Please don't let that factor into your decision. I don't need you to help me sail, okay? I can single-hand the boat. I just want you to come with me. I'll never push you into doing anything you don't want to do. I'm not an arsehole who'll force you to coil ropes and scrub the deck or whatever. I promise. You're not my slave, you're my love. Just having you there with me is all I want.'

I cast my eyes to the aqua water off the beach. Two cruise ships sit far behind our Gracie. I think of all the people on those ships, package-deal travellers rushed place to place on a preset schedule. I'm jealous of their safety and luxury, but I also know that it was the fear that made arriving here thrilling beyond anything I've ever experienced.

'The thing is,' I say, 'even though the passage was hell, when we passed those rocks at the bay, it was mind-blowing. Which makes me curious: what would it feel like to arrive at a tropical island twenty-six hundred miles away?'

'Torre,' Ivan says, taking my hands. 'Listen to me. I want to experience that with you. Come with me.'

I don't reply.

We walk along the beach in silence and I fret quietly about the decision I'm faced with. If I don't go, will Ivan just keep sailing the South Pacific islands like he planned before we met? Or will he sell the boat and give up his voyage to be with me? Both options suck.

This is my own mistake. I pursued a dreamer because I was attracted to his free spirit and his unique vision. To take my rare wild bird and stick him in a cage for admiring isn't an option. It would kill his soul. In order to keep him as he is, there's only one option: I have to tuck myself under the folds of his wing and soar into oblivion with him.

PART TWO
WATER

'Only a fool tests the depth of the water with both feet.'
African Proverb

The JOURNEY

Indonesia

AUSTRALIA

Society Islands

TAHITI > MOOREA > RANGIROA

Cook Islands

PORT VILLA

VAVA'U

AITUTAKI

BUN-
DABERG

Vanuatu

Tonga

MELBOURNE

*New
Zealand*

N
W   E
S

1000 NM

LOS ANGELES

CABO SAN LUCAS

USA

MEX

SOUTH
PACIFIC

Marquesas
HIVA OA > TAHUATA > NUKU HIVA

Tuamotus
?OAU > APATAKI > RANGIROA

of AMAZING
GRACE

EIGHT

THE ROLLING HILLS OF Mexico disappear into the boundless blue.

Today is my twenty-sixth birthday and I can think of many ways to celebrate the occasion, none of which involve deep bodies of water, but we're escaping Mexico in the eleventh hour of hurricane season and we can't wait any longer.

We're now on a one-way course through the most remote place a human can be. The Pacific Ocean will swallow us in her enormity and before we meet with dry land again, we'll have crossed more than one-third of the distance from America to Australia in one long marathon. 'Puddle jumping' it's called in the sailing world – an idiom designed to ease the idea of a month-long journey into the wild with nobody but each other to depend on, only the blue of day and the black of night; the rain, the wind, the waves and the ocean's moods, both loving and hostile.

I crave one last view of land but as we rise up on a tall wave, I can't see Mexico any more. I breathe in our first moment of aloneness and my knees weaken as this reality seeps in.

Down below in my berth, I nestle into the cocoon of my bunk. 'Happy birthday,' I tell myself, popping a seasickness pill to celebrate, and then I drift off into dreamland.

IF THIS WERE A Hollywood blockbuster, now would be the ideal time for Torre the character to overcome her disabling fear, grow a pair of sea legs and be face-to-the-spray at the bow of the ship, while a Hans Zimmer symphony reaches crescendo.

But this is real life.

And, unfortunately, the real-life version of me is no hero.

There is a breed of goats called 'myotonic goats' – or 'fainting goats' – who, when frightened, are seized by a sudden stiffening of their muscles, which causes them to tip over, frozen, despite being wide awake. I may share genes with these goats.

Nerves have weakened my muscles, numbed my emotions and turned reality into a peripheral fuzz. While this frozen-goat coping mechanism keeps me from a permanent state of fear, it also blocks pleasant feelings, like optimism and joy. So when Ivan tells me we've been a week at sea, my response is a brief glance away from my book and an indifferent 'Oh.'

'One week at sea. Isn't that great?'

'Yep,' I say in monotone.

Two days, three days, one week – I can't tell the difference. Days have become indistinguishable from one to the next and nights also resemble each other identically. Time fades in and out but seems to lack forward momentum and the days of the week have become a meaningless concept. The GPS is now our clock and time is measured in nautical miles – '1900 Nautical Miles to Destination,' it reads.

To release pent-up energy, my hands busy themselves by twisting rope into the knots I've studied to pass time. Bowlines, clove hitches, sheet knots, hangman's knots.

Meanwhile, my eyes stare up at the salon ceiling, studying its curves, corners, rust spots and screws. I'm familiar with all the leaks – one of them is impossible to ignore. It creeps in through the joint where the mast meets the ceiling, winds on a curvy path and stops to bulge into a droplet that drips – as though deliberately – onto my face. Day and night, rain and salt water drip on my forehead.

Together, Ivan and I patch the leak with rags and duct tape, but after a few hours, the rags engorge and the river floods, once again, on the same course to my forehead.

Splat. Splat. Splat.

I stop myself from expressing agitation the way kids do: by deliberately squeezing up the face muscles to pump out a few lousy, dry sobs.

More rags and more duct tape divert the river to my lower legs, which I decide is an acceptable compromise.

'FISH!' IVAN YELLS from the cockpit.

I go outside to inspect the commotion. The small waves surrounding our ship are tinted blood-red by the setting sun. Uninterrupted by buildings or mountains, the molten-lava sky is spectacular. For a second, there's nowhere else I'd rather be than under this roof of blazing fire.

'We have a fish!' Ivan says, reeling in the line, which has been trailing full-time since we left LA. His grin is drawn so tight with pride, I can see nothing but top gums. It's a rare moment of extreme self-satisfaction that reveals that this human is indeed a descendant of the caveman. *Me – man! Me catch fish!*

He pulls in a foot-long yellowfin tuna and it flips in protest, while its gills flex, seeking precious water. Not for long, though – its silvery head is bashed repeatedly with a metal winch handle. Ivan delivers several brutal smacks until the creature gives up the fight. Its tail quivers as its little eyes cloud over. Poor Mr Fish.

Red has spattered the white fibreglass and chunks of flesh cling to random locations, including Ivan's forehead. He wipes his head with the back of his hand, successfully removing the chunk while smearing blood in its place. I'm tempted to draw battle whiskers across his cheeks with fish blood.

I fetch Ivan a knife but all of our so-called stainless-steel knives have been rusted by salt exposure, rendering them blunt. Ivan tries his best to fillet the tuna, but the rusted blade won't slice the gelatinous meat. He resorts to biting nuggets directly from the skeleton, simultaneously filleting and snacking.

'Dinner doesn't get any fresher than this,' he says, licking at the blood in the corners of his lips.

'No,' I say, suppressing my gag reflex. 'No, it does not.'

Lining a plate with rows of chunky meat, Ivan presents me with my dinner. 'Sashimi!' he announces, proudly showcasing a dish that doesn't quite replicate the tidy art of Japanese cuisine.

I stare down at my plate of bludgeoned Mr Fish. I slide a morsel into my mouth and gulp it down. 'Mmm. You shouldn't have.'

A LOUD SLAPPING WAVE shocks me awake in the dead of night, lurching my heart into a fit, pumping adrenaline through my system. It's night – the time I dread because my guard is down and I'm no longer able to control the fear.

I take some deep breaths and squeeze my eyes shut, urging sleep to sedate me, but it's too late. Terror has arrived and the frantic anxiety has begun: *We're charging into darkness. What if we hit something? Running into a piece of debris would slice open our boat and we'd be swimming in the black abyss within sixty seconds. A single tree, that's all it would take. How many trees have been washed into the Pacific Ocean? A lot of trees! Wait. What was that noise? I heard a bang. Was that a tree?*

'No, no, just a wave,' I whisper soothingly to myself. My logic knows there's no danger, but I somehow need to communicate that message to the adrenaline factory inside my body.

Shh! *Listen! Can you hear that sound? It's water gushing in! We're sinking!*

'That's just water on the hull. We're not going to die.'

I heard something. Was that... a horn? Oh, shit, a ship's horn!

'No, it's just a rope rubbing against metal. Listen again... See? Just the normal sounds of the boat under a starry sky. Everything's perfect.'

But what if it was a horn? Maybe I should wake up Ivan.

I look over at Ivan, who is lying in his bunk, his lips parted as a little line of drool connects his mouth to his pillow, like he's plugged into his bedding.

'No, Ivan is sleeping. Leave him – he needs rest. If it's a ship, the radar will pick it up.'

The radar isn't on, remember? Ivan said we don't have the power to run it because the solar panels didn't collect enough sun today. I have to check the horizon. What if there's a ship out there?

I climb the stairs, poking my head through the hatch, using two hands to hold myself to the boat.

Holy shit, it's so dark. A rogue wave could sweep me off into deep space and Ivan wouldn't know I was missing until he woke up hours later. He wouldn't even get a chance to wave goodbye!

'*Shh*. Stop thinking about that. See the moon? It's the same moon you've always known. The same moon you see on land. We're not lost in deep space.'

I scan the horizon to make sure there's no Venus growing bigger on the horizon, coming straight for us, even though I know it's unlikely because we haven't seen anything at all for ten days. Standing up on my tippy-toes to see beyond the boat's windshield – the dodger – I circle the horizon two times. No tanker, no nothing. There are only wet sounds within the pure blackness.

'See?' I whisper to myself. 'Nothing to worry about.'

I wake up after dozing off again. It's still dark and Ivan is asleep in his bunk. I feel the rhythm of the boat changing, which always wakes me up, and I know that *Amazing Grace* is wallowing aimlessly. Whenever the boat falls off course, the swell changes direction and we dance to a new step. I check the GPS and it confirms that we're indeed heading nowhere.

'Ivan.' I gently shake him a few times before he snorts to life and smacks his lips, looking around.

'What is it?' he says.

'We've gone off course.'

He pulls himself out of bed and goes into the cockpit, where he disengages the automatic steering and takes the tiller in hand. Getting the boat on course is an intricate balance of wind, sails, speed, waves, compass bearing and – most importantly – charming the difficult Wendy.

Wendy, our aluminum wind vane, steers the ship. She stands tall at the stern, with a rudder in the water, a paddle in the air and two ropes joining to the tiller to correct the boat left and right to maintain a steady heading. Wendy guides the boat while we sleep, so we can continue travelling nonstop, day and night. However, Wendy is a hypersensitive lady and the slightest gust or extra large wave will toss her off centre and she'll steer us the wrong way. Then Ivan has to tweak the sails, adjust the course and pull out all his tricks to please Wendy.

Tonight, she's extra neurotic. After a lot of fussing around, *Amazing Grace* resumes the familiar dance steps of being back on course. But within minutes the waves change direction and Wendy's poor leadership takes us off step again. Ivan makes some adjustments – a little less canvas, a few degrees south – but Wendy refuses to cooperate.

This battle goes on for hours, until the orange of dawn melts through the dark horizon and light floods in through the hatches and portholes. My old friend, daylight, has arrived, and I can finally relax into a deep sleep.

When I wake up, hours later, I feel the steady canter of *Amazing Grace* on course and look over to see Ivan with a fresh string of dribble escaping his lips.

'WHEEE-WOOOOO.' The sound of Ivan whistling wakes me.

I have no idea how long I've been asleep. Is it today, or tomorrow? Is there really a difference anyway? 'Time is all one moment,' I mumble from my sleep delirium.

'Baby, come see,' Ivan says. 'We have whales!'

I open my eyes to find Ivan standing before me, nude apart from a life vest that hangs over his chest like royal-blue lapels. Utterly alone out here, clothes became useless some time ago and, while I'm used to seeing his bits hanging just below the whistle on his life jacket, I'm still continually amused at the sight. His face is covered in slapdash sunscreen, making him look like a mime: a naked mime, in a life jacket, shaking me awake.

'Quick, come see!'

Outside, the water mirrors the overcast sky. Four creatures as black and shiny as an oil slick weave through the water beside us. They're moving languidly, as though tired from a long ocean voyage. With their long bodies tapering into round heads, I recognise them as pilot whales. We have a pair of seabirds with us too; they've been following us for a week. Bob and Betty, I've named the duo. The lovers swoop and twirl around the mast, hovering close, as though their sole purpose is to keep sailors from loneliness.

Our animal friends charge my energy and pull me into the moment. The lovely air curls around my naked body and I notice it's warmer and more humid now. We've been crossing invisible lines into new time zones and climates. The world outside our boat

143

a stunning, welcoming environment, not the scary nightmare I see while huddled belowdecks in my cocoon.

'Hello!' I say to the whales when their heads poke up again. 'Where are you going?'

The whales sink and don't return. I wait awhile for them to reappear but it seems they've taken off and left us. 'Come back,' I say. 'Stay with us.' But they've continued on their epic crossing, leaving our sluggish boat alone in the void once again.

We're midway between the American continent and our destination: French Polynesia. To celebrate the halfway mark and two weeks at sea, we have hot, freshwater showers. I comb the jungle of knots from my hair. My skin is clean, my hair silky, and I spend at least an hour doing nothing more than lying back and enjoying the soapy smells on my body.

We've made it over the hump; from here, it should be downhill. The mood is high. Endorphins charge around the boat and Ivan and I chatter for hours, talking energetically about all the tropical fruits that await us on the other side of the ocean. Especially the mangoes.

To combat our cravings for fresh fruit, Ivan sips on his cup of maté, while I smother crackers with butter and Vegemite for us both. Ivan is the only non-Australian I've met who enjoys the salty taste of this thick, black yeast extract.

He offers me a cup of maté and I take it, masking the tobacco-like flavour with one of my crackers. I surprise myself – and Ivan – by asking for a top-up. As it turns out, Australia's most iconic spread mixed with Argentina's iconic beverage makes for the perfect flavour combination.

'It's really not that bad when you have it with Vegemite,' I say, sipping the tea.

'We're drinking maté together, baby!' Ivan says.

I suck down another mouthful and say, 'Ahhh,' which makes Ivan smile.

'That means you really *do* love me,' he says, earnestly.

I giggle at this. 'Of course I do.'

'Wheee-wooooo,' Ivan whistles. 'Come outside and look at all the massive squalls on the horizon. This has to be the doldrums.'

We've reached a band of unpredictable weather, a zone that sailors dread. In the doldrums, the winds of the Northern Hemisphere clash with the winds of the south, creating psychotic conditions. The ideal time for passing through this area was a month ago, but delayed by our lengthy maiden voyage down to Mexico – hauled up in Turtle Bay and Cabo San Lucas as I wrestled with committing to the crossing – the doldrums have swollen in proportion, and there's no telling how long it'll take us to break through to the trade winds on the other side.

Ivan has been strategising about when and where to cross the band at its narrowest point for weeks. If his guesswork is on target, we'll be through to the trade winds in four or five days. If he has it wrong, we could be trapped in these equatorial calms for weeks.

Out on deck, I'm chilled by the mood of the ocean. The horizon is dotted with black clouds squeezing into angry fists. Some have vertical streaks of rainfall, while others have the almost-horizontal lines of a downpour being blown by a violent wind. The heaviest squalls cast shadows as dark as night on the ocean beneath. A few bundles of clouds are alive with shocks of lightning that break free from the sky to lick the water's surface.

I look up at our metal mast reaching fifty feet high like an arm thrust upward by an excited child responding to the teacher's question: 'Who would like to get struck by lightning today?' *Oh, me! Please choose me!*

There is no way around it. Our destination is on the other side of that weather and the only thing we can do is batten down the hatches and touch wood – literally.

Weather comes and goes as though an evil finger is manning a switchboard of buttons: *Rain on. Rain off. Wind on. Wind off.*

From the cockpit, I watch the spectacular weather show. Fat droplets tumble down from dense clouds, pummeling the hood of my foul-weather jacket. Ivan fetches a bar of soap and scrubs down beneath nature's shower.

When the rain clears, the ocean becomes molten metal reflecting the sky and the humidity becomes dense and suffocating. Becalmed by the dead wind, Ivan starts the engine.

The old motor jackhammers day and night, wobbling our brains like jelly on the hood of a truck, pushing us forward through glassy stillness, which shatters into ripples as we pass.

FIVE DAYS AFTER entering the doldrums, fluffy cumulus clouds mark the beginning of the trade winds. After motoring through windless calm for five days, we're now gliding by the power of our sails once again. The engine's constant vibrations have been replaced with the Zen sound of trickling water. The delicious trade-wind breeze cools our bodies after days of sweating in the thick humidity of the doldrums. We've passed the equator. We're on the home stretch.

Ivan claps his hands together. 'Guess what? I have a surprise for you.'

'A surprise?'

'Yes. A really good one.'

'What?'

'Only five more days to go.'

'Really?'

'Really. We've been making great progress. We did one hundred twenty miles yesterday.'

I put down my book and a grin spreads across my face. 'So we're no longer in The Middle of Nowhere?'

'Nope. We're almost there.'

I smile wide. Civilisation is just one business week away. Excitement flutters in my stomach.

In the cockpit, I sit under the sun and groom my legs with a razor. The surrounding water is glowing a beautiful neon blue. I whistle a merry tune, feeling more awake than I've felt for a long time. We take showers with water warmed by the sun and I lather up all over. The breeze cools my wet skin and I feel happy. *So happy.* Now it's my turn to smile with gums showing.

Our birds are still circling the mast and, even though Ivan tells me they're different birds from the ones we had a while back, I still call them Bob and Betty. 'Hello!' I yell to them. They reply with a few elegant swooping circles.

I drift off into daydreams about arriving. More talk of fruit bounces around the boat – it's our favourite topic. We can linger on this single subject for hours, mulling over small details to pass the time. Mostly, we talk of mangoes.

'I like them sweet.'

'I like them tart.'

'I like the ones that are half green, half orange.'

'The yellow ones are my favorite.'

'Can you believe we'll be eating mangoes in just five days?'

We pass time by telling each other embarrassing memories from our childhoods, recounting personal stories both amusing and heartbreaking. When we run out of tales, we play stupid games, quizzing each other with pop trivia. Ivan dominates that game because – I'm stunned to discover – he's up to date with celebrity gossip and has watched every season of *Project Runway*.

When we get bored of trivia, we begin to make a French flag. At the salon table, I cut a rectangle from spare sailcloth, then I punch holes in the flag and insert rings to make eyelets. Ivan loads a paintbrush with red and I load up with blue. We take turns snapping photos as a record of this significant event. A French flag – a new country, culture and language – ready for hoisting in just *five days*.

It's only when we scan through the photos after the flag is done that we notice we're inappropriately dressed for the camera. We giggle at every shot, scrutinizing the images like a *Where's Wally?* picture book, spotting the dangly bits in each frame. Note to self: remember to put clothes on in five days.

'FOUR MORE DAYS' is the first thing I say to Ivan when I wake up the next day.

He frowns, looking tired, and then shakes his head dismally. 'I'm so sorry, I made a mistake. Still five days to go.'

My smile pauses, waiting for the punch line.

'We made very little progress last night,' he says. 'It was our worst night yet. We travelled only eight miles – about forty miles less than average. I couldn't get Wendy working, so I took a nap, and while I slept, the boat wallowed for ages and we were pushed the wrong way by the current.'

'Oh.' I do my best to conceal my disappointment.

'But don't worry because, guess what, baby? Five more days!' He claps his hands together, trying to resuscitate yesterday's levels of enthusiasm.

'Yay,' I say, shaking the restlessness from my feet and hands and turning my eyes back to the ceiling. 'Five more days.'

THE NEXT MORNING, Ivan's face is worn and his eyes are glassy. I know the news is bad.

'Let me guess… five more days?' I say.

'Another crappy night, sorry. Five more days. This time – *really,* five more days. We should get there on day twenty-six.'

He doesn't bother to follow up with a cheer. We both fail to conceal our disappointment and morale has dropped dangerously low. Five more days, as long as we don't drift backward or run into weather or sink or get struck by a plummeting UFO or...

I take myself belowdecks to roll around in a fresh, smelly pile of pessimism. In fact, I give up on the idea of arriving at all. It's less excruciating that way.

THE DAWN LIGHT of day twenty-six wakes me. The GPS says we've got eighteen miles to go, but we haven't yet spotted any real evidence of this fact, such as a big hunk of rock called land.

Ivan's been watching the horizon for hours with his face etched in worry lines – an expression of concern that I've never seen on him before.

'Why are you worried?' I ask him.

'I'm not.'

'You look like you are.'

'I'm not worried.'

'I know you are, I can read you. We've spent every single day together for five whole months. You're worried. 'Fess up.'

'All right, I'm worried.'

'Why?'

He breaks into inappropriate laughter, something he only does when he's nervous. He tries to stop the laughing by tightening his lips, but the nervous giggles break through. 'Never mind, honestly, it's nothing,' he says through his giggles.

Oh no, it must be serious. 'Please tell me?'

'It's nothing. Everything's fine, everything's good. Please.' He stares into my eyes with an expression that says he's hiding his worries for my own good. 'Forget it, baby. *Please?*'

We both go back to watching the horizon, waiting for Hiva Oa to appear like a mirage wobbling into existence. It hits me: We're not going to arrive today. That's what Ivan's hiding.

The day is dark and despairing and the clouds are restless with trapped energy. Spitting rain throws itself from the sky in suicidal droplets, while the waves build themselves up into summits full of hope, only to disperse back into nothing. The horizon is as empty as a dead man's gaze. I retreat to bed.

FRANTIC WHISTLING WAKES ME from my coma. '*Wheee-wooooo! Wheee-wooooo!* Baby, come see! *Wheee-wooooo.* Land ho!'

I emerge on deck and explore the horizon in the direction of Ivan's pointing finger. He looks giddy, choking up on his own short breaths. I search for a green outcrop with bendy palm trees and sandy shores, but I see only more emptiness.

'I can't see it,' I say, my voice quiet and shaky.

'Right there,' he says, pointing at empty horizon. 'See it?'

'No. Where?' I'm on the verge of tears. Is this a trick? Are there still five more days to go?

He pulls me into his arms and holds me against his shoulder, pointing straight along my line of sight. 'Right there. See it?'

My eyes linger on the spot where he's pointing. Something odd emerges from the clouds, like an accidental smudge of charcoal on a drawing. I stare for a long while, trying to make it out, and then it pops – the smudge is the top of a sheer mountain! The base of the island is shrouded in clouds, making it look like a pinnacle floating in the sky.

'Oh, yeah,' I say hesitantly, still pessimistic about ever making it there. My mind is full of anxious chatter: *Something could still happen. The wind could die. We could sink. We could get attacked by orcas!*

'Just a few hours – three at the most,' Ivan says, patting my back. 'We've almost made it.'

I take a deep, nervous breath and hold it.

Down below, Ivan turns on our stereo to see if we're receiving FM radio from the island. A tune peeks in through thick static and we get our first impression of this exotic Polynesian culture. Ivan tweaks the dial and a familiar song plays loud and clear. It's 'My Humps' by the Black Eyed Peas.

'*Hmm* – that's surprising,' Ivan says, flicking off the radio.

I WAKE UP to a change in the rhythm of the boat. Nerves knocked me out two hours ago, tipping me flat like a myotonic goat.

In the cockpit, Ivan stands tall with the tiller in hand. Behind us, large, lazy waves bulge into peaks and send us surfing down their slopes, doubling our speed. *Amazing Grace* carves up the water with a satisfying *chhhhhh*.

The charcoal smudge is now a colossal wall of rock to my right, an ominous island pushed up from the depths.

'Hiva Oa,' I whisper to myself, stunned by this fantasy island, this myth that has manifested right in front of me. Maybe I never believed it was real.

We watch the land in silence, awed. It seems to vibrate with energy, as though all the sailors who arrived here before us have left their collective sigh of relief lingering in the air. *Pheeeeeeeeeew,* says the breeze.

The sun breaks through the rain clouds and the island is revealed under a golden spotlight. Palms, dense jungle, jagged mountain ridges sliding down steeply to green valleys. Splotches of red hibiscus and pink bougainvillea pop out against the palette of intense greens.

I gasp in air, realising I've been holding my breath for some time. In fact, I haven't really let myself breathe in twenty-six days.

'Can you smell that?' I say.

'Yes, I smell it.'

I suck in air and slowly roll the scents over my taste buds. Wet soil, flowers and the sweet, pungent odor of nature's decay: that is the smell of land.

'Masts!' Ivan yells, spotting sailboats beyond the breakwater. 'That's Atuona Bay. Awesome, our navigation charts *are* accurate. They've led us to exactly the right spot.'

My mouth hangs open as I realise why he was so nervous earlier – he'd been afraid that we wouldn't find an island here! I'm glad he kept that fear to himself. Travelling twenty-six days into an abyss of blue, only to find more ocean where there should be an island, is one worst-case scenario that I thankfully never imagined.

Ivan steers us around the breakwater and into a small port, where a congregation of ocean gypsies hailing from around the world are anchored. People lounge in their cockpits, reading books, drinking beer or tending to their boats. An eclectic mix of flags flutter on backstays: Japan, Australia, Norway, USA. One man stops what he's doing to throw an enthusiastic greeting. *Welcome!* his long, sweeping wave says. *Congratulations!*

A tiny, brown-skinned Marquesan boy paddles past in an outrigger canoe, speedy and serious in his pursuit. We wave to him, and the boy, who is no older than four, offers a melodic *'Bonjour.'*

We find a place of our own in among the other boats. Ivan runs forward and releases the anchor into the olive-green water. *Amazing Grace* settles on her tether, a proud stallion that has kept her riders safe. She pulls to a gentle stop.

'We've jumped the puddle,' Ivan says. He looks at me and we stare at each other silently, breathing quick, shaky gulps of air.

I lunge toward him and pull him into a hug, squeezing tight, feeling both of our bodies shaking.

'We're here, baby,' Ivan says. 'We did it.'

NINE

THE DINGHY RUNS AGROUND on a rocky landing and we step out onto dry soil. My legs stumble like those of a newborn calf before they find purchase on the unmoving ground.

We're both too overwhelmed to string cohesive sentences together. Our chatter is a giddy back-and-forth exchange, like two birds communicating in lyrical chirps, clicks and whistles. My mouth speaks nonsense while Ivan replies in his own babble, yet we understand each other completely.

Wandering aimlessly, we take it all in. Dinosaurs wouldn't be out of place here. It's wild and steaming and green. The island is so fertile that the grass seems to grow right before my eyes. Untamed jungle lurks beyond roadsides, threatening to creep in and ingest power lines and paved roads the second backs are turned. Every so often, a roof made of tin or shingles is detectable among vegetation that's so thickly tangled, it probably needs to be groomed back daily, like a businessman's beard.

We made it! This realisation keeps shaking me lucid, slowly pulling me from the thick fog of a month-long daze. I stop to stare and marvel at the island of Hiva Oa, to smell the island's perfume of dewy rain on newly opened flower buds, to watch palms dance with the sultry breeze, swishing their fronds, flaunting their coconuts.

I turn to Ivan and see his eyes also fixed in a love affair with the landform. We chirp, click and whistle some more.

The wharf is alive with smiling, white-teethed Polynesians. Kids play at the water's edge, finding cool relief from the heat. Curvy women dressed in brilliant hibiscus-print dresses look like they've peeled themselves off Paul Gauguin's canvas. Tattoos are the norm here and everywhere I look they wrap around arms, climb up calves and, on some men, even decorate faces.

Ivan points to a man with the most striking tattoo I've ever seen. Interlocking black shapes form a bold design that cuffs around his arm and travels over his shoulder to his back.

'I want that tattoo,' Ivan declares, rushing forward to ask the man where he got it.

After a game of charades with the French-speaking islander, Ivan returns, out of breath with excitement. 'He said he got it done in Tahuata from a tattooist named Fati. We can sail there next!'

But for now, we have urgent business to attend to. *Find fresh food.* After eating nothing but canned foods for almost a month, my desperate craving for crispy greens may soon have me grazing roadside on all fours. Cooking is not a passion of mine, but I've spent days dreaming up elaborate recipes involving carrots, tomatoes, mangoes, eggplant, oranges, spinach, bananas, cucumber, beef and fish. *Fish!*

Craving fish when you're floating over an ocean full of them is particularly agonising. Ivan and I have come to accept that we're not going to win any trophies for fishing, except perhaps if there were a competition for longest drag of a hooked line without a single catch – for that, we'd be world record holders. Apart from a few small tuna early in our voyage, our lines have collected nothing but rust.

We wander into the island's main town of Atuona and find the biggest supermarket, which isn't much larger than a corner store.

The town has only a modest number of shops to service the small population: one bank, a couple of food markets, a few clothing stores and the occasional artisan gallery.

I quickly weave my way around the aisles, passing pyramids of cans, stacks of jars and rows of bagged grains. To my great disappointment, the only fresh items on offer are an afterthought sitting in the bottom of a wicker basket: garlic, onions and some potatoes that look like geriatric elbows.

I stand in the middle of the store and spin a few confused semicircles.

Ivan comes over with an empty shopping basket. 'I couldn't find any meat,' he says.

'They don't have fruit or vegetables either!' I cry. 'This island is covered in fruit trees – I've seen them everywhere. It makes no sense. And no fresh fish for sale either? The only thing I could find was Chicken of the Sea.' I hold up my shopping basket, rolling a lonely tuna can around inside.

'Well, I suppose people aren't going to pay money for something they can grow or catch in their own yard.'

'Damn,' I say. 'I didn't see this coming. I've been planning banquets in my head for weeks – minestrone soup with spring vegetables, mushrooms stuffed with fresh herbs, chopped onion, spinach and crumbled feta...' I pause to swallow the saliva gathering in my mouth. 'Medium-rare steaks, sliced thin, served on a bed of lettuce with lemony asparagus, and—'

'That all sounds really great,' Ivan interrupts. 'But we're in paradise and this is the trade-off. We're not in the city any more.'

'I've noticed that,' I say, hurt by his tone. 'Sailing twenty-six days through open ocean was a pretty good tip-off.'

'Sorry.' His voice softens. 'I want you to feel happy, that's all. I'm sure we'll find something soon if we keep looking.'

We walk along the roadside, searching for our Eden of edibles, getting rained on in bursts and then immediately dried by the hot sun. The island's tall mountains are magnets for engorged clouds, which release downpours in twenty-minute intervals, soaking the air and everything it touches. Sweating trees drip-feed the rainforest, which is alive with the sounds of crickets and birdsong.

I imagined these trees would be spilling with edibles – which they are – but something unexpected is getting in the way. Private property fences.

The fruit hangs inches beyond picking distance. I look around to see if anyone is watching before lunging for a banana that hangs a fraction of an inch away from my sticky fingers. There's no way to do this subtly; getting to the fruit will involve some degree of trespassing and larceny, making criminals of us, just so we can get our hands on a commodity that grows, quite literally, on every third tree.

Fallen fruits lie in the dirt, mocking us. I kick a few pieces around, looking for any edibles, but the birds have already claimed the good parts. The remainders teem with insects busy working the leftovers into a pulp. The smell of rotting fruit is intoxicating and, for a moment, I consider flicking the insects aside to sink my teeth into the sickly-sweet mush.

We keep searching, walking up steep hills and residential dirt roads, our atrophied sea legs shaking from exertion. We pass kids playing in the street and barking dogs, warning us away. Weaving along a desolate road, we come to an untethered bull blocking our path, staring us down with eyes that say, *Turn back now*. Intimidated, we U-turn, disappointed at our failed mission.

As we start back down the hill, a roadside sign catches my eye: *Fruits pour la vente*. We exchange smiles and take off cantering down a driveway toward the house advertising fruit for sale.

An elderly man opens the door.

'*Bonjour. Fruit, s'il vous plaît,*' Ivan says.

'*Oui, oui,*' the farmer says, gesturing for us to follow.

In his backyard, he grabs a clawed stick and plucks an enormous green citrus fruit from one of the many prolific trees towering above. He pulls out a pocketknife, slices the flesh open and offers us both a quartered chunk. '*Pamplemousse,*' he informs us.

It's a grapefruit on steroids – four times as big and light green in colour. I bite down and juice erupts, overflowing down to my chin and neck. It's fresh, tart and sweet – and without question the most exquisite food I've ever tasted. My eyes roll into my head and my cheeks flush as a deep longing is quenched.

I come to realise that I'm moaning aloud when I see the farmer shift in discomfort. He mutters something in French, probably translating to *Get a room, why don't you?* Between Ivan and me, the sight of us devouring fruit has become obscene.

We instruct the farmer to pluck as many fruits as we can carry in our backpacks, hands and the pits of our arms. From another tree, he picks a bag of fuzzy, golf-ball-sized rambutans that look like they are about to sprout legs and run away. Not on my watch.

He weighs the fruit on an old-style scale and taps numbers into a calculator. I have no idea what this will cost, but I have a crumbled pile of bills in my pocket, more than $100, which I'm willing to surrender for this fruit if I have to.

He holds up the calculator: $11. I pay the man and we scurry off with the fruit.

Beyond the fruit shop, on the side of the road, I spot a little market cart stocked with chunks of fleshy pink meat. Could that be…?

'Yellowfin tuna, six dollars a kilo,' the stall owner tells us. 'Caught this morning.'

We've already spent ten times as much on lost lures. Delighted with our 'catch', we take our slab of tuna back to the boat with the puffed chests of successful hunters, pretending for just a moment that we didn't buy our kill at a market stall. I have to restrain myself from posing in a catch-of-the-day photograph with the precious pink chunk.

On the boat, we cut our tuna steak into raw strips of sashimi, and, gobbling it down with far too much fruit, we get drunk on protein and vitamin C until we pass out, bloated, satiated and feverish with fructose.

THE SOUND OF CHIRPING BIRDS penetrates my dream world. It's morning and I notice that my cheek is sticky with dried fruit juice. There's no deep ocean swell rolling beneath us. Why can't I hear water rushing past the hull? *Where the hell are we?*

I remember. Smiling myself wide awake, I roll over to face Ivan. 'Good morning.' Happy kisses are planted over his lips. 'We're here. We're in the Marquesas.'

Craving another eyeful of the place we travelled through deep space to see, I get out of bed to peep outside. The sight chokes me up. A luminous rainbow arches over the bay's entrance, looking too vivid to be real. Stripes of colours form an arch almost palpable enough to swing from. One end of the rainbow rises up from the lush vegetation; the other end stops just off our starboard side. Spectacular peaks, born from the sea, steam with humidity in the background, and our painted French flag flutters in the foreground, completing a scene so eloquent that it seems contrived.

Ivan comes up on deck with the camera. He takes shots while I pose with the rainbow, then I remember I'm in a crowded anchorage and pants are now the expected standard. I hotfoot it below to dress, feeling thankful that at least I remembered my underwear.

HIGH ON FRUIT, fresh air and Marquesan culture for the sixth day, we soak up the sun on deck, while I cut Ivan's hair with scissors, trying to design his overgrown mop into the same styled look he used to wear in San Francisco.

'Hey,' I say, as I snip at his hairline, perfecting the cut. 'I heard a rumour about an island nearby called Nuku Hiva, which has an outdoor fruit and vegetable market on the wharf every Saturday. It starts at 4 a.m. A lot of other sailors are heading there next because it's the only place in the Marquesas with European vegetables. They have an internet café too. I was thinking we could head there after you get your tattoo in Tahuata and—'

'Nuku Hiva?' he interrupts. 'That's sixteen hours away. You really want to travel *sixteen hours* and get up at 3:30 a.m. for vegetables and e-mail?'

'Of course. Don't you?'

'Not really, no.'

I pause my snipping to stare at him, baffled. Doesn't he long for salads and spring vegetables? Wouldn't he, like me, trade a toe for a tomato? 'But, Ivan – don't you want fresh food? It's not like we have any other options around here.'

'Sure, but I don't want to go out of my way to run grocery errands. I'd rather go to a secluded paradise.'

My jaw dangles. 'A secluded paradise? Are you kidding me? This *is* a secluded paradise.' I throw my hands out to demonstrate our surroundings and tufts of Ivan's blond hair fall from my fingers, drifting away on the balmy breeze.

He shakes his head. 'The atolls in the Tuamotus are much more isolated. There are no airports on most of the atolls and there's nothing there but water and beach. Nuku Hiva is the most populated of all the Marquesas. They have lots of people, shops, restaurants and markets.'

I stare, blinking, confused as to why he's employing a negative tone to describe these fantastic features. Nuku Hiva may be the most populated of all the Marquesas, but located in the empty blue void between Hawaii and Tahiti, it's hardly a mecca of industry and tourism. It has *one* hotel.

I rub Ivan's hair off my hands with a towel and pack away the scissors. 'Ivan, they have an internet café in Nuku Hiva right by the wharf, so we can send e-mails and pictures and catch up with the world.'

He huffs. 'What's there to catch up on? The latest kidnapping? The crashing economy? How fuel prices have gone up? Maybe we could read up on the latest D-bag who's running for president. Fantastic! History always repeats itself and I don't see why we should travel out of our way to find out that the same old crap is going on in civilisation.'

'But, Ivan, I want to e-mail people and—'

'Knock, knock.' Tapping on the side of the boat cuts our disagreement short. An American voice chimes melodically from somewhere in the water. '*Ding-dong!* Hello? Yoo-hoo! Anyone aboard?'

I look overboard and see a deeply bronzed woman floating in a kayak alongside *Amazing Grace*. She throws an arm out and I shake her wet hand.

'Hi, I'm Leslie. What's your name?'

'I'm Torre. This is Ivan.'

'Oh, hey. What's going on? Just stopping by to say hello. I'm on that boat there.' She points to a sleek yacht named *Red Sky*.

She seems young to own a fifty-foot yacht. I saw her earlier today, stretched out on the foredeck, darkening her already crispy tan under rays amplified one hundred fold by white fibreglass and mirror-polished stainless-steel fittings.

'Come aboard, if you like,' Ivan says, but Leslie is already hoisting a leg over the lifelines.

'So, is that your boat?' I ask Leslie, while brushing the cut hair off Ivan's sticky skin.

'No, not mine. I'm crewing. Came from San Diego. Steve and Carol own the boat and they asked me to help them sail. They're really old, like, I don't know, sixty or something. They've been sailing forever, like forty years or something. They go to bed super early and stuff and they're *hella* boring, dude.'

Leslie sounds like she's in her teens, but she looks to be in her mid-thirties.

'I've sailed before, though,' she says. 'With Rusty – he has a yacht. Me and Rusty sailed the coast of Mexico in his boat. Rusty's a musician; he recorded an album. I brought some copies so I'll give you one later. He sings and plays guitar and he's, like, seriously awesome.'

'Rusty?'

'Yeah, Russell – he's my boyfriend. Oh, well technically my "ex-boyfriend", to be exact,' she says with air quotations. 'We're not together at the moment. Well, I guess since, hmm, three years. Rusty and I had such a great time in Mexico. We'd catch fish every day. I'd barbecue them. I had this great recipe—'

She pauses for a breath and a swallow, and I take the chance to break into the conversation. 'We did the same thing, actually. We just crossed over from Mexico and—'

'Things didn't work out so well with Rusty,' Leslie continues, 'but I really love sailing. So when Steve and Carol asked me to crew, I was like: *Hell, yeah*. It was boring as shit crossing with them, though, seriously yawn-worthy, dude. But anyway, I'm glad we're here now, how beautiful is it?'

'I know, I'm so happy we—'

'Hey, what are you doing later?'

'Going to the bank, checking in with customs and immigration, and then—'

'Rad. I can drop by later if you like? We can have some drinkies.'

'Oh. Well, we're—'

'Great, so, how about six then? *They* will be sleeping by then so I can take their kayak. They're so old and boring. I'm going crazy. Believe me, you guys, *I need young people*! Anyway, it's been great chatting. I'll see ya later on then, bitches. *Au revoir.*'

She gets in her kayak, paddles a few strokes, stops and turns back. 'You guys got booze, right? I'm all out, and normally I'd, like, totally bring something but I don't have anything left.' Then she adds in high-pitched singsong, *'I drank it.'*

'Yes, we've got some wine,' I tell her, and she drops her paddle to stab two enthusiastic thumbs in the air. In stow, we have ten bottles of red that have made the journey with us. They're an indulgent treat to help celebrate the milestones, like crossing the puddle.

It's been four weeks since we've conversed with anyone but each other and I'm desperate to socialise with anyone and everyone. Still buzzing from the high of our crossing, I'm brimming with tales to tell and experiences to compare. Even with Leslie, a get-together seems like a fine plan. Not that we really had much choice in the matter.

A LONG LINE of sweaty islanders stand behind us in the bank, fanning themselves with their fast-moving wrists. A tiny fan spins on the ceiling, offering no cooling effects, only squeaky noises. Ivan speaks to the bank teller in what he believes to be French, but she doesn't understand him. We're holding up the line.

Ivan's grasp of Spanish and English is perfect and, more than once, he shocked locals in Mexico when, as a fair-skinned, blond-haired gringo, he whipped out flawless *español* like a hidden sword drawn for battle. But in French Polynesia, his language sword is more of a bendy piece of celery. The best he can do is a mash-up of Spanfrenglish, delivered with a heavy American accent.

'*Où est la* bank check *intercambio trois mille dollars?*' he repeats.

A blank look washes over the teller's face. 'Ah… *je ne comprends pas.*' She doesn't understand.

We need to withdraw a $3,000 check in order to pay the required repatriation bond to the government. The bond – collectible upon exit – exists to discourage cruisers from retiring with their anchors embedded on these tropical sea floors. It's easy to understand why that's a common problem around here.

But communicating with the French-speaking bank teller is proving to be problematic, and if we can't withdraw the bond, we won't be able to check in with customs and immigration. While we've already partially explored the island and eaten its delectable fruits, we're not technically supposed to make ourselves at home here until our passports have been stamped. In fact, we're illegal aliens.

'What now?' I ask Ivan.

'Um—' Ivan taps the desk.

The people behind us fan themselves more vigorously and I shrug at them apologetically.

While in the States, I asked Ivan if he thought we should study French before departing, perhaps listen to *Learn While You Sleep* CDs in the hope of waking up miraculously fluent. Ivan insisted that learning French wasn't necessary because the language – he claims – is 70 percent similar to Spanish. He assured me that he could combine his native tongue with 30 percent English, add a dash of high school French to the mix, and then *voilà: je parle français!* It seemed like reasonable percentage-backed rationalising coming from an economics major, though I recall wondering how he'd know which words to put in which language. Now, I realise, he doesn't know either.

The teller raises an eyebrow at us and Ivan gives it one last shot in English. 'We need a bank check for three thousand dollars.'

'Oh, you'd like a bank check for your bond?' the teller says with a sigh of relief. 'No problem.'

The people behind us in line sigh in unison.

We're handed our bank check, as well as several colourful Marquesan bills, which look like play money from an oversized board game. They're almost too pretty to consider spending.

At the *gendarmerie* – the police station – we engage in a similar episode of Spanfrenglish mixed with an energetic game of charades to communicate complex nouns including 'EPIRB' and 'fibreglass'. Two puzzled policemen look on while Ivan first dials an invisible cell phone, then points an index finger at the sky (satellite phone). The officers' eyes light up with recognition and they scribble the detail into our official forms.

I watch on, giggling at this bizarre customs and immigration experience. It's far different from international airports, where I always arrive wondering if I'm going to get unlucky with a gloved hand.

Finally, the forms are completed, the bond is paid and our passports are stamped. We've just arrived in French Polynesia.

LESLIE ARRIVES right on six and she comes with armfuls of gifts. 'For you, madam,' she says, handing me not one but five copies of Rusty's CD. 'I've given you some extra copies so you can hand them around. And here's a Rusty T-shirt and a Rusty hat.' She pops the red cap on my head and pauses for my reply.

'Wow… thank you.' I've never owned so much branded merchandise in my life and now I am the number one fan of some guy named Rusty who used to date a woman I just met.

I slide the CD into the player and a country twang begins.

'Fantastic, isn't he?' Leslie says with a wistful smile.

'Yeah, really great,' I say, removing my Rusty hat.

After downing the majority of two bottles of red, Leslie starts to unleash. She's on a rant about her boat captain, Steve, and his wife, Carol, and her anger has reached boiling point.

'So Carol was all, "Please don't use that rice, Leslie, we bought that rice for sushi and we won't be able to find any more outside the US." Rice is rice, man, please. Was I not, like, cooking them a fucking meal? Give me a break, man.' Leslie's lips are surrounded in black wine sediment and her eyes seem to have lost the ability to see anything beyond her own lashes.

I check the time – it's 2:30 a.m. I let out a loud yawn and throw my arms up in a stretch. 'That's no good,' I say impassively.

'Totally, dude. That's what I'm saying. I'm so glad you get me. So Steve was all, "We would like you to leave the boat and fly home now, Leslie," and I'm all, "What the hell?" – you know?'

I snap awake. 'You're getting kicked off their boat?'

'Yeah, can you believe it? Arseholes. It's going to cost four hundred bucks to get a flight to Tahiti from here so I can get home. We were supposed to sail there but now that they're kicking me off, I have to fork out that money from my own savings.'

'Because you used the wrong rice?'

'Yeah, man. Can you believe it? Oh, and supposedly because I drank some of their vodka. Yeah, sure I did, but what else am I supposed to do to entertain myself on the Pacific-fucking-Ocean? I was totally helping them sail the boat over and they're freaking over two or three bottles of vodka.' She makes a dismissive *psssht* noise and spit flies from her mouth.

Leslie takes a swill of wine and tops up her glass with a third bottle that now resides far over to her side of the table. 'Major ball-busters, you know? I mean, I totally *helped* them sail, and now they're kicking me off. And then guess what happened?'

I look over at Ivan to help me out of this, but his head is leaning to the side and his eyes are closed. Is he asleep?

'They're accusing me of *stealing*. I didn't take their stupid money. Steve's all, "Where's our money, Leslie?" And I'm like, "How the hell am I supposed to know where your missing cash is, Steve?" I mean, seriously, what a prick. Accusing me of stealing four hundred dollars or some shit.'

I join the dots: $400 to fly home, $400 in missing cash... hmm, a real whodunit. Sick of listening to her lies, I call off the party. 'I'm off to bed now,' I say, collecting wine bottles.

Leslie looks irritated as she slams back the rest of her glass. I wonder if she's thinking, *Stupid boring old people.*

'I'll come by again tomorrow afternoon,' she says, getting in her kayak. 'Let's hang out again.' She paddles off and, soon after, I hear the ruckus of her colliding into Steve and Carol's boat, then lugging herself aboard.

Ivan finally wakes up from his 'snooze'.

'Now,' he says, 'you can understand why I don't want crew.'

I reply with a grimace. 'She's coming back tomorrow. What do we do? It's not like we can lock the front door and pretend we're not home.'

'We pick up anchor and move on,' he says.

I START THE ENGINE, take the tiller in hand and stand tall at the helm. Our next destination – the island of Tahuata and the home of the tattooist – is an easy two miles away, which would be a simple journey... if only we could get the anchor up.

Ivan tugs at the stubborn anchor using our only retrieval mechanism aboard: his arm muscles. Pulling in fifty feet of rope, chain and steel, he draws upon his upper body strength and plenty of primal grunting. '*Oughhhh,*' he yells, as though he's lifting a packed barbell over his shoulders. The line slips through his palms and four grunts of work drop back into the water. '*Ahhhh!*' he yells in frustration (not to be confused with his lifting noise of '*Oughhhh!*').

'You'll pop a hemorrhoid,' I warn from the helm, partly joking, but mostly concerned. I rev the engine to steer the boat upwind, easing the tension on the anchor's line, but Ivan is still in a tug-of-war.

'Is there a better way to do this?' I ask.

'No,' he snaps, growing impatient with my backseat driving.

Amazing Grace lacks the modern conveniences of most newer boats, such as an electric windlass – a simple system that sucks up the anchor like a vacuum cord. Most tasks on our decks have to be done the old muscle-and-grunt way. Though all the grunting comes from Ivan.

Eventually, a final '*Oughhhh-ahhhh*' brings the anchor on deck. The barbed flukes are smothered in a thick layer of volcanic sea floor mud, explaining Ivan's near-hemorrhoid effort in pulling up the weight. With the anchor up, we're adrift.

Sweaty, battered and speckled in mud, Ivan joins me in the helm and we steer away from our spectacular first landfall. I take one last look at the dramatic landscape, breathing in its smells of soil, frangipani and tropical fruit. I blow a goodbye kiss to Hiva Oa.

Outside of the breakwater, our boat meets the ocean's swell once again. *Amazing Grace* bucks on a strong current and as choppy waves pound the boat, I notice something odd: I'm not scared. For the first time since we left LA, the ocean doesn't frighten me. I've sailed one-third of the Pacific, I remind myself, so I'm an old salt now.

FLIPPING DOLPHINS PERFORM a welcome dance at the mouth of an empty cove in Tahuata. A dense population of palms ashore reflect off the glassy water and the entire cove glows emerald green. It's not our planned destination of Vaitahu Bay, but the gemstone water and resident dolphins seduce us into stopping for a night.

Ivan sets the anchor and announces he's going for a dip. He balances into a dive stance.

'Wait!' I catch him just in time. 'Look.' I point into the sea, which bubbles with life. It's nearing dusk and all members of the food chain have come out to eat. Jellyfish coat the surface with coloured tentacles, messing up the water like canned party string. Below the jellies, schools of fish swim in frantic circles, while bigger fish – visible by silhouette only – pace back and forth, planning attack. The water is too dense to see any deeper, but my logic determines that the base level of this food pyramid consists of the largest kind of predator.

'Are you thinking what I'm thinking?' Ivan says, before quickly running down below to busy himself. He slams a few cupboards and comes back up with a tackle box. The ocean is ripe and Ivan is going for the jackpot, baiting a three-tiered line with plastic worms from a packet that reads: *Now with a real worm flavour!* I'm tempted to find out what real worm tastes like, but I resist the urge to lick. Ivan loads on the sinkers, doing his best to aim for the intermediate layer where the dinner-sized fish are swimming.

'This is awesome,' he says.

'We're having fish for dinner!' I say.

I go down below to source some recipes from our book library. *Hmm, what should we have? Fish with caramelized onion, crumbed fish with lemon, fish with wasabi mayonnaise, fish with—*

'Assholes!' Ivan yells.

I put down the recipe book and go back on deck. I find him holding the rod in his hand, limp line at the end: bait gone, hooks gone, three-tiered system... gone.

'How can I *not* catch a fish in this teeming water?' Ivan says.

Unlucky fishermen stereotypically reel in an old boot, a rusty tin can or an emancipated goldfish, but we're not even that lucky. Our expensive lures are being stolen with the skill of a pickpocket on a peak-hour train. It's baffling and humiliating, and we're being mocked behind our backs with little fins poised in L-shapes.

As Ivan puts away the tackle box, I return the recipe books to the shelf and heat up some baked beans on the stovetop.

After dinner, we lie in bed together, discussing tactics for hooking one of those swimming fillets so we can show it who's smarter by way of a little butter and garlic drip torture, perhaps a chive and onion crown of thorns.

ON OUR SAIL to the tattooist's town, we pass a nirvana that beckons us to stop. It's straight out of a double-page spread from one of the cruising books that Ivan used to lure me here. The waters around the Marquesas, though stunning, are lined with volcanic sea mud, which tints the sea a dense shade of green. But this spot is unique: the sand is white and the water is a thirst-quenching turquoise.

Amazing Grace spins a few nesting dog circles and Ivan releases our mud-covered anchor into a water bath. Spotless, the anchor lodges on pure white sand a shallow twenty feet below.

There's a small collection of sailboats anchored here, including *Red Sky* – the boat that Leslie lives on, we note with alarm. But before we retrieve our anchor and escape, the 'old and boring' owners kayak over to welcome us. I know right away from their warmth and smiles that nothing we've been told about Steve and Carol holds true.

To our immense relief, we're told that Leslie flew home. 'Come by later for a cocktail,' Steve suggests and we gratefully accept the offer.

Just when you think life can't get any better, a sailor from a German boat stops by to offer us a heavy steak of wahoo, freshly caught. 'I've got too much,' he says with a shrug when we thank him.

'We hooked one!' Ivan says, holding up the steak in a catch-of-the-day pose.

I smile and run down below to get the recipe books.

THE WILD FOREST beyond the beach looks like a place where fruit grows in abundance and, with no private property fences to keep us away, we decide to go on another fruit scavenge. We jump into our dinghy – *Little Gracie* – and Ivan rows toward the beach.

As we approach the shore, the swell surfs us forward and delivers us onto the sand in one swift glide.

'Good work,' I say, and we pause to reflect on how beautiful our entrance was.

The stall costs us. The following wave bitch-slaps us with its wet, heavy weight, filling the dinghy with water. The ocean draws back and charges forward with another curling wave.

Crash. Another wave floods the dinghy.

'Oh, shit!'

We jump out and yank at her rope, but she doesn't budge – she's now over halfway full and as heavy as a beached whale. We don't know what else to do, so we keep playing tug-of-war with her rope, trying to coax the impossible weight beyond the waves. I attempt to bail with a bucket, scooping out frantic gallons of water, but the waves are faster than me, and she fills up before I can make a dint in the load.

Crash. She's full to the top and she succumbs to the water, dragging off the beach to be swallowed by the sucking tide.

'We've lost our dinghy!' I yell.

Ivan paces back and forth with his hands over his head, trying to figure out what to do, while I grip the tether as though her rope is the hand of a dying person. *Little Gracie* is taken out by the undertow and the ocean rips the tether from my palm, now pink and tender from our tug-of-war.

I feel like a fool. One week after our arrival, we're already shipwrecked.

'At least the engine wasn't on there,' I say. But it's a scant offering of positive thinking – what good is an engine without a dinghy to stick it on?

We stand and stare at our drowned boat, mouths agape.

'Check it out, she's coming back!' Ivan yells.

In one quick movement, *Little Gracie* is picked up inside a glassy swell, surfed back to the beach, dumped of water and then pounded before us onto the sand. She lies there flat, upright, intact, presented like a warning from the ocean: *Here's your dinghy back, but don't mess with me again!* We seize the moment, whisking her up the beach beyond the waves.

When she's out of danger, I tidy her hull, put the oars back in their sockets, coil ropes and pat her tenderly, thankful that she's still with us. 'I'm sorry,' I whisper to her. 'We'll be more careful with you next time.'

In the jungle beyond the beach, we get lucky again. Nestled deep in the vegetation, we find a tree glistening with bulbous yellow fruits: *mangoes!* Finally, the riches that sustained my morale for twenty-six days on passage. We bag mangoes in every shade from green to red. We pillage a lemon tree and collect green coconuts for drinking and brown ones for eating.

Choosing a waveless corner of the beach, we launch the dinghy back out to sea without incident.

THE MINUTE I STEP aboard *Red Sky*, I'm head over heels. She's a sleek and sexy fifty-foot Santa Cruz: a race boat, Ivan tells me. The interior looks like a nautical loft apartment with an open-plan space large enough to host a disco.

Steve serves us cocktails on the rocks and I have to touch an ice cube to make sure it's real. I'm instantly jealous – beverages are served only one way on *Amazing Grace*: room temperature.

'So…' Ivan says. 'We want to get something clear with you. Leslie told us a bunch of weird stories. Just so you guys know, we don't believe anything she had to say.'

'Oh my God, what a nightmare,' Steve says, and so begins their version of the story in which Leslie features as a drunken crew person who didn't know how to use a compass. Steve discovered this after finding her in the cockpit, lounged on a towel, cocktail in hand, bikini straps untied for minimal tan lines… while the boat was charging in the direction of Japan.

Over several cocktails, I fall for Steve and Carol. Contrary to Leslie's opinion, there's nothing old about these people. Carol is tall, slender and athletic, and her blue eyes draw me in with the magnetic presence I'm seeing in many lifestyle sailors. Steve is handsome and muscular, with the relaxed mannerisms of a surfer. They both have salt-and-pepper hair and the faint lines of age in the corners of their eyes, yet their personalities are frozen somewhere around thirty. Clearly, the ocean has preserved them.

They tell us that, for almost forty years, they've lived aboard, docked all over the world. Along the way, they've earned money in odd jobs – skippering, cashiering, boat refurbishing – but, recently, an unexpected inheritance gift allowed them to buy the beautiful quarter-of-a-million-dollar *Red Sky*. In their years, they've raised two boys on the ocean, now grown men living in the United States.

The Pacific crossing was their longest voyage to date and Carol says she spent the whole time lying flat in bed, too unnerved to do anything but sleep and read. 'I didn't move in twenty-four days,' she explains. 'Steve sailed the boat. I couldn't get out of bed. I was so seasick and scared out there.'

'Me too!' I confess. I relay my own experience of being frozen in terror for the better part of twenty-six days and we laugh at our similarities.

'You know,' Steve says, 'I've met a number of solo sailors whose wives refuse to go on the ocean at all. Some fly out to meet their partners, while others wait at home. I don't mind managing the boat on my own, I'm just happy to have Carol aboard with me.'

Ivan nods in firm agreement.

It's energising to recognise myself in Carol and to see that an indomitable shell isn't necessarily required for this kind of lifestyle. Enduring the long, scary passages comes with majestic rewards for the mind and soul, and Carol – with her athletic body and oozing happiness – is living proof of this. She's shown me that even experienced adventurers are not always fearless. They just don't run from fear.

It's 1 a.m. when we say good night and row back to our boat.

'I adore Steve and Carol,' I say to Ivan as he paddles us through the darkness.

'Me too,' he says. 'Do they remind you of anyone?'

'Yes, they remind me of us...'

'... when we're older,' he says, finishing my sentence.

'Wow. Can you imagine sailing for that long?' I ask.

'Of course! That's how I always envisioned this trip.'

I laugh, until I register that he's serious. The next forty years adrift on the ocean? *That's* his dream?

TEN

'SHARK!' I YELL. A notched fin cuts through the water beside us.

'Probably a hammerhead,' Ivan says. 'The Marquesas are full of them. They come here to breed.'

I let out a noise – half gag, half whinny – and slap at the sensation of a thousand spiders crawling over my skin. The menacing fin dips underneath *Amazing Grace* and out of sight.

We leave the sharky depths behind us and steer into the deep green water of Vaitahu Bay, Tahuata, home of Fati, the tattooist. The village ashore looks tidy and quaint, with a church made of stone, wood and stained glass creating an architectural centrepiece. Beyond the red steeple, the jagged peaks of the island jut up with all the drama of a fantasy-film backdrop.

The town is inviting a closer look, but getting to shore is a problem. Leaving the dinghy tied to the wharf all day isn't possible because it'll monopolise the only dock, and since a powerful swell pounds against the boulder-strewn beach, landing there is also out of the question. We've come all this way to get Ivan's tattoo, but it seems there's no way ashore. Unless…

'We swim,' Ivan says, verbalising my thoughts.

I look down at the opaque water and decide that it's now or never to face this. I can't let fear stop me. *I'm an old salt,* I remind myself. *I can totally swim with breeding hammerheads!*

I stand tall, forearms flexed, voice lowered, and say to Ivan, 'Let's do it.'

We tie the dinghy to a mooring ball halfway between our boat and the shore – about 200 feet off the beach. Ivan splashes overboard and begins to swim, and, without overthinking it, I plug my nose and jump overboard.

The second I hit the water, my mind screams, *Shark!* and I take off sprinting. *Don't splash!* I tell myself. *Keep cool. Splashing provokes sharks.* But this thought only gives me a logical foundation to know that I'm clearly being trailed by sixteen hungry hammerheads. *They're coming after me!* I begin thrashing like a madwoman, clobbering the water with violent kicks and fists, leaving a frothing jacuzzi of bubbles between the dinghy and the shoreline.

Miraculously unscathed, I stagger onto the beach, breathless. Ivan bodysurfs in on a wave minutes later, refreshed after his leisurely breaststroke. 'Gee, you swim fast,' he remarks.

Dripping wet but still alive, we go looking for the tattooist.

The town of Vaitahu is full of happy children. Some are playing with boogie boards in the river; others are kicking a soccer ball on the street. I wonder if there is a better place on earth to be a kid. Dogs lie under trees to escape the heat of the day and locals – dressed in tied sarongs or board shorts – welcome us with melodic *bonjour*s. We approach them with one question: 'Tattoo?' and they smile and point toward Fati's place.

Fati welcomes us into his humble parlour and I'm relieved to see a professional-style tattoo drill, not the sharpened matchstick that I've read is common in these parts. 'Where do you want it?' Fati asks.

Ivan glides his finger along the skin of his arm, tracing an invisible sketch for the artwork. 'Maybe nobody will ever hire me again,' he says. 'Not that I have a problem with that,' he adds.

His finger journeys up his shoulder in the direction of his neck. 'Imagine if—'

'What if you put it here,' I say, stopping his straying finger – and imagination – short. I draw a circle the size of a basketball that begins at his shoulder blade and wraps around to make a sleeve on his arm. 'It'll be nice and big, but you can always hide it under a shirt if you need to.'

He agrees, and I'm relieved. Watching Ivan transform from a corporate professional to a tattooed sailor is exciting, but I'm not yet open-minded enough to encourage facial tattoos and throwing away a career.

Fati begins to design directly onto Ivan's skin in pen, explaining that his tattoos are inspired by each person's unique soul.

The sketch takes two hours. When Fati is ready to start drilling, Ivan pulls out a vial of our strongest opiate painkiller, Vicodin, and shakes a pill into his hand.

'I'm sure that our doctor in LA wouldn't be comfortable with this,' I joke.

'Bottoms up,' Ivan says, swallowing the pill down with a sip of water.

Ivan can solo sail a boat across an ocean. He can lift a heavy anchor until his hands bleed. He can endure twenty-foot waves crashing over his fearless skull. Yet a tattoo requires opiate assistance? The man is a walking contradiction who never fails to surprise me.

After an hour of drilling, it appears that the Vicodin isn't offering a great deal of relief for this kind of pain – Ivan's face scrunches up every time the drill's needle connects.

He pauses to take another Vicodin pill and Fati gets back to work, using the needle to drill black ink into bloodied flesh. As I watch that relentless drill on the growing open wound, suddenly the Vicodin seems somewhat justifiable. But still, Ivan's face scrunches up in agony. The only effect the opiate is having on him is an ecstatic outburst of affection. 'I love you, baby,' he sings when the drill pauses. 'I love you soooo much.' His eyes are soft and adoring for a microsecond before they go crossed-eyed again in pain.

After hunching over his design for six long hours, Fati declares his artwork complete. He washes the tattoo down under a cold tap and, for a few short seconds before the black ink and blood begins to weep, we see the design. It's magnificent. Pink, puffy and no doubt sore, but truly magnificent.

Cream is rubbed over Ivan's bleeding flesh. Fati lists off the instructions for care: 'Do not pick at the scabs, apply cream twice per day, and absolutely no salt water for two weeks.'

I turn to Ivan in alarm, my eyes saying it all: *We swam here! How are we going to get back to the boat?* Although it's a moot point at the moment, really, as Ivan is far too stoned to do anything but sing, 'I love you *soooo* much.'

WE STAND ON THE BEACH, looking out at *Little Gracie* bobbing on her mooring several hundred feet away, trying to solve the dilemma like a riddle. *A farmer has a bag of grain, a chicken and a fox...*

'Eh!' someone yells to us. 'Come, come.'

I follow the direction of the voice with my eyes to find a woman lazing under the shade of a tree with her two kids and her husband. 'Tattoo,' she says, pointing at Ivan's weeping arm. She makes a swimming gesture. 'Tattoo. No swim.' She has intuited our dilemma.

The woman slaps her smallest boy on the back and speaks a few abrupt words in Marquesan. The kid gets up and walks over to an old kayak, which he drags by a tether into the water. Sitting on his knees and using a piece of driftwood as a paddle, he heads out to *Little Gracie*, unties her from the mooring and reattaches the rope to his kayak. From there, he travels to the concrete wharf, far away on the other side of the bay. His slow progress means we have plenty of time to walk around the perimeter of the bay to meet him at the wharf.

The boy presents *Little Gracie* to us, like a valet. We shower the kid with *merci*s, which he shrugs off, forcing me to wonder if he does this with all the freshly tattooed sailors. He turns his kayak around and heads shoreward at a snail's pace with his little driftwood paddle.

BACK AT THE BOAT, I inspect Ivan's new body feature from every possible angle. Abstract patterns portraying manta rays, stars, waves and turtles interlock into a dense, detailed design.

I rub the wound with antiseptic cream, as per Fati's instructions. 'What a nice souvenir,' I say. 'You can always remember this trip, but you can always hide it under a shirt if you need to.'

'Maybe I should've gone a bit bigger,' he ponders. He turns serious as he slips into a private thought. 'I should call my parents. It's been over a week since I last called; I know Mum will be worried.'

'So why not call now then?' I retrieve the satellite phone from its cubby, extend its thick aerial and hold it out to Ivan.

He sits on the sofa and crosses his arms over his chest. 'Got nothing to say.'

'Huh? You just got a massive tattoo today.'

He tightens his jaw and looks away. 'I'm not going to bother telling them about the tattoo.'

I can't help but laugh at this. 'Are you kidding? You're an adult.'

'Exactly. But you know what will happen? Mum will *freak out*. She'll be all, "Ivan, you'll never get a job again with that tattoo. Blah, blah, blah." Not that I care, it's just irritating. I don't want that negativity bringing my mood down.'

His mood, it appears, is suddenly down all on its own.

'Don't talk about the tattoo. Speak about something else.'

'Like what?'

'I dunno, other news.'

'We have no news. That's the point of this trip! To get away from the news. Our latest headline is: "Man Catches Wahoo, Gives Some to Us."'

'Hey, that's pretty funny. Tell them that.'

'No.'

'But if you don't call soon, won't your parents get worried?'

'I don't want to call my parents. Okay?'

'Fine, whatever, you brought it up,' I say. 'Suit yourself. Don't call them.'

'I won't.'

'Good.'

'Fine.'

I hold off for as long as I can. 'But you haven't called your mother in over a week and she'll be freaking out right about now. She'll think we've sunk.'

'That's her problem.'

'That's cruel, Ivan. She won't sleep if you don't call her.'

'But why is that my problem? I never even wanted the stupid satellite phone aboard anyway, but she had to go and buy it for us. The whole point of this trip was to disconnect and now I'm expected to check in with my mum like a five-year-old?'

They say you can tell a man's character by how he treats his mother, and Ivan, quite frankly, is a jerk to his. 'Why are you being so hostile?' I ask.

'It just shits me, you know? I used to read Moitessier and think about how, when he was sailing around the world, the Cold War was going on but it didn't matter one bit to him. All he was worried about was catching fish! He was disconnected from current affairs and all that bullshit. That was one of my biggest motivators for doing this trip – to get away from that. I don't want all the mess that goes on in the world to affect me, and I don't want other people's stress to affect me.'

I shrink into a corner of the sofa, withered by his outburst. 'I don't get why you're so angry,' I say quietly.

'I'm not angry!' he says, gritting his teeth. 'I just don't want my parents serving up some crap about how I'll never get a job in corporate America again because of this tattoo. I want to enjoy being here in these islands and I don't want their opinions bringing me down. So what if I never get a job again? Is that a reason not to do this trip?'

'But nobody has said anything yet, you're just—'

'Do you know what my dad said right before we left? He said, "What are you planning to do when you get back, Ivan? Do you think you'll get a corporate job again?" I was, like, "Who cares?" Is that a reason to not fulfill a dream? Because of fear of the unknown? Can't I just do a trip like this without everyone imposing their irrational fears?'

I go quiet for a while, guilty over my own truckload of phobias. Will he eventually lose patience with me too?

'Your parents care about you, Ivan, that's all. Why is that a bad thing?'

'I don't need them to, though.'

'But that's just what parents do.'

'I didn't ask to be born. Why can't they just leave me alone?'

'Please calm down. I'm not sure why you're so—'

'I don't get it! *All I want is to be left alone!*' He gets up off the sofa and stomps outside. I don't pursue him – I don't wish to further aggravate a man who clearly wishes to be isolated, possibly for the next forty years.

LOVE WITH A CHANCE OF DROWNING

SINCE WE'RE COEXISTING full-time in a space smaller than most standard-sized bedrooms, our arguments need to resolve quickly. All our waking hours are spent in each other's company and at night we crush together in a small bed, our bodies tightly pressed, intimate with each other's sweat and breathing and heartbeats. We never fight over whose turn it is to do the dishes, make the bed or rinse the decks with buckets of salt water. Chores get done without arguments because we've developed a natural rhythm for these things. When the boat arrives into a new anchorage, we begin an organised dance of securing, tidying and coiling. Petty disagreements would only throw off our steps.

When I announced my sailing plans to friends in San Francisco, a colleague confessed that if she were stuck on a boat with her fiancé, chances are, she'd push him overboard. While insisting that she loved him dearly, she declared that being stuck on a boat with her betrothed all day was not a romantic fantasy, but her personal idea of hell. I couldn't help but wonder why she was intending to marry a man whom she couldn't stand to be alone with.

But perhaps her feelings were not so unusual. I once read researched statistics that found that average couples spend around two and a half waking hours together per day (including weekends). The majority of this time is spent watching TV, doing housework and eating, meaning that even the measly one-on-one time is shared partaking in tasks either practical or distracting. One would assume that the figure for retirees would skyrocket, yet somehow these couples still avoid each other for all but four hours per day, on average.

Ivan and I spend *every waking hour* together: around fourteen hours per day, or thirteen if we apportion a generous amount of time to toilet breaks. Occasionally we go about our own individual tasks: I may write on my laptop inside while Ivan writes in his journal ten feet away outside, but it's impossible for us to be more than thirty-two feet apart at any given time. In other words, for twenty-four hours per day, seven days per week, we're close enough to hear each other's sneezes and farts.

In six months, we've already clocked in more than two years of 'average relationship' one-on-one time together. By the end of the year, we'll have essentially been married for five years in 'land time.'

But unlike a normal marital environment, we don't have the luxury of escaping behind a slammed door if an argument fires up or the tension mounts. There's no room for a private cry in the bath, a venting phone call to a friend or a temporary escape into the world of sports. *Amazing Grace* doesn't have the space to host disagreements.

Instead, our differences need to be worked through regularly, treated in the same way that one might iron the laundry: carefully tending to each problem, pushing out the wrinkles and folding it all away in a neat, resolved pile. Without jobs, social engagements, television, gardening, bill-paying, family obligations and other time-hungry commitments, there are no distractions to turn to. There is only the sea, the sky, the boat and the relationship. So when we're not speaking, it's awkward beyond words.

All it would take is one of us wishing for time out, even if just for a day, before the flesh-against-flesh intimacy of living in a boat could no longer be tolerated.

After forty minutes of not speaking, as I'm showering under cold water in the bathroom, I overhear Ivan chatting to his parents on the satellite phone. I can't understand the Spanish conversation, but it's light and good humoured. He's happy now, but the anger that was in his voice earlier still rings in my ears.

When he's done, he comes down into the salon and hugs me over my towel.

'Guess what? My parents said they've booked flights to come and see us in a few months' time.' He says this through a smile, which I take to mean that whatever was upsetting him was resolved.

'Great. So you're happy about that?' I eye him dubiously.

'Yes, I'm happy. I miss them. I know we fight and stuff, but I do love them. They're my parents and, you're right, they care about me. I'm just a brat. Sorry. I love you. We can go to Nuku Hiva for vegetables and internet too. I don't know why I got so upset about that before. I'm a jerk sometimes. There must be something wrong with me.'

I reply with a cheeky nod.

He laughs and then he peels the towel away from my cold, damp skin and holds my flesh to his.

AFTER AN OVERNIGHT JOURNEY beneath sinister overhanging storm clouds, we sail into Nuku Hiva, feeling humbled by the cathedral-like walls of rock that encase the bay's entrance. The anchorage of Taiohae Bay opens up to a yawning mouth, over a mile wide, and it's dotted with more cruising boats than I ever imagined we'd be sharing this experience with. So many people have journeyed incredible distances to get here, through storms and rainbows, calms and squalls. We've reached a mecca of ocean vagabonds, and I couldn't be happier to be in the company of so many people.

I locate an old alarm clock, set it for 3:30 a.m. in time for the market, and we go to bed early.

At 5 a.m. we wake to darkness. The old, salt-corroded alarm clock didn't chime and we overslept. We dress fast and load into the dinghy, paddling through black water. Ivan rows with lazy strokes toward the bright lights of the market half a mile away. I hear the turbulent splashing of nocturnal feeders beside us, but I'm too tired to fret. Ivan almost collides us with three anchored yachts, invisible in the darkness until the last moment. Sleepily, he turns the dinghy and continues toward the lights.

By the time we get ashore, it's 5:30 a.m. The crowd has thinned out and the market sellers are stacking empty crates into the back of their cars. The only remains are a few stray leaves of lettuce and a bunch of bruised bananas. My stomach makes a warped, self-pitying gurgle.

'Don't worry,' Ivan says, reading my slumped shoulders. 'Steve told me there's an isolated anchorage on the north side of this island called Anaho Bay. It can only be reached by hiking or by boat, so we can go there and come back in time for next week's market, okay?'

'Thank you,' I say, lunging at him with an appreciative hug.

We find the internet café and I'm whisked away to another world. Each letter in my inbox is a present that brings me close enough to hear people's voices, to see loved ones with my mind's eye. I attack the keyboard with an epic four-thousand-word e-mail to my mum, walking her through my life down to the small details, like how many mosquito bites I've collected so far. Everyone else gets a thousand words each, including Anna, who already seems a lifetime away.

I leave the internet café with stiff fingers and a beaming smile.

We eat sweet pastries with coffee for breakfast at a small café. At an artisan store, I buy a new lime-green sarong, and then we stock up on canned staples at the market.

On the long row back to *Amazing Grace*, we pass a yacht called *Sea Dream* and a man in his late forties gives us a wave. 'Howdy. How y'all doin' today?' he says in a Texan accent.

The man is tinkering with hardware on deck. Behind him, a US flag the dimension of a king-sized sheet flaps in the wind. I stare longer than I should because he's unexpectedly clad in a metallic turquoise Speedo, tight enough to suffocate the life from his family jewels. His hair is a scraggly mullet and blond fluff grows all the way down his chest, along his bulging belly, until it tucks down into his shiny Speedo.

'Look at that man,' I whisper. 'Where did he get that bathing suit?' We both have a giggle. 'He must have kept it from his heyday as a muscle man on Venice Beach.' More giggling.

Then the Texan turns around to reveal the backside of his get-up and I gasp and nearly lose my breakfast. As he bends down to wrench something on deck, the 'T' of his metallic turquoise G-string wedges so far up his crack that all I can see is a tropical heat rash. A large white moon face returns the stare. This man is up on deck at seven in the morning, tending to the hardware of his topside in nothing but a stripper's thong.

He turns around and spots us staring, mouths agape. 'The name's Wayne,' he yells, tipping an invisible cowboy hat.

Ivan lowers his voice. 'I've heard about this guy. He runs some sort of escort service. Women pay him to take them to exotic destinations, and this guy, Wayne, gives 'em a little somethin' extra on the side.'

'So he's a gigolo of the sea?'

'Guess so.'

'It's an original business model, that's for sure.'

Ivan picks up the rowing pace.

To get to Anaho Bay from our current position, we have to forge into a strong headwind, which our sailboat takes to with the elegance of roller skates on sand.

After a lengthy battle, we arrive in an L-shaped retreat, with *Red Sky* the only other boat in sight. Tall pinnacles, green with palms, buffer every breath of wind, leaving the water as smooth as an ironed silk sheet.

In fact, the water is so flat, we're inspired to do chores that rougher waters have kept us from tackling. I scrub down the boat and use linseed oil to polish the teak inside and out until it shines, while Ivan fills our drinking water tanks – a task that involves rowing to shore to fill jerry cans at the closest tap, which is sometimes far from the shore. He fills the cans, carries them to the dinghy, rows back to the boat, lugs them aboard, and then funnels the water into our tanks. Performed six times over with three jerry cans on each trip, it's a labour-intensive task, and acquiring water this way gives us both an appreciation for the precious liquid so that every drop is rationed. We have a watermaker aboard, but it's so slow and power-hungry that using it means going without lights or our one allocated laptop charge per day.

Ivan returns from a water run and calls me outside. 'Come see this.'

Up on deck, I follow Ivan's pointing finger to look at the water. Mixed schools of fish surround the boat, decorating the shallows with silvery stripes and sparkling red skins.

'Check this out,' Ivan says. He takes a cracker in his hand, crumbles it, and throws it overboard. The fish go into an eating frenzy, aggressively competing for a nibble. Schools of stripy convict fish mix with black surgeonfish in a writhing mass, but it's the red snapper that always win the fight. One foot long, they're fast and aggressive and can gobble down every crumb microseconds ahead of the smaller fish.

'I guarantee you we'll catch one of those snappers,' Ivan says, springing into action with his rod and tackle box.

Just as he's about to throw the line, he stops and peers out toward the beach. 'Hey, look.' He points to some kids playing with a little white boat. 'That dinghy looks just like *Little Gracie*.' He loses interest and goes back to prepping his fishing rod.

My eyes stay fixed on the kids' boat. It is suspiciously similar to ours: white, wooden, same paddles, same black bailing bucket inside, shoes identical to mine. I look to starboard and notice that *Little Gracie* is missing. 'That is our dinghy, Ivan,' I say.

He takes a second look. 'Oh, yeah. She must have gotten away.'

I put my hand on my hip and glare at him. 'And just *how* did she get away?'

'Oops. I just feel really relaxed here. Must have forgotten to tie her up.'

I try to maintain my stern face, but I can't help but smile at his clumsiness. It's as though, in these calm waters, he expected the dinghy would stay put like a bike resting against a tree.

The three island kids row over to return *Little Gracie*. Aboard, there's a girl of about twelve and two boys who look ten and eight. They're all giggles and white-toothed smiles.

Come aboard, I gesture, and they don't hesitate to accept the invite.

Though we don't share a common language, the kids seem happy to just hang out and watch us do our thing, giggling and chatting among themselves in French.

While I draw pictures with the kids, Ivan throws the fishing line overboard. He instantly snags a greedy foot-long snapper. He baits and throws another line, dragging up a second fish moments later. To his audience of four, Ivan acts all nonchalant, as though effortlessly plucking seafood from the ocean is nothing out of the ordinary for this master fisherman.

The young girl volunteers to help clean the catch, so we watch and learn. She grabs a fish from the bucket and gets a neck-hold by wedging her fingers into its gill region. It flaps around in self-defence and she responds by taking a balled-up fist and punching it square in the head. *Bam!* The fish is stunned to stillness.

She takes a knife and begins scaling the fish alive. When it starts to wiggle again – *bam!* – another hook to the head. After she's done with the scaling, she slices it from the gills to the tail. The fish, still alive, lies motionless, apart from the occasional dismal tail flip. She goes in with her fingers to retrieve a white organ that is coveted enough to cause bickering among the kids. They settle on parting it three ways. I have no idea what it is, but I'm not going to squabble for a taste.

The second fish meets the same island-style fate: a punch to the head, followed by a live scaling and gutting. We coat the now-dead fish in a little garlic and lemon, then wrap them in foil and cook them on the small barbecue mounted to our stern railing.

When the meat is cooked, the five of us enjoy a lunch of snapper meat dipped in mayonnaise.

'This is awesome,' Ivan says, sucking the last morsel of meat off the bone. He tosses the head overboard, and the awaiting fish go crazy, thrashing in the water over the food. 'Check that out. They're cannibals.'

'This place is teeming with fish,' I say.

'Finally, baby, we can have fresh fish for every meal!'

THAT EVENING, as I sit alone on deck after a satisfying day, I relax and watch the brilliant orange sunset. Turbulent splashes of water just off the boat catch my attention and I jump up to investigate. Our gilled companions are in a feeding frenzy. *Strange*, I think, *we haven't thrown them any food, so what are they eating?*

I move closer so I can peer over the railing. The light is dimming, so I squint to make out the shapes in the water. The fish are thrashing and gobbling from a speckled, murky cloud of something I can't identify. I hang my head overboard for a closer look, baffled by the mystery food that's driving them into a fit of excitement.

Ivan emerges from down below, tightening the drawstring of his board shorts. 'What are you looking at?' he asks, seeing me with my head hanging over the rail. 'Is something down there?'

'Check it out.' I point to the water. 'The fish are getting a good feed. But I can't figure out what they're eating.'

Ivan moves in to investigate and his face screws up. 'I just flushed the toilet. *They're eating my poo!*'

For dinner that night, we don't eat barbecued red snapper. In fact, shit-fed red snapper is off the menu for good.

WHILE HIKING AROUND the mountains of Anaho Bay, we encounter a friendly local named Thomas, who is one of the few fluent-English-speaking Marquesans we've met. Thomas invites us to his house for some beers and, there, we chat with him about Marquesan culture, his life on Nuku Hiva, our travels and our lives back home.

He tells us he loves life in this place because he doesn't need money to get by. 'People in the cities, like Tahiti, they're poor,' he tells us. 'You need big money to live in the city. Here, money is not important. I have everything I need – a fish garden in my front yard, a coconut garden in my backyard. I'm a happy man and I'm rich.'

He brings out a baggie stuffed with green herbs. 'Smoke?'

Apparently, Thomas has another kind of garden as well. Though neither of us are pot smokers, we accept the invitation, not wanting to turn down a cultural experience with this kind man.

The joint is rolled and passed to Ivan, who takes a toke and coughs it down.

'What happens if you get caught with marijuana here?' I ask Thomas, exhaling smoke.

'Not good,' he says, turning serious. 'You go to jail. Sailors can have their boats taken away. The *gendarmerie* here is very strict.'

I break into a coughing fit.

Thomas then invites us to a small party of locals on the beach. The group is drinking Hinano beers and playing music with makeshift instruments. Fish cook on embers made from coconut husks, while friendly dogs join the party, jostling for affection. All the family pets feast on coconut and fish scraps, which seem to keep their coats shiny.

Ivan and I are handed empty beer bottles with spoons so we can tap percussion along with the traditional songs and, without speaking, we sit with the gathering for an hour, connecting through music.

When the time comes to head back to the boat, Thomas stops us. 'Before you go,' he says, 'let me give you something.' He pulls a knife from his pocket and runs into his garden, cutting down a bunch of bananas that's half my height at least. He hands them to Ivan and then disappears into another part of his garden, returning with a handful of green leaves. I have no idea what it is at first, but when I inspect it up close in the darkening light, I see that I'm holding a bud-covered bouquet of marijuana.

'HELLO? ANYONE ABOARD?' Ivan stands in the dinghy, knocking on the shiny hull of *Red Sky*. Steve and Carol emerge.

'Hi, guys, what's up?' Carol says. She's wearing a black one-piece bathing suit with peepholes in the torso that shows off her slender swimmer's body. Carol is one sexy sixty-year-old.

'We're wondering if you'd like some of this?' I hold half the bouquet out.

Steve's eyes light up. 'Where did you get *this*?'

'A kind stranger in the mountains.'

'Oh, wow,' Steve says, taking the gift. 'Oh, fantastic. Why don't any locals ever give us handfuls of pot? How did you guys get so lucky? We must look too old or something. This is awesome. Oh, wow. Thank you.'

'We have something for you too,' Carol says. She runs below and comes back with a bag of fish steaks. 'Wahoo. On the way over here, we caught a fish bigger than you, Torre.'

We thank them and then return to *Amazing Grace*. I tuck the stash of pot into a plastic container, which I bury within our deepest cupboard.

I marinate the wahoo in onions, balsamic, garlic and herbs and serve it with mashed potatoes.

'This is incredible,' Ivan says, with a forkful of fish in his hand. 'So much better than shit-fed snapper. I have to say that when I dreamed of sailing the South Pacific, I honestly never anticipated I'd be out here trading marijuana for wahoo steaks with sixty-year-old best friends.'

THIS MORNING, Steve and Carol pulled up their anchor with the push of a button and sailed out of Anaho Bay twenty minutes ago to make their way back to Taiohae Bay for the island's market tomorrow. Ivan has been grunting up our anchor ever since.

'OUGHHHH!' Ivan's yell makes all nearby birds scream off in fright.

I've been stewing over the problem of our anchor system for a while, because Ivan's muscle-and-grunt method doesn't make sense.

I go forward to inspect the hardware. There's a large piece of apparatus in the bow, which looks like it belongs with the anchor. 'Could you wrap the chain around that winch and crank it with the handle?'

'The winch is not for chain, it's for rope,' Ivan says. I ignore his condescending voice.

'Why don't you just try it? It might work.'

'Look, I know what I'm doing, okay?'

At the risk of rubbing him the wrong way with my persistence, I give it one more shot. 'Try it once. Please?'

He lets out a loud, frustrated breath and then obliges to please me. He wraps the chain around the winch and cranks the handle with his other arm. The anchor starts to retract effortlessly into its locker. 'Oh, look at that,' Ivan says. 'Wow!'

I tighten my lips to conceal an erupting *Told you so!*

'I totally didn't think that would work,' he says in shock. 'Thanks, baby, of course that's what the winch is for, geez!' He keeps cranking, retracting the anchor by the power of steel cogs, stopping every now and again to let out another surprised 'Huh'. This new method requires no grunting whatsoever.

I walk back to the tiller with confidence in my stride, wondering if I'm getting the hang of this whole sailing thing after all.

A SUDDEN, VIOLENT SQUALL slams the boat, waking me from a deep sleep. Despite the screaming wind in our rigging and the fact that the boat is tipping from the wind's angry force, we're safely anchored in the crowded bay of Taiohae, and there's nothing to worry about. Is there?

I remember that my new green sarong is hanging outside and I jump out of bed to save it. As I'm unpinning my sarong from the lifelines, something enormous and white catches my eye off the starboard side. I glance up and take a moment to register what I'm seeing. My hair stands on end.

We're about to collide with *Red Sky*!

When we went to bed, we were anchored one hundred feet away. Now we're one squall's breath from ramming our friends.

'Getting kinda close there, aren't you?' Steve says. I realise he's standing in the cockpit. There's no need for him to yell out, we're almost close enough to shake hands.

'Yes, far too close! Are we dragging anchor, or are you?'

Ivan hears our voices and comes up into the cockpit. 'Oh, shit,' he says.

'Hey, Ivan,' Steve says in his usual laid-back surfer voice. 'Your anchor is dragging. I've been up watching for a while and with that last big gust, you guys sure took off flying. I've been hanging up on deck for about an hour, keeping an eye out.'

Red Sky is an S-class Mercedes to our 1979 Volvo station wagon. I'd be watching us too. Few sailors can afford to insure their boats out here, since the annual premium for offshore cruisers is half the total cost of the boat. I'm amazed that Steve is still keeping his cool. If that were my Mercedes, I'd be sitting on my horn and extending not one but two middle fingers.

Steve picks up *Red Sky*'s anchor with the push of a button, while Ivan slowly cranks in our chain. When we're a safe distance apart, we go back to bed for some restless sleep. My days of blissful ignorance are over; I now know that, even at anchor while we're sleeping, a strong wind can send us wherever it likes.

IN THE DARK HOURS of the morning, we row to the market and fight through an early crowd to get our fresh produce. We return to the boat with overflowing bags of hard-earned booty.

'Are you happy to see me?' I say to Ivan, holding a long green cucumber suggestively.

Ivan pushes two enormous grapefruits to his bare chest and says, 'Oh yes, I am.'

Our roaring laughter is disproportionate to the quality of the joke, but we're giddy with euphoria over this simple pleasure. We've come a long way to get it.

Without refrigeration, our produce won't last, so our only option is to eat it all now and get our fix before we head toward the sandy, barren shores of the Tuamotus.

While gobbling down a mound of salad, we get to work planning our voyage to the Tuamotus. We're both edgy. Travelling on the ocean always feels like a mad dash through a bullet field, particularly when you're heading into a zone nicknamed 'The Dangerous Archipelago'. Even seasoned sailors get nervous travelling through this archipelago and, while many decide to skip the area entirely, those who brave the journey into this 215-nautical-mile zone of coral hazards do so with trepidation. Impossible to spot from afar, the scattered coral reefs accumulate shipwrecks on shorelines like sandcastles on a beach after a busy summer day. Boats of all sizes – from skiffs to tankers – go belly up, scattering the world's largest chain of atolls with rusty metal skeletons, decomposing wood and fractured fibreglass bodies.

The ring-shaped atolls have a passage just wide and deep enough to allow a boat to travel into the centre lagoon, but these narrow channels generate strong currents as tides push water in and out. With currents of up to twelve knots, a poorly timed attempt at entering an atoll pass could leave our meek boat forked on a reef.

There's no room for clumsiness; our seamanship has to be impeccable. Which is why we've spent the entire day doing research.

At the island's internet café, we print tide times for an atoll called Manihi, chosen for its rumoured ease of entry. Rummaging up as much information as possible, we study three guidebooks for particulars, reading up on hazards and strategies for anchoring. Ivan charts our course on his laptop, creating a dotted route for *Amazing Grace* to follow from here to the next safe retreat.

We're as ready as we'll ever be to depart, but I'm dragging my feet, feeling nervous about heading into this remote corner of the earth. It's easy to stall in this beautiful place, so we sit in the cockpit eating from our huge stem of bananas for breakfast while gazing out at the scenery.

A familiar boat is missing. 'Where's *Red Sky*?' I ask.

Ivan looks around. 'That's weird. They were here earlier.'

I scan in circles, thinking perhaps I'm somehow not seeing their unmistakable fifty-foot yacht. 'They said they weren't going to leave for a few more days. Strange. Did they just... leave?'

'They must have.'

My heart sinks. Our 'friends' have left without even a goodbye. I guess they wanted space from clumsy amateur sailors who drag into them during the night.

'Damn it,' I say. 'I really loved those guys.' Even though I adore Ivan's company, I long to be connected to a community, to have friends to share stories with over meals and drinks. When it's just the two of us for weeks and weeks, our stories begin to fade, like a sun-bleached Polaroid.

Ivan pats my back. 'Don't worry. We'll make new friends.'

But I'm not convinced, because our next destination is Ivan's remote paradise.

ELEVEN

OUR SAILS ARE FLUFFED to a perfect convex by a steady breath of air, taking us on a direct course toward the Tuamotus. I lie in the cockpit, half asleep, enjoying the rhythm as though I'm riding bareback on a horse through a flat, open wilderness. This is trade-wind sailing at its best.

The wind is fresh and warm, twirling pleasurable circles around my naked body. The two of us have been lazing about, relaxing far too much for sailors who are manning a ship on an ocean passage. It's been days since Ivan has touched the sails. They're trimmed just so, harnessing the breeze, which pushes us along at our top speed of six knots. We've made our record distance of 143 miles in twenty-four hours without even lifting a finger.

I'm excited to see the Tuamotus. The archipelago is an expanse of seventy-eight atolls, each made up of a string of perfect islets like a necklace of pearls. The lagoon within the necklace is a sheltered oasis – a picturesque lake in the middle of the Pacific – and many of the sparsely inhabited atolls can only be accessed by boat.

Ivan switches on the SSB and tunes in to the Coconut Net to hear the daily forecast. Broadcast by sailors in the area, the station announces daily weather and provides a forum for contact and support among cruisers. We take note of the weather report, and then—

'*Amazing Grace, Amazing Grace.* This is *Red Sky.* Do you copy? Over.'

Taken by surprise to hear our boat name over the radio, and with a mouth full of banana, Ivan dashes to the SSB to answer the call.

'Ivan and Torre, where are you heading?' Steve says through the radio's static.

I smile wide, overjoyed to learn that they didn't ditch us after all. Ivan thumbs the radio's talk button. 'Hey, Steve. We're going to Manihi.'

'Change course now, guys. We're in one of the most incredible locations we've ever seen. You need to come here as soon as you can, this place is spectacular.'

With forty years of cruising experience, Steve and Carol know what spectacular looks like. I'm all ears.

'Where are you, Steve?' Ivan says.

'In one of the Tuamotus, nearby to Rangiroa. We're in a place called Anse Amyot in Toau. You guys have to see this place.'

Ivan's thumb lingers on the SSB talk button, waiting to give a reply. 'What do you think?' he asks me.

'Sounds great, but we haven't done any research. Our tide times are for Manihi. Ask Steve what the pass is like. We need more information.'

Ivan pushes down the radio talk button. 'Steve, what is the pass like in Toau? Do you have the tide times?'

'This place is unaffected by tides,' Steve says. 'Guys, I tell you, it's so easy. It's nothing like all that hair-raising stuff you read about going through dangerous passes.'

Ivan and I stare at each other skeptically. 'This goes against everything we've read,' Ivan says to me. 'How can this one atoll be unaffected by tides?'

'Not sure, but Steve's experienced. He knows what he's talking about.'

Ivan presses the radio button. 'So, Steve – we really just come in at any time?'

'Yeah, that's right. There are five other boats here and nobody had an issue getting in.'

'Five other boats!' I squeal, celebrating with jazz fingers and a little jig.

My happy dance makes Ivan smile. 'Sounds great, Steve,' he says.

'When you get close, a local guy called Gaston will come out in his boat to guide you to a mooring. Only one family lives here and they love getting visits from sailors. They'll all come out and meet you when you arrive because it's pretty isolated here, so any new company is a big deal to them. These people are unbelievably warm and they'll adopt you immediately. They've installed a bunch of solid moorings in the lagoon, so just come right in and pick one up right outside of the family's homes. Don't worry about the difficulty of arriving here – that part is easy. If anything, you should worry about the difficulty of *leaving*.'

Easy. That's a relief. I nod to Ivan and he nods back.

'Okay, well, I guess we'll see you tomorrow, then.' Ivan signs out and hangs up the radio receiver.

We check the guidebook for information. There's only one entrance into Toau's lagoon and it's called the Otugi Pass. Ivan replots our course on the GPS.

'This place is a little harder to get to than Manihi,' he says, 'so we'll have to do a bit of weaving between other atolls at night. If all goes well, we'll be there tomorrow around four in the afternoon.'

I STIR IN MY BUNK, kept awake by the jackhammer sound of the engine running high. The perfect breeze we've been treated to over the last four days has waned and we need to use the engine's power to make progress.

We're on a tight deadline – we need to make Toau tomorrow before sundown. If we arrive just thirty minutes late, the light will dim and our vision will be poor. Having enough daylight to enter the lagoon is vital because, by night, the ocean is a pool of toneless black with no definition between water and reef.

The hope of a good night's sleep sometimes seduces otherwise rational sailors into taking stupid risks, like entering a port at night, and boats are often lost because of this impatience. We have a rule aboard: no port entries at night, no matter what. If we arrive late, we'll be forced to turn the boat around and wallow in darkness for fifteen hours.

Navigating through the reefs by night is stressful and there's no margin for error. Ivan watches the GPS nonstop, double-checking numbers against his charts to be sure the currents are not side-sweeping us toward hiding shorelines, which quietly wait for the chance to add another boat to an already impressive collection. But watching the numbers on the GPS becomes Ivan's peculiar obsession. No matter what he's doing, cooking, eating or trimming sails, his saucer-like eyes are fixed to the LCD display, ogling the monitor with the same slack jaw and vacant gaze of the infomercial-addicted.

TOAU IS A MODEST SIGHT from sea, little more than a thin layer of green vegetation on the horizon. It looks like a light refraction that will evaporate once we get close. Palm trees appear to grow directly from the water's surface like tufts of green hair.

As we close in right on time at 4 p.m. we're both stunned to silence. The pass doesn't look like I imagined when Steve described it. I pictured a wall of palm trees to either side with a riverlike waterway running between. But there is no visible pass, just turbulent water crashing against exposed reef. The waves look like a sloppy surf break and I have no idea which parts are deep water and which are jagged reef.

'Is this it?' I ask. 'It looks really rough.'

'Yeah, it does. I'll check in with Steve.' Ivan picks up the radio receiver. '*Red Sky, Red Sky,* this is *Amazing Grace.* Do you copy? Over.'

He tries three times, but only empty static responds.

'Any yachts in Toau, this is *Amazing Grace,* is anyone copying this? Over.'

Nothing.

Ivan hangs up the radio receiver. 'Weird. Steve mentioned there were five other boats with them in Toau. Why isn't anyone responding?'

'It could be our radio antenna. Or maybe nobody has their radios on?'

'Maybe.'

'So should we just... go through the pass?'

'I guess?'

'Steve said it was easy,' I remind us both.

The light is dimming and our opportunity to spend the night in a calm lagoon is closing in fast. A decision needs to be made.

I double-check the guidebooks and Ivan checks his navigation. There's only one passageway into Toau's lagoon and we're looking right at it. We can only trust the data on a GPS, which right now is telling us to head directly into agitated water on the fringe of an exposed shoal.

'Remember, Steve said it was easy,' I say again, my voice now trembling.

Ivan revs the engine and points the boat toward the mayhem. 'Here we go,' he says.

Amazing Grace works herself up into a fit as she meets the choppy waves. My balance becomes unsteady and I find something to hold on to with both hands.

Ivan holds the tiller firm in his hand, doing his best to meet what's thrown at us. His face shows an emotion I rarely see on him: worry.

Waves are coming from all angles; the water is as confused as we are. *Amazing Grace* surfs, then slams into a contrary wave, which smashes the cockpit with a cold, salty spray. All around, dolphins are breaching, using the waves to boost their acrobatic propulsion. As another wave slops overboard, dousing us both, I grow concerned that I may end up with a dolphin in my lap.

'This mustn't be as hard as it seems,' I mumble to myself.

Our slow progress forward tells me we're pushing against a strong current. It's pinning us in the turbulence. All we can do is keep pushing forward: if we turn around now, we'll be side to the waves, which are looking vicious enough to roll us.

'Shallows!' Ivan yells.

Without warning, we're over the top of pale blue water and I can make out colours and shapes of coral heads on the sea floor. *We're going to hit!* I suppress the urge to panic – freaking out will do no good. I look around for a safe place to swim. There's a reef platform but it's being washed over by angry waves. Far off in the distance, to either side of the pass, there are sandy islets, but swimming would be futile anyway: the outgoing current is too strong and we'd be tossed to the sharks like meat to dogs.

Suddenly, the waves peel away. The water levels out to dead flat. We're floating in a tranquil expanse of turquoise blue.

'We're in the lagoon!' Ivan says.

We've popped into a new dimension and we hug in a clammy embrace.

'So much for easy,' Ivan says.

'I was pretty sure we were going to drown.'

'Yeah, totally.' Ivan releases a shaky laugh.

'Where's *Red Sky*?' I say, scanning the empty lagoon.

'Wasn't someone called Gaston going to meet us?'

'This is weird. Let's try the radio again,' I suggest.

To my great relief, Ivan summons Steve on the radio.

'Where are you guys?' Steve asks. 'We thought you'd be here by now.'

'We just made it through the pass, Steve. Wow, that was a hairy ride in, I don't know if I'd call it "easy", myself. We can't see you guys. Where are you anchored?'

'Hang on,' Steve says. 'Exactly *where* are you guys? You can't be here.'

'We just came in the pass, we're in the lagoon.' Ivan scans the horizon for the mast of *Red Sky*. 'Can you see us?'

I rubberneck the horizon, twirling circles until I'm dizzy.

'Ah, no, definitely can't see you,' Steve says. 'Ivan, what's your position?'

'Just a sec...' Ivan checks the GPS. 'We're at 15° 55.5' south, 145° 52.8' west.'

'Ah, shit,' Steve says. 'You went through the Otugi Pass?'

Ivan's eyes linger on mine as he slowly squeezes down the radio button. 'That's right.'

'Oh, Ivan. Oh, dammit. You're in the wrong place. *Completely* the wrong place. We should have given you more information. I'm so sorry, guys. We're not actually *inside* the lagoon, we're in a place called Anse Amyot, probably twenty miles or so from where you are. It's in a little cul-de-sac, buried in the reef that you get to from the outside of the lagoon. You'll have to go back out the Otugi Pass to get here.'

I'm almost ready to cry. I hear Ivan's voice lower an octave, no doubt battling with his own dismay. 'Well,' he says, 'I guess we'll catch up with you tomorrow, then. It's getting dark and the pass is really rough right now. It would be suicide to go back out with those waves. We'll head off tomorrow sometime, it'll take us four hours or so.'

'I'm so sorry, guys,' Steve says once more before the conversation ends.

I check our sources again, opening a guidebook to the dog-eared Otugi Pass page we've been referencing. On the opposite page, in bold, painfully obvious capital letters, is a heading that reads 'Anse Amyot'. Under the heading it mentions that Gaston is an inhabitant of this sheltered anchorage. *'Gaston will guide you in on his boat,'* Steve had mentioned. Our guidebook had been marked up by its previous owner and there's a pencilled warning alongside the Otugi Pass, which we notice belatedly: *Pass considered dangerous by locals!*

Ivan and I look at each other in disbelief.

'We just forced our way into one of the most dangerous passes in the Tuamotus!' I say.

'In the wrong tide!' he adds.

'So much for all our research.'

'So much for my promise to play it extra safe. I'm an arsehole.'

'I'm an arsehole,' I say, holding up the guide I've had my nose buried in for days.

'Steve's an arsehole,' Ivan quips. 'Gracie's an arsehole.'

'The Otugi Pass is an arsehole,' I say, playing along.

We giggle and our tension diminishes.

'Shit, that was close,' Ivan says, scratching his stubble.

I CAN BROOD like no one's business. Instead of appreciating my first look at an atoll, I roll around in the mud of my disappointment. I refuse to enjoy the papaya-coloured sunset or its reflection off the water. I ignore the warm breeze that kisses apologetically at my crossed arms. I will not let a sky full of stars and galaxies, of moonlight illuminating the water's surface, dislodge my mood.

Nope. I'm committed to ride this sulk until we're back through that dangerous pass.

'Do you think we're going to have to beat back through those waves in the pass?' I say. 'We don't know the tides for this place.

We need to check online, but for some reason my laptop isn't getting a Wi-Fi connection,' I mock, gesturing to the desolate shore.

'Maybe those people know?' he says, pointing to the only other boat inside the lagoon with us. He gets in the dinghy and rows over to the yacht, which flies an Italian flag.

Thirty minutes later, he returns with a single piece of paper, marked up in pencil.

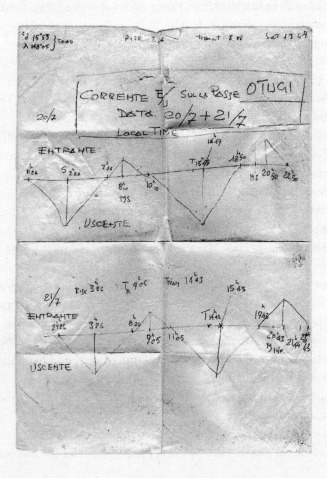

'He drew this up for you?' I ask.

'Yep – right there on the spot. Helpful, huh?'

'Really helpful. Unbelievably helpful. *I have no idea what any of that means!*'

'Me neither. It looks impressive though, doesn't it? Anyway, he said 8:26 a.m. is the start of high tide.'

'Great. Who's on that boat, anyway? Stephen Hawking?'

We laugh hard together, but deep down I'm wondering if we're the only sailors out here who don't know how to get by without Google.

AT 8:26 A.M. where once there were violent waves, there is a flat passageway out of Otugi. We glide through glassy water and I feel even more foolish about our bucking-bronco entrance.

In four hours, we're outside of Anse Amyot.

We meet the infamous Gaston and Steve greets us from his kayak. 'Welcome, guys, you finally made it. Great to see you.'

As we're guided to a mooring, I grin so hard it hurts. I catch an eyeful of Anse Amyot and I see exactly why we were ordered to change course. It's a U-shaped pocket in the reef that forms a protected womb, as though Mother Earth designed it just for sailors. The anchorage is a deep pool carved into the electric-blue shallows, which stretch out until they meet with the cerulean sky. Along the horizon, sandy islets with wispy crops of palms obstruct the palette of blues, rising just above sea level. The islet nearest to our boat has a few modest homes and thatched bungalows, built directly onto the beach overlooking one of the best views in the world. It's as idyllic as an island paradise can get.

'I can die happy now,' I declare, and then I leap from the boat and pin drop into the blue.

TWELVE

'WELCOME,' SAYS A SMILING Polynesian woman with her arms outstretched. The resident family has been waiting for us ashore since we arrived, ready to greet the new arrivals to their tiny island home.

We step out of the dinghy and she pulls us into her embrace, squeezing tight to mash us against ample folds of flesh. Stark white against her dark skin are two overjoyed eyes and a set of pearly teeth, one of which is missing. She has the powerful physique of a sumo wrestler, but she moves with a graceful elegance that is unmistakably female. 'I'm Liza,' she says, squeezing both my hands. 'You?'

'I'm Torre, this is Ivan.'

'Welcome, Torre! Welcome, Ivan!' she says in her French-Polynesian accent, showering us with more physical affection, like we're her long-lost children. I melt into the motherly snuggle.

'Come!' Liza says, ushering us away from the dinghy dock and onto her island.

Small puppies run alongside, licking our ankles, and I pull one up into my arms. He has black fur with little caramel eyebrows and I'm immediately in love with him. He gently gnashes my hand with puppy teeth until I pat his pudgy belly. Everyone is well fed on this island, it seems.

Outside their beach home, Liza's family waits to greet us. She lists off the names: Snow, the husband; sons Jean and Tamatea, both in their twenties; her gorgeous teenage daughter, Vaea; and an eleven-month-old boy named Ari'eh, a solid little tank with brown doe eyes and a wet smile that showcases his few teeth.

Ari'eh, we're told, is Liza's grandson. His mother lives on a neighbouring island but Ari'eh will live with Liza until he's five. With the limited resources and wealth of many of the islands' inhabitants, it is not uncommon to hear of this type of arrangement.

Liza's mother, Violet, has her own house on the island, as does Liza's sister, Valentine, and her husband, Gaston. When Liza talks of Valentine, her face scrunches up with disapproval, making no effort to hide their sibling rivalry. As the islet's sole residents, if the family's differences got wildly out of hand, I imagine, this place could quickly turn into a scene from *Lord of the Flies*.

VAEA WASTES NO TIME inviting us to go snorkelling with her in the pass, so we jump into the dinghy, motor out toward a deep shade of blue and throw the anchor. While I've paddled reluctantly in sandy shallows here and there, this is the first time in my twenty-six years that I've snorkelled over a reef. Peering overboard, I look ten feet down to the coral-dotted sea floor. The limpid water looks so refreshing, but the dark, wobbly shapes on the bottom bring flashes of teeth and blood to mind.

'Okay?' Vaea asks.

'I'm afraid of water,' I confess.

She stares at me, utterly blank, and I realise how absurd that must sound to an islander. I may as well be telling a New Yorker that I'm afraid of cabs.

'Go!' Vaea demands, and she rolls overboard. Ivan follows, and I sit alone on the boat, listening to my rapid breaths being amplified through my snorkel. I count down from three, let go and drop backward into the deep water.

Beneath the waves, I enter a turquoise world. Sunlight shatters into fragments that flicker across skin, sand and sea life. All around, I hear crunching sounds from busy creatures nibbling at coral and sand for a feed.

Vaea swims past, twisting and somersaulting for the joy of it. She's a classic Tahitian beauty – all long, sculpted limbs and thick ropes of black hair. She belongs on the seabed with the bouquets of coral and the waving sea grasses. I hover near the surface, watching the Tahitian mermaid dive to tease a coy fish from its lair. A technicolour parrotfish, startled by her arrival, dashes behind a twig of coral – a poor excuse for a hiding spot. Taking up the offer for a game of hide-and-seek, she goes after it.

Come, she beckons with her hand, but we're stuck near the surface because neither one of us can dive that far down. Vaea shows us how to depressurize our ears by pinching our nostrils closed, then forcing trapped air to *pop* through our ears, relieving the pressure. This technique frees us up to go deeper, and soon Ivan and I are reaching the bottom and coming back to the surface with handfuls of sand to prove our new skill.

Vaea is our tour guide, showing us the underwater attractions. Deeper and deeper we go, testing our abilities to reach the ocean floor, gaining confidence with each dive. I pin myself on the bottom and then relax, allowing the natural buoyancy of my body to slowly drift me to the surface. I gulp a mouthful of air before eagerly diving straight back down, forgetting my earlier unease.

We hover close to enormous coral clusters, which become busier with inhabitants the deeper we go. In a metropolis of sea fans, coral brains and twisted, bony branches, fish of every colour parade the district, making a grand show of their gaudy costumes. An irked moray eel peers out his front door when a peak-hour throng of yellow fish zoom past, invading his personal space – *Hey! Get oudda here!* A neurotic puffer fish treads water on the outskirts, eyeballing his surroundings for any excuse to blow up.

Out of the blurry blue, I notice something approaching from the abyss. I can only make out three key details: it's steely blue, it's bigger than me and it's heading straight for us.

I freeze.

Vaea pulls me to the surface and removes her snorkel to shriek, 'Manta ray!'

She dives back under to pursue the ray, which must be six feet wide. She grabs onto the creature's wings and rides it through the water. Its huge wings move in languid flaps, unperturbed by Vaea hitching a ride. For an impossible stretch of time, without the need for a breath, Vaea clings on until she disappears with the creature into blurry depths.

I look at Ivan eyes, which are, like mine, bulged in disbelief behind the glass of his mask. We communicate with excited eyebrows, gestures and bubbles.

I can't believe this!

She's riding the wings of a giant ray!

We've discovered an incredible new world beneath the waves.

SEVERAL SMALL ISLETS surround the lagoon in Toau, called *motus* by the locals. They're small reef outcrops with white coral beaches, too salty and exposed to grow anything apart from dense clusters of coconut trees. Liza's home sits on one of these *motus*, but many more islets surround the horizon, most of them uninhabited. They collect flotsam and jetsam on their tideline, delivered there from mysterious origins. Picking through the treasure is what people do for fun around here, and why not? Who knows what will show up next?

We take the dinghy to a deserted *motu* for some exploring. Walking around through sharp coral, we step over piles of driftwood, headless palms and a thousand castaway coconuts. In the centre of the *motu*, Ivan finds several fallen green drinking coconuts, which he loads into the dinghy.

Back at the boat, he decides to crack into one of his collected coconuts to drink the sweet water and flesh. He takes the machete in one hand and holds the coconut with the other. His fingers clasp around one end of the nut, while the other hand strikes from high up with manic hacks, hitting his target one time out of four.

I notice something gravely wrong with his technique. The machete comes down hard and fast, often inches away from his very useful, much-needed left-hand fingers.

Whack, whack, whack.

'You'll chop yourself,' I warn him, like a nagging mother.

He tells me I'm always worrying. It's true. I have to let go like a good mother would: let him learn on his own.

Whack, whack: 'Shit!'

I bandage up Ivan's left thumb, tenderly wrapping gauze around a pea-sized chunk missing from his nail and the flesh below. I'm good at this – Ivan has given me several opportunities to practise my first-aid skills. He's always recovering from one injury or another.

'You were right,' he says. 'You're always right.'

I return a thin smile.

'TORRE – ARI'EH has dirty pants. Clean him!' Liza yells.

I obey the matriarch and collect the small boy in my arms, carrying him outside to change him the island way: by hosing him down under an outdoor shower. He squeals and laughs when the cold water hits his pudgy behind.

After one week on their island, Liza has all but signed adoption papers declaring us her legal children. We get ordered around like we're her kids and, frankly, I'm honoured. We have a home here.

I prop the cleaned, naked boy onto the sand and he scuttles away on all fours, with yipping puppies following in his trail.

'Ivan, Torre – lunch,' Liza yells from her kitchen in a voice powerful enough to cause an avalanche on the other side of the world. Garlic-scented puffs of steam pour out of the open-plan house. The house is modest and run down by the elements, but, built on the beach and facing the incredible view, any lack of modern luxury doesn't matter.

We sit down at the outdoor meal table and help ourselves to fresh fish prepared in a range of ways. Everyone is here: Liza, Snow, Tamatea, Jean, Vaea, Ari'eh and Deek – a newly arrived family member. Deek is the brother of Liza and Valentine and he just got back after being away for the last twenty years. In prison, we're told.

Mealtime with the family has become a twice-daily event, so I'm grateful when there is a chore I can carry out to give something back. It still feels out of balance, but I shrug off the guilt and enjoy the food with my new Polynesian family.

Every new arrival on the island sides with either Liza's family or her sister Valentine's family, depending on who manages to adopt them first. We have no idea what the argument is about, yet Ivan and I maintain a doglike loyalty to Liza. Most sailors have sided with Valentine and Gaston, including Steve and Carol. We see them around and stop by one another's boats for regular chats, but most of our time is spent with Liza's family. We help them with a couple of chores and, in return, we're fed meals of fresh fish and taken exploring.

'COME, TORRE,' Vaea says, after our fish lunch is finished. 'No, Ivan.' She gives Ivan a gentle push on the chest to let him know he's not invited. The language barrier may prevent flowing conversation, but with gestures and a few demanding English words, Vaea has a way of getting exactly what she wants.

She helps herself into the driver's seat of *Little Gracie*, pulls the engine cord and steers us through the lagoon, navigating around the coral head hazards at top speed. Although I'm ten years her senior, sixteen-year-old Vaea has decided we'll make perfect new best friends. She pulls me along by the hand, showing me all the riches of her island home.

Today, it's something in the water. We gear up in flippers, masks and snorkels.

'Go!' she says, with a gentle shove as she urges me to roll backward.

I do as she says.

'Now you come!' she says, taking a big breath and tugging my hand. One single flap of her feet propels her elongated body through the water in a dolphin-like glide. I stop at the surface to recharge breaths, something Vaea doesn't need to do quite so often, and each time I pause, my hand is given another yank. 'Come quickly,' she says.

I follow her down to the base of a coral head the size of a Kombi van. Vaea points and urges me closer, so I make my way around to her side of the coral. I wonder if it's pearls. I know the families harvest a modest amount of pearls in Toau. Black-pearl farming is the main source of income for many inhabitants of the remote Tuamotus atolls. Whatever is there, Vaea is excited about it.

At the base of the coral, I spot the big attraction.

I let out a bubbly underwater scream.

A giant moray eel with a head the girth of a football is poised in full territorial stance: mouth wide open in a silent hiss, electric-blue gaze daring us closer. Needle-sharp teeth are drawn, ready. Most of its body is tucked inside the coral, but judging by its torso-thick girth, it's longer than me. Moray eels are territorial and will strike if they feel their home is being threatened. They attack by lunging at prey and, with teeth engaged, their muscular bodies twist on flesh until they tear off a chunk. The strength of their bite and the sharpness of their teeth can chip bone.

And right now, I'm in a stare-down with *the mother of all eels*.

With a crazed flapping of limbs, I jet to the surface. I peer down to see Vaea hovering beside the eel and I wonder for a second if she's planning to coax the gnarly beast from its cave to ride it like a horse.

AFTER AN HOUR of underwater sightseeing, we take the dinghy back to shore. As we get close, we see a commotion on the beach. Islanders and cruisers are circled around a pale and anguished figure in a chair.

Ivan!

I jump out of the dinghy and run along the pier to the beach. Ivan is staring blankly ahead, lips thin, eyes wide, muscles rigid. Liza is behind him, rubbing milk straight from a coconut onto his back. I notice his flesh is covered in straps of red, like he's been whipped.

'Jellyfish,' Ivan spits through clenched teeth before I have a chance to ask.

I race the dinghy back to *Amazing Grace* and find our medical kit. I return to the beach with a little bottle of ammonia gel. I rub it over his back and instantly see by his relaxing shoulders that the gel is working.

'I also got stung here,' he says, pointing to his stomach. 'And here, and here, and here,' he adds, marking out zones of flesh from his toes to his nose. His whole body is inflamed with red welts and whip marks.

'Did you swim into a whole colony?' I ask.

'No. Only one,' he says. 'I think I spread the poison with my hands because my skin started to sting and I thought I was being attacked by thousands of bees. Bees! How stupid. So I just started slapping myself all over. That's how it got everywhere.'

'Your nose, too?'

'Yeah, I used my hand to wipe away boogers. I'm an idiot.'

'Maybe just a little clumsy,' I say, rubbing ointment into the raw corners of his nose.

'Yeah, but something else happened too. Something worse.'

'Worse? What could be—'

'I shot Deek. With a speargun.'

'You mean Deek the ex-con?'

'Yeah, that Deek. I didn't mean it.'

'Oh, shit… you shot Deek?'

'Yeah, kinda. I didn't even know about it, I was in too much pain to notice. Someone only just told me.'

'What the hell happened?'

'When you were out with Vaea, the men asked me to come spearfishing. I jumped in their skiff with my snorkelling gear and they handed me a speargun. I thought we were just going fishing in the lagoon, but we went out into the ocean. It was really deep and the islanders were all diving down really far to get the fish. I knew there was no way I could do that, so I started to make my way back to the skiff. While I was swimming back, I saw this huge shark underneath my feet and it distracted me, so I didn't see the jellyfish before I swam right into it. I didn't know what was happening to me; I was stinging all over. *I thought it was bees.* Bees in the water? Man, what was I thinking?' he says solemnly.

'So anyway,' he continues, 'I wanted to get out of the water – fast. I didn't know anyone was aboard the skiff when I threw my gun in and climbed up. I was in so much pain, I didn't even know I'd shot someone. I found out later that it fired the spear into Deek's hand.' Ivan looks over at Deek's hand, which is bandaged and seeping blood between his index finger and his thumb.

'Nobody taught me how to use the gun,' Ivan says. 'So I didn't know you are supposed to, like, disarm it, you know?'

I turn to Deek, who is hovering silently ten feet away. 'Okay?' I ask, gesturing to his hand.

'*Oui*,' he says. 'No problem.'

Deek looks mildly amused. Everyone is giggling a little now that Ivan's no longer pale and quivering.

'Hey, I'm really sorry about that,' Ivan says to Deek.

'No problem.' He waves off Ivan's apology with his punctured hand.

'Of all the people out here,' I say to Ivan out of the corner of my mouth in a whisper, 'you had to go and shoot the jailbird?'

'DON'T BE STUPID. You clean clothes here,' Liza snaps at me.

It's laundry day and Liza has insisted that we use the family washing machine. When she first offered, I was reluctant to accept because we're almost living with these people as it is – I just need to put a toothbrush and a box of tampons in their bathroom to seal the deal. However, Liza refused to accept our gracious refusal. Her generosity is offered with the aggression of a linebacker.

I load up the machine, which is about a thousand years old in washing-machine years. It functions for a family of six, running full-time during daylight hours, and is powered by the only source of electricity around here – a diesel generator. Lidless, it sloshes half its water all over the laundry floor, but this is acceptable, because that's just how things go in places without washing-machine technicians.

I press the start button, which is no longer a button, but an exposed toggle with wiring visible behind it. A strange feeling runs through my body – an uncomfortable tingly sensation that reminds me of a time during my teen years when I climbed a fence to pat a cow and felt inexplicable pain where my leg touched the fence. *Why is the fence hurting me?* I remember wondering. It didn't immediately occur to me that I was getting electrocuted.

Just like now.

I pull my hand back and dash out of the puddle on the floor, alive, intact and unharmed. The washing machine begins its cycle, banging violently from wall to wall like a straitjacketed loony. I back away slowly.

I help Vaea peg the family's laundry on the clothesline. Worn, sun-bleached clothes in all sizes blow in the hot breeze and are turned crispy dry in less than an hour. I fold the clothes with her and then help to sweep their house.

Ivan is out collecting sand with the men. On another islet, they filter the sand through a mesh screen, sifting out debris. The plush, white sand is transported back to the family's beach, which is also their front porch.

AN ACTION FILM PLAYS on the TV, booming loudly through bad speakers. It's dubbed in French with no English subtitles. I have no idea what the plot is, but we're not here for the movie anyway.

The living area is small. Lazy bodies drape over the room's few chairs and spill out onto the floor, occupying the cushions and mattresses that are tossed about the room. A huge bowl of buttery popcorn does the rounds. Ivan and I lie on the floor alongside Vaea. Ari'eh's body slams me with his full Polynesian baby weight and I raspberry him for punishment. He giggles and crab-crawls to Ivan, who also gets body-slammed in exchange for raspberries. I look around the room at everyone's eyes flickering in the dark, engrossed in the movie. The islanders' brown faces camouflage into the darkened room, while Ivan's skin glows from the TV's reflection, despite his deep tan, and I'm reminded that we're not a part of this family, though it's easy to forget this. We spend every waking hour with these people. In the morning, we're awakened by Liza yelling onshore, calling us over for breakfast. We eat, clean dishes and then go out snorkelling, or fishing, or exploring.

I do chores with Vaea. We help keep an eye on Ari'eh, grabbing him when he reaches the shore, attempting to go for a swim like the grown-ups. Sometimes Vaea comes over to *Amazing Grace* and we listen to music together or swap clothes like teenagers. She doesn't stay long because, funnily enough, she gets seasick aboard our boat.

I bake cakes with Vaea in their kitchen and together we prepare lunch from the fish the men have caught. Meals are shared around a big family table on the beach under the shade of an old tree. Sometimes other cruisers come along, Steve and Carol or sailors from the five other boats anchored here, but most often it's just us. Afterward, we play ping-pong and volleyball together and then go for a swim to cool down. We race to see who can swim the fastest and we're defeated, of course, by everyone except little Ari'eh, who can't swim yet (but he's probably not long off beating us too).

After our long days spent in their company, we thank them profusely for the meals and entertainment and then we return to *Amazing Grace* so the family can have their space. But now they're inviting us to their movie nights as well.

In this cut-off place, these people have become our surrogate family. And, in some way, I can't help but think it is mutual because, after all, it's the family who invites us over for a French movie, despite knowing that we don't speak the language.

Ari'eh flops into my arms, curling up to settle down. Vaea hooks her arm around my elbow. Liza sits on the couch, her puffy cheeks forming a serene smile. How are we ever going to leave this place?

THE MOVIE HAS ENDED and we've said good night. Outside, the weather has turned nasty. The shrieking wind kicks up a feisty chop, while rain spits from the sky in horizontal torpedoes.

We're thoroughly soaked by the time we reach our boat.

I'm restless in bed, unable to sleep with the boat bouncing on her mooring. Plus, I'm worried about *Little Gracie*. I can hear her slapping about outside, getting kicked around by the chop. I know I should get my brave face on and check on her myself, but I'm terrified on nights like this, when the moon is blocked and the wind is howling and there is nothing but blackness out there. I'm certain I'll be swept overboard like a flying piece of office paper, propelled into the black void, never to be seen again.

'Do you think the dinghy is okay out there?' I ask Ivan.

'Fine,' he says in a snappy tone that means: *You'd better not be asking me to go and check it.*

'Will you come out with me to check it?'

'It's *fine*, baby.'

I'm good at worrying and excellent at nagging. At times I can be like an oversensitive smoke alarm, screeching loudly at any whiff of possible danger. I'm aware of this defect, but I don't know how to turn it off. 'Please? Can we check it? I can't sleep.'

Ivan lifts the covers abruptly and I follow him outside.

Little Gracie is thrashing violently on her tether and, in the pitch black, we can only just make out that our gear is still in there – reef shoes, wooden oars, gas tank, two sets of snorkelling gear – all of it bouncing up and down with the chop.

'Do you think we should maybe—'

'No.'

'Get the gear out so that—'

'No.'

'But what if it—'

'No. It's fine. *Stop worrying so much.* Let's go back to bed.' He's clearly tired of talking about it, so I drop the issue.

In bed, I listen to the wind scream while rain comes down even heavier than I thought was possible. I toss, turn and worry, intermittently sounding my oversensitive alarm and waking Ivan, which he responds to by pressing my mute button.

'IVAN, TORRE, WAKE UP – your dinghy sank!' a voice yells from outside our boat at the first light of dawn.

I look at Ivan with slits for eyes that say exactly what I want them to say: *I told you so.*

We rush out on deck and see Steve in his kayak with a grim expression. *Little Gracie* sits below the surface with the engine still clinging to the stern, fully submerged and looking as pathetic as a television at the bottom of a swimming pool. Made from wood, *Little Gracie* can't sink to the bottom, but the waves and torrential rain flooded her in the night and she can no longer sit above the water. Still connected to the boat by her tether, her violent bouncing has ceased. She hovers defencelessly below the surface.

Ivan jumps overboard to recover the drowned engine, working at a manic pace as though getting it out of the water quickly will make everything okay. But there's no point: the engine is in the blue-lipped rigor mortis stage and far beyond resuscitation.

Our gear's gone. Everything is lost – my one pair of shoes, flippers, masks, snorkels, oars and *Little Gracie*'s wooden seats. I'm wondering how we'll move this useless chunk of wood from A to B without an engine or oars. That's if we manage to get it back on the floating side of the water.

Without *Little Gracie*, we're confined to the boat. Without snorkelling gear, we can't explore the water. Without shoes, I'll struggle to walk around in the atolls, which are covered in sharp coral shards. This is a big loss.

Woken by the commotion, all the other cruisers stand on their decks, watching and shaking their heads at our mistake. I see now that everyone else pulled their engines on deck last night and some even hauled their entire dinghy out of the chop.

We hide inside our boat until noon, embarrassed by our mistake and demoralised by our loss. It's not like we can leave the boat even if we want to: we're surrounded by a moat. If the weather weren't so foul, it would be possible to swim, but, for now, we're boat-bound. Tucked in our cabin, we brood for hours.

A young French sailor, Elise, stops by to donate a pair of shoes. They're a size too small, but small shoes are better than no shoes. I'm touched by her thoughtfulness.

Liza and Vaea then stop by to tell us we're welcome to use their snorkelling gear whenever we like, and Tamatea and Jean tow our dinghy to shore and get it floating again. They flush our drowned engine with water and tinker for hours under the hood. I'm shocked when I hear it roar back to life.

It works! But with one small catch: it only runs at full throttle. So now, getting around in *Little Gracie* involves squatting in an empty, seat-less hull at full speed. Unable to slow the engine, we now collide abruptly with our destination: *Bang!* 'We're here!'

I WAKE UP in the morning to urgent yelling coming from right outside our boat. 'Ivan, Torre, wake up. Your dinghy is gone.'

This can't be happening again. This happened yesterday. It's a joke. Or I'm not awake yet.

Outside, the island family floats beside *Amazing Grace* in their skiff, looking grim. This isn't a gag. Liza's yelling has woken the entire anchorage and now everyone is up on decks peering over to the commotion, once again centred on us. This is mortifying.

'Your dinghy got away. It washed up on the reef,' Liza says, pointing to a neighbouring *motu*, the one on which we found the drinking coconuts. I squint and see a tiny white fleck on the distant beach. *Little Gracie* has become the latest piece of jetsam to wash ashore.

We jump in the family's skiff and they race us over to the site. On the shoreline, *Little Gracie* is being pounded against dead coral by the surf. She looks like a rundown castaway, her paint scratched up all over, her wood pummelled into pulpy bruises.

'Guess I didn't tie her up properly,' Ivan says, his voice so thick with sadness and regret that it makes me want to cry.

The islanders avoid our gaze. I know what they're thinking. *How could you do this to your* Little Gracie?

The family tows our dinghy back and we notice that she now leaks in several places. She still floats, but only just.

Once again, we hide inside *Amazing Grace*, avoiding other people. Drowning the dinghy and losing all our gear was unfortunate, but having the dinghy wash up on a distant reef the very next morning is unforgivably moronic. I wonder if today the community of sailors is gossiping about how the hell we've come this far without accidentally killing ourselves. That's what I'm wondering, anyway.

IN EXCHANGE FOR TYING *Amazing Grace* to one of Valentine and Gaston's moorings, we've been politely asked to attend a dinner at their restaurant for $25 a head. It's an excellent deal: for that price, we get a mooring in paradise for as long as we want and an all-you-can-eat seafood buffet.

Gaston – apart from being a builder, organiser and all-round workhorse – is a master fisherman. His sculpted, sinewy body is a sign of his daylong hard work. After he brings home the seafood, Valentine turns it into a delicious feast. Her ingredients are limited by what is available on the atoll (coconuts, fish) and the staples they receive every month from a visiting supply ship, but, despite this, she manages to create an array of flavours in her dishes.

A platter piled high with lobster is going around the dinner table. I pass. Saying no to lobster feels criminal but I've already eaten a whole one myself, in addition to four kinds of fish. Everyone is passing: there's simply too much food.

Outside Gaston and Valentine's house, a forty-something man wearing a wetsuit approaches and I recognise him as a new arrival. All the visiting sailors become part of the island's family, so when there's a new arrival, it's big news.

He extends a hand to introduce himself. 'Hi, I'm Doctor Glen. I'm a surgeon,' he says in an American accent, with his lips drawing like curtains to display perfect white teeth.

I wait, anticipating him to follow up the formal intro with an embossed business card drawn from his wetsuit breast pocket. *Doctor Glen – Surgeon.*

'Hi, Glen, I'm Torre. I'm... a graphic designer?'

His introduction throws me. The only time I can envision 'Hi, I'm a *surgeon*' as a fitting introduction is if I were on a gurney in a stark white room and a man wielding a scalpel was standing over me. Plus, it's been a while since we've talked careers with anyone. Jobs are rarely a topic of conversation any more – they exist in a place and time too far away to seem interesting. 'What do you do?' is not a question asked to define someone, because out here we're all working the same jobs: yachties, mechanics, navigators, weather readers, fishermen, adventure travellers, storytellers. We don't talk about projects, clients and bosses; we talk about places visited, shipwrecks and jellyfish attacks. We compare experiences or we exchange long-life food recipes. We talk about Ivan's latest injury – and we never run out of material.

But Glen, first and foremost, is a surgeon. He wants to get that clear, just in case he gets confused for an ordinary sailor in a wetsuit with a pink snorkelling-mask line circling his eyes.

As he walks away, squelching in his wetsuit, I can't help but think there is something off-key about Doctor Glen.

WORD SPREADS QUICKLY on a small island, especially when someone has been hurt. Gaston, we've been told, has dropped a large piece of coral on his foot and crushed his little toe.

Gaston is okay, but Doctor Glen has taken a look at it and is adamant that the toe will need surgery. As it turns out, he happens to know the perfect man for the job.

Glen is collecting drug donations to help with the surgery and cruisers are contributing everything from Tylenol to morphine. Glen has also requested lamps and torches to light his 'operating theater,' which is going to be Gaston's own bedroom.

I wonder if anyone has asked this sailor for a résumé?

Maybe Glen is a qualified surgeon and perhaps operating is the best solution, but, either way, Gaston and Valentine have given the green light.

Hours later, Glen spreads the word that Gaston is recovering well after having his toe removed all the way down to the first joint that connects the bone to the foot.

'He's a little groggy,' Doctor Glen says in a tone one octave deeper than his normal voice. 'But don't worry, he'll make a recovery over the next week or two. Meanwhile, I've offered to stand in his place until he can function again. I'll be catching the fish and lobsters for the restaurant buffet dinners and helping Valentine prepare the meals.'

Altruistic? Or a case of *Sweeney Todd* meets *Single White Female*?

A CONCH SHELL SOUNDS three times: an island tradition to announce goodbye to a departing boat. A yacht is leaving Anse Amyot, heading west for new destinations.

Aboard the departing yacht is a good friend of Liza's who's been here a month: a Norwegian woman whom Liza opened her heart to with reckless abandon, despite knowing that this sailor would inevitably leave like all the others. They've shared meals, laughs and stories through the challenge of a language barrier.

People always leave her, and yet Liza still loves with the intensity of a mother or a best friend. And her heart is shattered every single time someone goes.

On the dock, I spot Liza sitting with her legs dangling over the edge. She's crying. Her tears are slipping from her cheeks in volumes, dropping into the same water that separates her from the rest of the world.

'We have to leave soon too,' Ivan says to me in a wretched voice.

I've been waiting for this moment. We've been here three weeks and, while we'd both love to stay longer, soon we're going to meet Ivan's parents nearby in Rangiroa, one of the only atolls that offers a safe place to anchor outside of a nice resort.

Just yesterday Liza said to us, 'When you first came, you were both city people. Now, you're just like us.'

We can't deny that, in this place, we've both emerged from our city skins to learn the ways of island living. I've been swimming in deep water with Vaea, overcoming my fear. And it's been *one whole week* since Ivan hurt himself or another person.

We make our rounds, saying goodbye. We give hugs to Steve and Carol, who are heading to Tahiti and beyond. Our awkward farewells are laced with the knowledge that we might not ever see each other again because that's just how things go in the vagabond world. We exchange e-mails and home addresses and promises to see each other again one day.

Then we head to Liza's home to break the news of our departure. I feel like I'm telling my mother that I'm running away from home forever. I give Vaea a painting I made for her. 'It's time for us to go,' I say.

Vaea takes my hand in a firm grip. 'No!' she demands.

'Liza,' I say, 'you've done so much for us. What can we do for you? We'd like to give you something but you have to tell us what you need. We have food from America: sauces, pastas, maple syrup. We have clothing and fishing gear. We have DVDs and music. We have hardware, ropes and screws, glue and epoxy. Please, tell us what you can use. We want to give you something you need.'

'No!' she snaps. 'Get that out of your head. You're like my children. I don't want anything from my children.'

Liza takes my cheeks in her hands and draws me close to her face. 'You are young people, so I'm not sad. You'll come back. There is much time. You will come back.'

We tell Liza we'll come back one day because I need to give her that hope. Promising to return makes leaving easier for everybody.

Vaea grips my hand until the last second before we get in our dinghy, board our boat and throw our mooring back into the spectacular blue water.

At sunset, we sail out the pass into the ocean, and I hear the conch shell of this secluded paradise trumpet three times.

THIRTEEN

'ARSEHOLE!' IVAN YELLS.

I've got no idea who he's yelling at – we're out to sea, alone, with ten miles of ocean between us and our destination: the atoll of Apataki. If I didn't feel so nauseated, I'd go outside to see what all the commotion is about. I'm lying low, sick from a swell that is rolling the boat from side to side.

'That was my fish, bitch,' I hear him saying.

He comes charging down the companionway, stomping his heavy weight on each step. 'A shark stole my tuna,' he says, as though I'm the mother and I need to step in as diplomat between him and said shark. *Now, now, boys, cut that out.*

'I had a tuna. Then a big shark came along and just chewed it off the line. He took my best lure!'

'Don't worry,' I tell him. 'There are plenty more fish in the sea.' Though with a fishing track record like ours, I'm wondering if all the good ones have already been taken.

Fishless, we arrive at the pass of Apataki, which is easy to spot because it looks like a deep river running between cleared palms. We glide easily through the entrance into water that looks like facet-cut sapphire.

Within the tranquil lagoon, my stomach finally settles. While Ivan hand-steers the boat, I begin my normal routine of coiling ropes, fastening loose equipment, throwing dead flying fish back overboard and restoring the boat to its normal, tidy state. At the bow, I unfasten the anchor and get it ready for tossing. With bare feet, I climb the mast, curling my toes and fingers around the steps to cling fifteen feet up. I untangle a snagged rope and, from my high vantage point, I scan the encircling lagoon. There are no other sailboats in sight. We're alone.

I climb back down and perch myself on top of our beat-up dinghy, which is roped upside down to the foredeck.

'Baby,' Ivan yells, 'can you keep a lookout for coral heads? The guidebook says this lagoon has a bunch of uncharted hazards.'

I nod at him in the cockpit from my bow position and turn and look out into the water ahead. It seems far too deep to have any stray coral heads. I've become skilled at estimating depths by reading the shade of blue. My guess is we're over sixty feet of water right now.

'What's the depth here?' I holler.

Ivan casts his eyes forward to the depth sounder. 'Sixty-two feet,' he yells back.

I smile and relax back onto the upturned dinghy. The sails are out and the wind is pushing us along at a nice pace. With no rolling ocean swell beneath us and no rumbling engine hammering into the silence, gliding along the water feels exquisite. I lace my fingers behind my head, stretch out my tanned legs and turn my face into the breeze. It tangles my hair and wraps itself around my limbs, warming my skin with a thousand salty kisses.

This is what sailing should be all the time: a flat lake, a ten-knot breeze, a clear blue sky, a hazardous outcrop of coral directly ahead. *A hazardous outcrop of coral?*

'Coral head!' I shout just in time.

I'm the coral-head watch girl, but nobody should entrust me with this job on a day like today. If you combine a sultry breeze with a wayward imagination like mine, it's like employing a dementia sufferer as an air-traffic controller.

Ivan yanks the tiller and *Amazing Grace* swerves around the enormous stony outcrop beneath the water's surface.

'Sorry about that!' I yell. 'I'll pay more attention.'

I carefully survey every square inch of water ahead for coral or pearl-farm buoys that indicate taut ropes below the surface, which might tangle with our keel or propeller. But the day is magical, the breeze sensual, and distractions ashore pull me away from the job. My mind takes off, skipping down a deviated path, smelling roses, playing with butterflies, scrawling *I heart you* into imaginary trees. I remember the coral heads and slap my cheeks to stay focused.

Coral heads. Look for coral heads. This is serious. Look, look, look, look. Hey… look at that palm tree over there. It's so bendy. I wonder how it got like that. It looks like it's doing a yoga bridge. Ha ha. Yogi tree. 'Howdy, group, I'm a yogi tree and I'm going to teach you some yoga. Now, watch me do a Downward-Facing Dog.' Man, that's funny. I love—

'Torre! I said is that a pearl farm right there?'

Oh, shit. 'Pearl farm, twelve o'clock.'

Across the lagoon, we find a deserted islet to anchor alongside. A glaring white beach – made of bleached, broken coral pieces – encircled by a forest of palms. Behind the islet we can see the ocean crashing against the protective reef of the lagoon. There are no other boats in sight.

'This place is absolutely perfect!' Ivan exclaims as he tosses the anchor onto the white sand bottom.

He's right – it is the postcard image of paradise. I stare at the scenery and notice that, despite the jaw-dropping beauty, something important is missing… but what?

'Can you believe we got here by boat?' Ivan says. 'Our very own island. There's only one thing – no, *two* things that could make this better. Cold beer and pizza.'

'Can't help you with the cold beer,' I say, 'but I might be able to improvise a pizza.'

In the kitchen, I mix dough into a bowl. It rises and I pour the contents into a frying pan on the stove. After forty minutes, it's a thick, fluffy base. I rub it with olive oil and garlic and then decorate it with a confetti of Italian herbs. I smother on canned tomato paste in thick spoonfuls and spread a layer of packaged olives. A blanket of grated long-life cheese melts over the top to seal the deal.

'*Voilà!* Boat-style pizza,' I say, delivering it to Ivan in the cockpit. We're both equally amazed that I've managed to reinvent the same old dry ingredients from our stores. However, no amount of creativity can change the fact that we're still eating a diet of pure carbs. My body, specifically my small intestine, isn't so thrilled with the pizza. What took an hour and a half to make will take five minutes to eat. What takes minutes to eat will take days to digest. After months without fresh food, I don't just need fruit and vegetables – I need Dyno-Rod.

'Doesn't get much better than this,' Ivan says, leaning back in the cockpit, munching on a slice of pizza. 'We have our very own paradise in the South Pacific. I feel like I'm home.'

I smile. 'I'm so glad you're happy.' I swallow my bites of pizza with sips of room-temperature water, hoping to coax the doughy ball through my system.

'In my original plans, I never envisioned I'd have you here with me. We have this view all to ourselves. Hey, do you ever think about what's happening on land?'

'What do you mean?'

'Like right now there's gang violence and AMBER Alerts going on, armed robberies, wars, people sitting in traffic on the 405, grey office cubicles, all of that. But we're here, on our boat, with all of this to ourselves.'

'You're being awfully smug.'

'No. I'm saying that it's, like, weird, you know? Because that used to be me. I'd sit there in bumper-to-bumper traffic and dream of this deserted island in the middle of the Pacific. But now I'm here, and it's like I teleported myself to a different world. It's as though, at any given time, there are alternate universes taking place. We just have to decide which reality we want for ourselves.'

I find myself wondering what Anna is doing right now in the alternate universe of San Francisco, and I realise what is missing from this otherwise perfect isle: people. It makes me think of that philosophical question: *If a tree falls in a forest and no one is around to hear it, does it make a sound?* Without a circle of connections to share experiences and observations with over coffee, telephone or e-mail, something about this seems non-existent, like the sound of that falling tree.

'You know,' Ivan says, drawing me away from my thoughts, 'for several years, Moitessier lived in Ahe, an atoll like this one only forty miles north of here. He talks about it in his book, *Tamata and the Alliance.* This place looks exactly the way I imagined it when I was reading that book.'

'Several years,' I marvel, returning to deep thought to consider what it would feel like to live here for years. Sure – this place is beautiful, but once our eyes have had their fill, isn't it just a pretty place to be lonely in?

I look over at Ivan as he goggles our surroundings and suddenly I'm plagued with guilt over wasting the moment to yearn for friends and vegetables instead of enjoying this experience. *Be present, Torre,* I remind myself. *Live for now.* I relax my pensive expression and return my attention to the conversation. 'So what did Moitessier do all that time? I mean, how did he fill his days?'

'He made a project of trying to grow a range of food here, which was thought to be impossible because of the saltiness of the islets and the lack of fertile soil. He was determined to create a system for growing fruit and vegetables on the *motus*, which he could then teach to the Polynesians.'

'Ha! So I'm not the only one who's preoccupied with veggies.'

He grins. 'Guess not.'

'Did it work?' I say, hopeful that Moitessier's pumpkins, tomatoes and zucchinis are hiding out somewhere in the palm forest ashore.

'Yes and no. He brought soil from Tahiti and he made compost from things like fish guts and rotting palm fronds and his own pee. He put a lot of hard work into honing the system and optimising the compost, and eventually he managed to create fertile soil. He tried to get the islanders to adopt it, but he said they were lazy and they couldn't be bothered with the work. In the end, Moitessier realised that the islanders were not lazy at all – they were wise. They knew how to be content with what they already had, like fish and coconuts. In their spare time, they knew how relax. After his attempt, the Polynesians gave him the nickname *Tamata*, which means "try".'

'*Tamata*,' I say, repeating the word aloud, remembering why I teleported myself to *this* alternative universe.

Ivan turns and combs his fingers through my hair, stopping short as he snags on the tangles. 'I'm so glad you're here with me. You look so beautiful right now.'

I smile faintly. This lifestyle looks far better on Ivan – the messy hair, the stubble, the tattoo, the worn clothes and his serene expression. Rugged fits him so perfectly that I can no longer imagine him any other way.

'LOOK!' I SAY, peering out the porthole while waiting for my morning coffee to brew. 'Sailboats!'

Two white specks are visible in the distance, heading north under sail. I recognise the boats as *Hilda* and *Sirius*. We may be in one of the most remote places in the world, but, as it turns out, running into familiar faces isn't out of the question.

We met these sailors briefly on Toau. A ravishing young French couple owns *Sirius*, while *Hilda* belongs to Lisbeth and Lasse, an energetic and highly adventurous couple in their sixties, from Sweden.

'Let's follow them,' I say, flicking on the engine's battery bank and thumbing the ignition before Ivan has barely had a chance to rub the sleep from his eyes.

A few hours later, we drop anchor by *Hilda* and *Sirius*. Our three boats seem to levitate over crystalline water near a beach just as beautiful as the one we've come from.

Lisbeth and Lasse stop by *Amazing Grace* in their dinghy to welcome us. 'We had a successful afternoon catching fish,' Lasse says in a melodic Swedish lilt. He holds up a large, duck-billed snapper that is frozen in rigor mortis with a petulant look on its face. *Goddammit*, the fish's face reads, *this just isn't my day.*

'We want to know if you'd like to join us and the French couple tonight for a barbecue on the beach?'

'Sure,' Ivan says with excitement in his eyes. A beach barbecue is his chance to set great mounds of wood aflame.

'I'm pretty sure this fish is okay to eat,' Lasse says. 'But it is quite large, which might be a problem, especially because these fish are known for having ciguatera.'

I laugh, waiting for the punch line.

There isn't one.

'You really think it might have ciguatera?' I say, knowing that the only way to test if a person has ingested too much of this accumulative poison from a reef fish is *after* the onset of neurological symptoms (numbness, headaches, muscle aches, ataxia and hallucinations), which, if they don't kill you, can take decades to abate. Ciguatera poisoning is frequently misdiagnosed as multiple sclerosis and the poison is rife in the larger reef fish of these atolls.

'I guess we shall see, eh?' Lasse says.

'Really?' I say, still hoping for that punch line.

'Ah, yes, yes, well, *so is it,*' he says in Swedish singsong before motoring off.

'So is it?' I say, turning to Ivan. '*So is it?* We're just going to eat fish and see who winds up paralysed?'

'I'm hungry,' he says to the horizon, immune to any worry, as usual.

As THE SUN IS GOING DOWN, we drive the dinghy to shore, carefully motoring around coral-head hazards that lie on the sandy bottom like sleeping hippos. It would be wiser to row rather than motor and risk colliding the engine into coral but our oars were sent adrift on the Pacific when the dinghy drowned.

While I prepare food, Ivan disappears into the bushes to forage for firewood. Three minutes pass when I hear a sharp crack from nearby, followed by a blood-curdling scream that I recognise as Ivan's voice.

'*Wheee-wooooo!*' I whistle.

I wait several seconds and hear no reply, so I take off running into the scrub. My headlamp shines a tiny circle of light into the darkness and I climb through dry undergrowth and fallen palm fronds. Where is he?

I finally find him standing in the dark, holding his mouth with both hands. His eyes are wide with fear.

My heart thumps. 'Are you hurt?'

He doesn't speak. He just holds his mouth. I guide him by the arm, out of the scrub and back onto the beach.

'Ivan. What happened?' I'm panicking now.

He doesn't reply. He just stands there, motionless.

'Did you get hurt? Did you see something horrible? What?'

He speaks, but both his hands are clamped firmly over his mouth, muffling his voice. 'Ehsink elip emeotoff.'

'What?' I say.

He shifts his hands a little. 'I said think I ripped my lips off. I think… they're hanging off my face.'

'What?'

'My teeth. Oh no… I'm missing teeth!'

This is bad. We're eighteen miles from the atoll's one and only town. We can't go anywhere until morning; the lagoon has too many hazards to consider sailing at night. We're completely desolate. Here it is – the moment I've been afraid of: a medical emergency in the middle of nowhere. Shit. What do I do?

Something rushes through my body and I shift from panic to survival. I have to help him. I'm the only one who can. First, find out what the damage is.

'Okay, Ivan, move your hands. Let me see.'

'No. I can't. My lips are hanging off!'

'Listen. Move your hands; I have to see how bad it is. You need to let me help you.' I take his hands and coax them gently from his mouth.

He loosens his grip.

I illuminate his face with my headlamp, preparing myself for the worst.

His lips throb under my spotlight. They're blood-flecked and engorged to twice their normal size, but everything is still attached to his face, including all of his teeth. The injury looks painful but superficial, like he's been punched in the mouth with an angry fist.

I breathe out, relieved that I won't have to cross-stitch a face tonight. I let go of his hands and they spring back to his mouth as though propelled by rubber bands, attempting – in his mind – to keep his severed lips in place.

'Don't worry,' I tell him, 'your lips are still there. They're split and very swollen but they're one hundred percent attached to your face. Your teeth are all fine too.'

'Oh,' he says, exploring with his fingertips. 'Oh, man, I really thought I'd torn my face. That was really violent.' His engorged mouth spreads into an embarrassed smile.

Laughter explodes around us. Only now do I realise that the other two couples have been watching the whole drama. Ivan the klutz strikes again! These friends have already witnessed several of his antics on Toau.

'Well?' I say when the giggles settle. 'Are you going to tell us what happened? Who punched you?'

'Yes, was Deek waiting for you in the bushes?' Lasse says, hiccupping back his laughter.

'A branch,' Ivan says, laughing. 'I tried to snap a branch for the fire, like, a really big one because I wanted to get one branch, the mother of all branches, to put on the fire and keep it burning all night, you know? But the thing wouldn't break; it was solid. I was pushing on it with all my weight and then suddenly, it broke halfway down and then swung back and smacked my mouth. Oh, man, I'm so glad my lips are still there.'

The sound of six people snorting with hysterical laughter echoes out into the empty lagoon.

'How do you do it?' I ask, when the hysterics settle. 'Three minutes. That's how long it took for you to get pummelled by the shrubbery.'

I look around at all the laughing faces and realise I'm the only one suppressing worry behind my giggles. *I have to sail in a boat with this man!* I've lost count of his accidents to date. Ivan can find dangers in even the most unassuming environments.

'Do you want to go back to the boat?' I ask. 'Get cleaned up with some antiseptic?'

Ivan turns to the gang and tells them we'll be back shortly. We get in the dinghy and Ivan yanks back on the engine cord. The engine revs at its one speed: full-throttle. The dinghy flies forward. We run directly into a coral head. We whiplash like crash-test dummies. The engine is dead on impact. Not even a sick cough – dead.

I look at Ivan. What just happened?

I turn to face our group of friends gathered on the beach only six feet away. They've all paused, mid-action, to stare at us, astounded. Nobody utters a word. I hear someone's throat clear. Everything else is silent.

Accident one: hilarious.

Accident two: a real shame.

We step out of the dinghy into two feet of water and walk *Little Gracie* back up the shore. Wordlessly, we carry on with getting the barbecue ready, doing our best to pretend we didn't just perform the most idiotic chain of slapstick mishaps before an audience.

I'M GRATEFUL that the punch-and-crash isn't mentioned again throughout the night. Our prior mishaps are ignored and, apart from the unavoidable vision of Ivan's mouth, it's like nothing ever happened.

Instead, the mood is light, conversation flows and everyone gets full on barbecued fish. Nobody shows symptoms of ciguatera poisoning, which is a relief given that accidents always happen in threes.

When the night comes to an end, I walk around the beach, cleaning dishes and tidying up. I stand on something hot – very hot – and pain travels through the soles of my feet and up my bone marrow until it reaches my scalp, turning it to gooseflesh. Only now do I remember the barbecue embers that were covered by a thin layer of sand that I'm now standing on.

Too humiliated to scream – having completed a full hat-trick of accidents in one short night – I quietly go cross-eyed and stagger to the water's edge to snuff out my feet.

FOURTEEN

CLUSTERS OF GALAXIES sprinkle the sky not long after we exit Apataki's pass. The length of our voyage to the Tuamotus atoll of Rangiroa has been calculated so that in sixteen hours, on the dot, we'll be on time to enter the pass during slack tide. Ivan's parents will soon be arriving on Rangiroa to stay in the Kia Ora Resort. Located right next to a protected anchorage, it'll make an ideal meeting spot. It's only an overnight sail away, but we're both nervous about getting there unscathed and on time. We've travelled close to 4,000 miles without a major incident and – just as Ivan is set to prove his seamanship to his parents – now would be a particularly devastating time to run into trouble.

I sit with Ivan in the cockpit under the faint light of the moon and listen to waves passing the hull, knowing that only miles from our position these same waves will break onto the sharp coral reefs that surround us. I try not to think about it too much. Behind us on the horizon is the tiny mast light of *Hilda*. By coincidence, Lisbeth and Lasse are heading for the same place.

The wind is strong, shoving us along from behind, and at this speed we'll get there too early. Ivan puts a reef in the mainsail, which pulls the reins in on our galloping boat. *Whoa, girl.*

At dawn, Ivan brings the boat down to a crawl, slowing our speed to ensure we'll arrive on schedule. It's a fine balance of speed and timing and Ivan is a skilled navigator. We're still an hour early when Rangiroa comes into sight, the largest and most touristy atoll of all the Tuamotus.

We survey the wide-open mouth of the pass from sea. Rangiroa has two passes and, while the one we're staring at – the Tiputa Pass – is right next to the Kia Ora Resort, our guidebook tells us it can have dangerously strong currents as the large lagoon empties and fills with the tides. The good news is, there's a second entrance a few miles downwind, the Avatoru Pass, which is rumoured to have much gentler currents. Since it's referred to as the 'easy pass' in our guidebook, selecting a point of entry into the lagoon seems like a no-brainer to me.

Hilda overtook us in the night. We watch her dart through the mouth of the Tiputa Pass.

'Why are they going through the hard pass?' I ask.

Ivan shrugs. 'I guess they have a more powerful engine than we do.'

Hilda bounces on the rough waves of the pass and then breaks through to the lagoon without a hitch. She disappears behind the other side of the islet toward the hotel anchorage that resides behind a wall of palms blocking our view into the lagoon.

We don't want to take any more chances after the Otugi Pass. We turn away and charge downwind on the strong breeze, cutting through water like professional racers, headed for pass number two.

It takes thirty minutes to reach the second pass and as soon as we arrive, I'm questioning the decision. Two sobering sights mar the mouth of the entrance: a sailboat lies sideways onshore, half buried with sand, and on the opposite side of the pass, another cruising yacht has been washed up on the reef, forever pinned under smashing waves. The vision snaps me wide awake. 'So, this is the easy way in?' I squeak.

A nervous laugh escapes Ivan's throat. He rolls in the sails and starts the engine. My heart pumps as he turns the tiller and angles *Amazing Grace* to align with the GPS points.

Once inside the river-like strip of the pass, the palm trees buffer the wind. The water is still, the current gentle, and we glide through, congratulating ourselves for our responsible decision-making. We now need to travel back upwind to get to the resort.

But inside the lagoon, the trees no longer block the wind and we're slammed in the face with twenty-five knots. Beneath us, the lagoon water is a hair-raising shade of shallow brown. I check our depth: ten feet. The waves are kicked up over the shallows by the strong wind, creating a vigorous washing machine of slop and foam. We're stuck right in it.

I check the GPS. 'We're not moving,' I yell above the wind.

Ivan nudges the throttle, attempting to squeeze more power from the engine, but we're already vibrating at top speed. We bounce on the waves and as gravity slaps our six tons down, I fear our keel is going to connect with the reef below. All it would take is one extra-large coral head and we'd come down on it like a fat man slamming pavement from the thirteenth floor.

'We're overpowered,' Ivan yells. 'We have to go back out to sea and go through the first pass!'

We made the wrong decision to attempt the 'easy pass.' If we'd followed *Hilda*, we'd be anchored in front of the hotel by now. We have to backtrack to the first pass, which may take hours against the wind, and if we're not there in an hour or two, we'll miss our chance to enter the pass and be forced back out to sea, a safe distance away, to wallow through another night.

'Tack,' Ivan yells, and that's my cue to release the jib rope and wind it around the opposite winch.

Together, we manhandle the boat upwind in perfect synchronicity. We'd make an excellent professional sailing team if not for the fact that, in between winching ropes, I'm unleashing a shameless tantrum. There's something intensely satisfying about letting it all out when a strong breeze is sweeping the howls right off my lips.

I can hear the Sydney to Hobart commentators in my head: '*Well, it looks like* Amazing Grace *is flying along at the front of the line. But – hang on – I'm getting something from our guy on the scene. What's that, Jim? The first mate is pounding her fists into the fibreglass? She's yelling at the ocean, calling it a "stupid piece of shit"?*' This is when my sponsors would get on the phone to my agent.

WE ANCHOR OUTSIDE the resort four and a half hours later. Going through the Tiputa Pass, as it turns out, was the easiest part of our morning.

'What took you two so long?' Lisbeth from *Hilda* asks, when we arrive looking puffy-eyed, ratty-haired and salt-encrusted.

'You've been missing for a very long time,' Lasse says. 'First you were right behind us, then you were gone. We've been very worried. We don't understand.'

I let Ivan tell the story.

Our clumsy ways are no surprise to these people. In our short friendship, they've been present for: a jellyfish stinging, the accidental shooting of an islander, a macheted thumb, a sunken dinghy immediately followed by *losing* our dinghy and, last but not least, the punch-and-crash. There is nothing uncharacteristic about our judgement error. We may as well rename our vessel *Amazingly Graceless* to give other sailors a heads-up to steer clear.

Wearing sympathetic expressions, Lisbeth and Lasse patiently listen as Ivan explains our morning.

'So anyway,' Ivan says, bringing the story to a close, 'that was pretty stupid, really. We should've factored in the headwinds and come in through the Tiputa Pass from the start.'

'Yes, yes,' Lisbeth agrees in her thick Swedish accent. 'It was definitely stupid.'

'But, oh well, *so is it*,' Lasse says.

THE RESORT GIVES US our first taste of modern civilisation since Cabo San Lucas. Honeymooners, wealthy lovers and classy singles relax in $400-a-night luxury, as beautiful accents flutter between couples. French, Italian, Spanish: the romance languages. Statuesque women lie poolside wearing designer sunglasses, flowing resort wear and elegant wide-brimmed hats. Some are bare-breasted, with only a tiny thong to keep them covered. Equally beautiful men lounge alongside, taking intermittent breaks from their cocktails to plunge into the infinity pool. The scene belongs in a Ralph Lauren ad.

In our dilapidated *Little Gracie*, we approach the dock, which leads directly up to the resort and into the pool area, like a runway cutting through a crowd of European fashion critics. The spotlight is on us.

We pull up alongside the dock, coming to our usual collision-style stop, whiplashing our heads in graceful unison. We strut in slow motion side by side and the crowd turns to watch us.

Report from the scene: The male wears a pair of stained and frayed pants that sit stylishly low around his midriff, exposing a controversial flash of bushy hair. Riding partway up his back, his shirt has been shrunken and bleached by the elements. His bee-stung lips are decorated with blood-red lacerations, and his forty-day-old stubble complements the relaxed look of his DIY haircut.

His partner sashays alongside and, in line with the collection, her hair is windswept and ratted and her shorts and T-shirt have been adorned with gorgeous grease-and-rust polka dots. On her feet are a pair of truly original reflex blue Neoprene shoes that are one size too small, allowing her fashionably unkempt toenails to hang over the ends. These shoes cannot be classified as either sandals or sea booties but a creative mating of both, capable of taking a woman straight from snorkelling to cocktails. Dazzling, but not showy, this collection brilliantly combines effortless glam with castaway chic.

We disrobe down to our bathing suits and help ourselves to the lounge chairs by the infinity pool. I pick up the cocktail menu: twenty bucks for a piña colada. I put down the cocktail menu. I pick up my book instead.

A resort employee notices us from afar and stops what he's doing to make a beeline for us. I'm hoping he's coming to take our order, but he looks stern. I start to get nervous – I hate getting in trouble.

'*Excusez-moi*,' he says. 'What is your room number?' His upturned nose tells me he already knows the answer to this. Dammit, how can he tell?

I race through a list of creative lies, but Ivan answers before I can come up with anything. 'We don't have a room here,' he says with no hint of shame.

'Well, then would you mind removing yourself from the pool lounges? This area here is for paying guests only.'

I grab my clothes and begin to shift, red in the face.

Ivan stays put on his lounge, stubbornly splayed in a relaxed position. He makes direct eye contact with the man over his sunglasses. 'Listen, *sir*. My parents are flying from the US for the sole purpose of meeting up with us here. We chose this resort for them to come to and we sailed a long, challenging distance from Los Angeles to get here – almost four thousand miles. My parents, who are spending in excess of six thousand dollars on their vacation, would not be travelling to *this* resort otherwise. When they arrive, we will be eating regularly in the hotel's restaurant together and drinking your overpriced beverages. I'm sure you can understand that, while we do not have a room at your resort, we are – for all intents and purposes – paying guests.'

The man clears his throat. 'Fine, then,' he says before turning quickly on his heels and marching off elsewhere.

Ivan goes back to his book, unperturbed.

'I'm so glad you're such an arrogant arse,' I tell him as I settle back into my lounge, both proud and mortified to be associated with him.

'LOOK AT THIS PLACE you've sailed to,' Ivan's mother, Monica, says in her strong Argentinean accent. '¡Qué linda! You're so lucky.'

I flashback to our series of recent mishaps. 'Yep, we're real lucky people,' I say in monotone.

Inside Monica and Jorge's hotel bungalow, I marvel at all the luxuries I've missed: among them a hot shower, a fridge and a flushing toilet. The bed is large enough that two people don't have to choreograph their spooning throughout the night like Ivan and I have learned to do.

'Feel free to use anything in our room, guys,' Monica offers. 'You probably want hot showers with soap, so, please, help yourselves.'

I can tell that Ivan is waiting for his parents to notice his tattoo. He's shirtless, arm poised in their direction, eyeballing them expectantly. Neither one of them has said a thing. The bowling-ball-sized decoration on Ivan's body remains unacknowledged. Perhaps his parents are hoping the black mark will dissolve with a little hot water and soap?

Monica presents us with two enormous suitcases. 'Here's everything you asked for,' she says.

I open the first bag to find piles of gear we requested from the US: flashlights, replacement shoes, boat hardware, batteries, rice wine vinegar, throat lozenges, DVDs and a ridiculous quantity of crackers (because Argentineans will eat anything as long as there is a water cracker wedged underneath it). Monica tells us how she spent time running from place to place after work, trying to find everything, even though she didn't know what she was looking for: *telltales, radar reflector, anchor roller, rail mount anchor bracket.* Not a single item we asked for is missing; she gathered up everything right down to the last screw.

Jorge has thoughtfully bought Ivan new lures, a filleting knife and a handsome red fishing reel, which is like gifting a bicycle to a man with no legs. The lures will make expensive chew toys for the fish after they're cast overboard and never seen again.

It's hard to ignore the other bag they've brought for us – it's a rolling suitcase that could be used for people-smuggling. Monica keeps referring to it as 'The Dead Body.'

'The Dead Body was so hard to travel with,' she says, in an exasperated voice. 'It was horrible, guys, so horrible.' Monica explains all the issues they had trying to import the oversized bag from LA. Hearing the details makes me feel ashamed that we requested they bring such a thing on an airplane.

'Well, thank you so much for bringing it,' I say, unzipping the eighty-pound bag. 'You don't know how much this means to us.'

I catch a glimpse of grey rubber. I smell that new toy smell. My heart starts pounding. *Little Gracie II* is beautiful.

On the beach, we pull all the parts out of the bag and put her together by stacking the wooden-slat floorboards, inflating the tubes and installing the plastic oars. When she's floating, we stare at her like proud new parents. She's a sturdy and majestic Zodiac, and with her large inflatable tubes, no midnight storm can sink this little girl.

At night, after many water crackers and rounds of maté, we get up to leave Monica and Jorge's bungalow to go back to *Amazing Grace.*

'Guys,' Monica says as we're leaving, 'do me a favor when you get back to your boat. Can you flash a light five times, please, so I know you made it back there okay? It will help me sleep because I will not have to worry all night long.'

'No,' Ivan says. 'We sailed all the way here from Los Angeles. The wind is blowing onshore, so the worst thing that could possibly happen is we'll wash back up on the resort's beach.'

'Ivan, please, I—'

'Ma! Stop! We are capable of travelling one hundred feet back to the boat in our new dinghy.'

Maybe not in the old dinghy though, I think.

Not even a day has passed since Ivan's parents arrived and tension is already thickening the humid air. It's only a matter of time before a fiery Latin fight erupts.

'But it's so windy out there tonight, Ivan. Please,' her voice is both stern and tormented, demanding and pleading. 'Please, Ivan, I'll worry. You have no engine. I won't sleep all night. *Please.* Do this for me.'

'No.'

'But, why is it so difficult for you to—'

'No!'

Then, while Ivan is in the bathroom, Monica quietly asks me to flash a light so she can sleep. 'Please, Torre, flash the light for me. That's all I'm asking. I get so worried.'

How can I say no to her when she's talking in that pleading tone? She's always so generous with us. Dragging The Dead Body halfway across the world for us is only a fraction of it. It's not a big deal for me to flash a light. If it helps her sleep, I can give her that.

Standing in our cockpit, I flash a spotlight directly at Monica and Jorge's bungalow five times, as promised. The beam is so powerful, it can suck through four double-D batteries in less than five minutes.

'What are you doing?' Ivan asks, catching me standing outside in the dark, clicking the light on and off, illuminating the entire sleeping resort with my strobe.

'Your mother wanted me to flash the light.'

'Yeah, but I'd already told her no. You agreed?'

'I couldn't really say no. I mean, it's no big deal and if it helps her sleep, then—'

'Dammit! She went behind my back to ask you to do it. I can't believe this. I'm not five years old. We sailed this far and, now, in the most touristy, safe place we've been, we have to take part in her stupid safety procedures? No. This is ridiculous.'

'I know. But you know what Monica is like, she worries, and I guess I can relate. If it helps her sleep, then we should just—'

'We should just *nothing*. You don't know what it's like. She thinks I'm going to sink and drown off a five-star resort in six feet of warm water? I'm thirty-two years old.'

'Yeah, but you take it too personally. She cares about you, and in her mind it's dangerous.'

'But I don't need my mother to tell me when I'm in danger. We sailed across the Pacific already and she *still* doesn't believe in me.'

'She's just scared.'

'Well, don't agree to that stuff any more,' he says. 'She needs to sort it out on her own. I can't make decisions in my life just to pander to her fears.'

I lie awake in bed, upset by the conflict. In my family, I do whatever I can to keep the peace. I don't like fighting. Saying no to such a simple request goes against my nature, but now I'm stuck in the middle of a conflict that I don't understand.

First thing, when we arrive at their bungalow in the morning, Monica asks why we didn't flash the light. 'I could not sleep, it was so horrible. I thought you were dead.'

'I flashed it, though,' I tell her. 'Five times. A giant orb of light right at your bungalow.' *Then argued in your defence.*

'Well, Torre, I didn't see it,' she says, slightly indignant. 'And I did not sleep all last night.' She glares at me with suffering eyes, waiting for… what? An apology?

'Sorry, Monica,' I tell her.

'Well, tonight, can you please call me over the VHF radio to let me know you've arrived back to the boat?'

'Uh… Ivan doesn't want me to,' I say, scolding myself for giving Monica a handheld VHF so we can call them from the boat and arrange meeting times.

'Ivan, please, let Torre call me over the radio.'

'No!'

Then a fiery Latin fight breaks out right on schedule. I stand by, shifting awkwardly, understanding nothing.

LUCKILY, THE ARGUING IS KEPT to a minimum. We spend more time talking and laughing, as we lounge by the pool, eat in the restaurant and have breakfast on *Amazing Grace*. Monica and Jorge are here for a short time and it seems everyone wants to make the most of it.

For Ivan's thirty-third birthday, Monica and Jorge take us out to a seafood dinner and then, as one more surprise, they upgrade their bungalow to a $600-a-night villa with enough space to fit all of us. For one glorious night, we're treated to a plush, king-sized bed that overlooks the lagoon. The word 'luxury' does not begin to describe the incredible indulgence of this short respite from our salty nomad life. I feel like I'm in the penthouse at the top of the world.

Ivan and I take long hot showers with handfuls of soapsuds, lathering away all the accumulated grit. Afterward, we stand nude in front of the full-length mirror, studying our appearances. Ivan's shoulders and forearms are brawny from rowing and lifting. The fine hairs on his body and hairline have turned to golden strands that grow from the shadows of his tan.

The glossy brunette haircut that I had in the city has become long, wild and sun-bleached with streaks of amber. My limbs are still slender, but my hips and breasts have grown, turning my girlish frame into a woman's hourglass. I turn this way and that, admiring my curves.

In the king-sized bed, alongside Ivan, I flap my arms and legs, making angels in the silky, clean sheets. Ivan lies supine in his own snow-angel pose.

'Ivan?' I whisper into the darkness. 'Why are you always so angry at your parents?'

The room is silent. I can hear the tide rolling up onto the coral beach just outside our room. Moonlight spills over the bed but I can't see his eyes. *Is he asleep? He must be.*

I roll onto my side to settle into sleep and then, as I'm drifting off, his voice interrupts the silence. 'I don't know, I guess I just feel like my parents don't support this trip. That makes me sad.'

Rolling to face him, I drape my arm over his chest. 'But they're here visiting you. That's support, isn't it?'

'It just pisses me off when they're not happy.' I feel his heart start thumping in his chest as his anger resurfaces.

I regret bringing this up. We're in a luxury villa for one night only – we should be enjoying it, not sorting through melodrama. But the bitterness is upsetting. Watching Ivan fight with his parents is disturbing and I need to know what's behind his frustration with them. I can't ignore this issue any more. 'Why are you angry, though?'

Under my arm, his heart slows its gallop. 'I guess because when they're not happy, I feel like it's my fault.'

His reply takes me by surprise. 'But… *what* is your fault?'

A long spell of silence takes over. I see him reach up to wipe his eyes.

'Are you okay?' I ask.

'Do you remember how I told you about the dictatorship we had in Argentina?'

'You mentioned it, but I don't know a lot about politics.'

'When we lived in Argentina, we lived under a harsh dictatorship. About thirty thousand people were "disappeared" by the government – abducted, tortured, raped, killed. All it took was one rumour, one sniff that you were a "freethinker", and the military would come and take you on your way to school or work. They took people from their beds at night sometimes. If you had long hair during the dictatorship in Argentina, that was enough to get you arrested. We lived a few blocks from a military base, which I guess you could call a concentration camp. People in the neighbourhood would hear screaming. Friends would speak of family members who just disappeared. We all knew why. We knew where they'd gone and we knew they were never coming back. I was scared for my life there. I was scared for all of us.'

'Shit,' I say, staring out at the moonlit lagoon with wide eyes.

'And my family... we're atheists from a Jewish background, with a Russian last name. So we had *three* targets on our backs. I was always afraid that the next person to disappear would be my brother or my mum or my dad. Or me. That's just the way it was. Even when the dictatorship ended, I still didn't feel safe there because history always repeats itself and I felt like it was just a matter of time before the next dictatorship took over.'

I think back to my naive childhood: playing on the street, bike-riding around the neighbourhood, building sandcastles at the beach, blissfully unaware of politics and human atrocities.

'I decided to leave when I was seventeen,' he continues. 'I knew I didn't want to live in Argentina any more, so I told my parents

I was going to the US. I said, "Come if you want." I was ready to go alone but they decided to come too. They left everything behind and it took us years to find our feet. All because I wanted to leave, you know? Sometimes my parents seem unhappy in LA, like they miss Argentina. They don't have many friends and Dad still struggles to speak English. I feel pretty bad about that.'

'So you carry all that weight.' An image of Ivan sitting at the bar the first night I met him flashes across my mind. A man alone at the bar, pressed beneath the incredible weight of an invisible backpack. I tear up.

'We immigrated to the US to be free, but I began to realise that you're not truly free there either, you know? I mean, if you get a speeding ticket, they could decide to send you back to your home country... just like that.' He snaps his fingers. 'I was terrified they'd send me back to Argentina. I'd have nightmares about it. When I was in college I'd get pulled over by the cops all the time for driving a Camaro! If you don't look and act the same as everyone else, you must be a criminal. Refuse to wear a business suit to work and you're some kind of freak. Grow some fucking facial hair and you're a goddamn terrorist. You're never truly free. Not in Argentina. Not in the States. Not anywhere in society.'

I look over and see the moonlight catching on his beard and his overgrown hair, turning it to silver threads. My throat constricts. 'I'm so sorry you went through that.'

'So anyway,' he says, brushing off my pity, 'I decided to buy a boat and go sailing to be free – truly free – and now it just feels like, I don't know, like my parents don't support this trip. That makes me sad. They haven't said anything about my tattoo or even acknowledged our voyage at all. Nothing. No questions, no congratulations, which is strange, right? But then I think about how the four of us immigrated together. We suffered and fought so that we could have a better life in the US. My parents are *still* suffering. All because I wanted to be free and I thought I'd find it there, and...' He lets out a heavy, shaking breath. '... And now I've abandoned them.' He buries his face in his pillow.

I grasp for the right thing to say, but there is nothing to say. Instead, I snuggle up close, spooning him, holding him tighter than I ever have before.

When the morning light pours in, I wake to find the two of us in the same position, tightly crunched together, flesh on flesh, huddled in the centre of the crisp-white king-sized bed.

FIFTEEN

'How can this be happening again?' I mumble to myself.

Huge waves, almost breakers, charge toward us in the Tiputa Pass. We rise up sharply and then rush down the other side, slamming our bow into the trough. Everything in the cabin lurches with the impact and items that aren't strapped down get tossed to the pointy end of the boat.

We said goodbye to Ivan's parents and left the safety of our anchorage for a two-day sail to Tahiti. Now, just ten minutes into the voyage, we're already in trouble.

The dive shop insisted that 4 p.m. is slack tide. I check the time again: 3:58 p.m. So why is this going gravely wrong?

Even with the engine revving at full power, our speed is a nerve-racking two knots. We're close to being overpowered and if that happens, we'll be pushed backward into the reef. I peer over my shoulder and take note of the tiny distance between our boat and the coral shelf where fishermen stand in ankle-deep water collecting sea life in buckets. If we try to turn around, these waves will knock us down or roll us over.

A powerboat crowded with tourists makes a beeline for us. They must be coming to help! The captain will toss us a rope and use the large engines to tow us to safety.

But when the tourist boat nears, people begin laughing and pointing cameras at us.

'They're treating us like zoo animals!' I say.

Then I notice there are dolphins all around us, flipping acrobatically. The tourists are here for the animals, not for us. The dolphins are excited by the waves and the camera flashes are firing like mad. I wish they'd go away and leave us to shipwreck in peace. *Please don't let this end up on YouTube!*

When I realise we're alone in this, I click into survival mode. I check the GPS: 1 knot. We're not going to make it out of this.

'Keep going,' I tell Ivan.

His eyes dart around, full of worry.

'We're almost through this,' I say. 'Hang in there!' I don't believe a word of it but when all else fails, there is nothing left but to become annoyingly cheery.

But we're pinned to the spot by oncoming waves.

I remember hearing advice for swimmers stuck in a rip: swim perpendicular. Fighting is futile and that's what we're doing – beating into the current with tired arms. We need to swim sideways to the current.

I tell my theory to Ivan and he shifts the angle of the boat. The GPS reading is still at 1 knot and I have no idea if it's working. Is that 1 knot forward or backward? I keep my eyes on the LCD display: 1 knot turns to 1.2… 1.7… 2 knots – it's working! – 2.1… 2.6… 3 knots. The waves are diminishing. We're breaking free.

The dolphins disappear and the tourist boats fall behind us. The reef fishermen are now distant specks. My breathing returns to normal when we reach the navy blue of deep ocean.

'Why are we so gifted at getting it wrong?' I ask Ivan.

'I'll have to get back to you on that one.'

Our laughter dissolves the tension as he steers *Amazing Grace* into the blue expanse toward Tahiti, invisible beyond the horizon. I notice something peculiar: the farther we get from the treacherous shore, the more I relax.

LOVE WITH A CHANCE OF DROWNING

THE TWO-DAY JOURNEY to Tahiti is difficult, marred by grey clouds, spitting rain and erratic weather. But as we approach the island, the sky is shaken clean like an Etch A Sketch.

We enter the fringing reef and follow a path of deep blue that cuts through aqua shallows. Mother Earth has taken the majestic mountains of the Marquesas and stuck them in the centre of the lagoons of the Tuamotus. It has all the beauty of jungle-covered pinnacles with the safety of an encircling lagoon.

'We made it to Tahiti!' Ivan pulls me into a hug, squeezing with his tired arms.

I'm so proud – arriving at this world-famous centre of French Polynesia is a milestone achievement. It may be just a tiny dot on a world map, but Tahiti is enormous in the imaginations of tropical dreamers. It's the archetype for the South Pacific fantasy, a place where honeymooners come to live out once-in-a-lifetime experiences of romance in paradise.

I take in the sight of Tahiti. Peeking above the palm heads is a set of golden arches – another corner of the world marked by a corporate hind leg. Sounds of traffic drift from the shore and buildings stipple the hills. There's no denying that, after dropping off the planet for months, we've arrived at a bustling city.

Tahiti is the Bangkok of the South Pacific and it has all the grievances that sailors go to sea to escape. This place has contracted a disease that's turned Gauguin's vivid paradise into a sprawl of grey concrete spotted with franchise stores, malls, traffic jams and pollution.

Which is exactly why I'm *thrilled* to arrive here. Shopping, people, internet, restaurants, art – all the big-city features I've been missing. It's a retreat from the seclusion of the South Pacific, a holiday from the peace and quiet, a breath of not-so-fresh air.

We squeeze in among a dense population of boats, dropping anchor in water coated by a rainbow slick of spilled fuel. I spot *Hilda* nearby.

'It's so crowded here,' Ivan says flatly.

My eyes are wide and excited. 'I know!'

'Let's go back to Apataki,' he says with a joking laugh.

I know he's not really joking, but I try to avoid dwelling on it.

WE WALK ALONG the main artery of the island in search of a supermarket. Traffic is dense and exhaust fumes stick to the humid air in one oppressive mass. I suck it in like a pack-a-day smoker, nostalgic for the smell of a busy city. It excites me.

Everything is moving at high speed. Cars zip past, one after the other. Old run-down buses tear by, roaring obnoxiously, leaving puffs of black smoke in their trail.

The heat is stifling. The world is rushing past in fast-forward. I follow the traffic with my eyes, my head turning left, right, left, right. My nerves shift into overdrive, jumping at every car horn. The traffic noises start to resemble a chainsaw and, clutching my spinning head, I realise I've sucked in too many fumes.

I look at Ivan and, like me, he looks like a lost dog: hyperaware and bewildered by every noise and movement. 'Everything is moving so fast,' he says, his head turning left, right, left, right.

We find an American-sized supermarket called Carrefour. We are greeted at the entrance by ice-cold air-conditioning, fluorescent lights and rows of food extending beyond the horizon. This is going to be good.

Pursuing the smell of vitamin C, we head straight to the fresh-produce section. Succulent fruits of every description are lined up in neat, misted mountains. I stand and stare and smile until it hurts. If this were the musical of my life, I would break out into song and dance right now, cavorting among the fruits, poking the pears and juggling the mangoes to the lyrics of a camp song. There would be little people dressed as fruits, doing acrobatics, really bringing the production alive.

In the deli section we discover a selection of cheeses that reveal how many French expats reside in Tahiti. There's an impressive collection of delicately packaged cheeses, creamy parcels of pure joy waiting to be unwrapped.

'This is the best day of my life,' I say to Ivan, caressing a soft, creamy Brie.

When we check the time, we realise we've spent *three hours* exploring the supermarket. Almost every item has been inspected, prodded, sniffed and poked at in our slow-motion slack-jawed stupor.

After we've stocked up on fruits and veggies, cheeses, red meat, yogurt, juices, wines and salads, we return to the boat to prepare a meal fit for kings... or perhaps just normal people.

A WI-FI CONNECTION is broadcast around the anchorage and I can check my e-mail a hundred times a day. I've been tapping my keyboard with manic strokes, relaying stories, reading updates, catching up. We're surrounded by a mountainous tropical island, a destination that people pay big bucks to visit on honeymoons, and all I want to do right now is stare at my laptop screen and be transported by e-mails.

Monica has been e-mailing from America, prodding us to get a new engine. Ever since the drowning incident, our dinghy engine has been making gurgling sounds of impending doom. Now it refuses to start. We have a beautiful new dinghy but, with no engine, it is only half the vehicle it could be: a Porsche powered by a desk-fan engine.

I can hear Monica's pleading tone, even through e-mail. 'I can't sleep at night knowing you have no engine.' Attached is a researched list of retailers and prices. She's even phoned engine-sellers in Tahiti to negotiate prices, which are included in her e-mail. This woman can move mountains when she wants.

Ivan does something out of character and decides to take his mother's advice.

We wait by the side of the road for the local bus into town. I have become obsessed with saying the term for bus – '*le truck*'. There is a satisfying hacking sound in the pronunciation of *truck* that sounds as though you're trying to push a hairball from your throat while cursing. So, of course, I say it as often as possible. 'Here comes *le truck*'; 'Let's get on *le truck*'; 'How much is the fare for *le truck*?'; '*Le truck* has arrived!' By the time we reach the main city of Papeete, my throat is chafed and I need a lozenge.

I take in Papeete: slums, markets, huddles of teens, homeless beggars, new developments, artisan stores, colours, smells, graffiti. It's a slice of urban society in the tropics, offering all the gritty ugliness that I adore in big cities.

The boating store showcases a range of shiny engines, lined up in a row, ranging from tiny to behemoth. A 275-horsepower engine looks like it's about to give birth to a litter of twenty newborn engines in the size we're looking for.

We spot a piano-black five-horsepower Suzuki that looks handsome enough to adopt. It has all the right stats and it puts our scrawny two-horsepower Honda to shame. Armed with Monica's negotiated prices, we make the purchase.

For fun, we plane through the water at exhilarating speeds with our new engine, taking joyrides around the lagoon. Powerful enough to take us much farther afield, it lets us explore places we couldn't go in our old dinghy.

Sometimes, though, we get in the dinghy and, without untying the tether from *Amazing Grace,* we sit stationary for hours, drinking beers, chilling out, breathing in the greatness of our new vehicle. No doubt, we look as strange as a couple hanging out in a parked car for the sheer joy of it.

Since we have no need for *Little Gracie* the first, we tie her up at the dock and abandon her like an unwanted pet. She bobs there for a few days and is eventually picked up by a loving stranger who doesn't mind caring for a ramshackle dinghy.

'WE SHOULD GET moving soon,' Ivan says: five inevitable words I've known were coming.

I look up from my computer to shoot him daggers. 'We just *got* here.'

'Ten days ago,' he reminds me. 'I was thinking we could go to another island nearby? There are lots of beautiful anchorages in the Society Islands.'

'But this is beautiful. We're having so much fun here.'

'It's been invaded by the western world.'

'So? I like the western world. We have delicious meals available, we get to e-mail every day. And there's really, really good cheese! *French cheese*, Ivan. Everything is so... practical here.'

'"Practical" and "spectacular" are not usually two words that go together.'

'Don't be cheeky.'

'Look, I know you're having a good time. It's crowded here. There are better places we could be, secluded places. Let's keep moving.'

'But—'

An Air Tahiti Nui plane flies by, loud and low, ascending into the overcast clouds. We both go quiet, waiting for the plane to pass. It's been a long time since I saw a plane – I almost forgot they existed.

I wonder where the plane is headed, and then I drift off into a daydream of flying back to Australia. In my reverie, I sip cold beers with friends, I go to art exhibitions, I chat with my mother in her kitchen, discussing life. I wonder if my nephews and nieces will remember me.

We still have half an ocean to cross before I'll see Australia again. And what if something bad happens before then? What if I never get to—

'Torre?' Ivan says.

'Yeah.'

'Did you hear what I just said?'

'No, sorry.'

'I said, how about we go to Moorea? It's only four hours away and the guidebook says the anchorage is safe and beautiful. There's a market with fresh food and a hotel with internet. If you need anything here in Tahiti, we can just catch the ferry over. I think you'll like it there.'

I'm suddenly gripped with incredible guilt for dreaming about home. I'm in paradise with a wonderful man – I should be overjoyed.

'Okay,' I say. 'Let's go to Moorea.'

'PITY ABOUT THE VIEW HERE,' Ivan says, sarcastically.

'A real tragedy.' I giggle.

From the cockpit of our anchored boat, we gaze lovingly at the spectacular vision that is Moorea. Tall, green pinnacles are the centrepiece of this anchorage, jutting up behind a blue lagoon.

A sea-wanderer's life seems to be a continual pursuit of the next idyllic hideout to call home. With so many beauties to choose from, it's easy to get picky. Which island has the whiter sand? Which lagoon has the clearer shade of aqua? Then there's the anchorage to consider: the cove needs to be protected so you can sleep without worrying you'll wake up pinned to a rock face by surf waves. Having friends nearby scores highly: there's nothing like a sunset drink shared with company while you laugh about misadventures. If you have all of these things *and* good scenery – the kind of beauty that makes you want to weep like a sentimental old man on his deathbed every time you catch a glimpse – then you've found the perfect place. *Opunohu Bay,* I think to myself, *is exactly this.*

I'm doing laundry in the cockpit, filling buckets with water from jerry cans to soap and stomp dirt from fabric. Laundry is a constant task. The humidity soaks everything inside, embedding dampness into fabrics. Towels are the worst: they retain a clean smell for two days after a hand-wash and then something biologically horrible happens. In a matter of a few short days, towels go from rainforest-breeze to dead-animal scented. Once they reach this stage, I can't be in the same space as them unless I'm dousing them with scoops of washing powder.

Ivan doesn't smell it since he's nasally challenged. He gets out of the shower, soapy and fragrant, and rubs himself down from head to toe in dead animal, transferring the odor onto his clean skin. He snuggles up to me in bed smelling of sickly-sweet decay: a reminder that it's time to do the laundry again.

While I lather up the towels in a bucket, Ivan declares he's going to clean the bilge. It's a rare sight to see Ivan performing boat maintenance while we're anchored; he's more commonly seen drinking beers in the cockpit, thumbing the pages of a novel or staring blankly at the horizon in the kind of unresponsive stupor that's common in psychiatric hospitals. He likes to work hard and play hard, and after his devoted efforts at sailing the boat from place to place, he deserves to play. For him, maintenance is only a priority when something is gushing water or crackling in flames.

Cleaning out the bilge is as ambitious as boat maintenance gets, because it's a territory where no living creature should ever have to venture. We call it The Dark Zone. Running up the centre of the boat, the bilge is a hollow space beneath the floor that collects runoff and overflow from multiple sources: shower water, engine spills and salt water. If the boat sprang a leak, many gallons of seawater would collect in this space first, preventing the cabin from flooding straightaway. An automatic pump empties any collected fluid overboard, but there's always an inch of greasy liquid that lines the bottom, which tends to putrefy into a thick, black funk. Four wooden panels along the floor of our living space cover the bilge and when we lift them up to peer into The Dark Zone, the boat's interior is defiled with an overbearing fart bomb of eggs, beans and motor oil.

Determined to make the smell go away, Ivan lifts the lid and goes in up to his elbows. I can see where his face has become itchy in the last twenty minutes by the smudges of black goo around his temples, left eyebrow and chin.

Partway through the big clean, he washes his hands and face off and takes a break from the stink, joining me in the cockpit. We chat as I wring clothes, squeezing the cool water onto my legs.

'Do you know what would be better than this?' Ivan asks.

'What?'

'Nothing.'

I smile.

'Actually,' he says, 'this place and a baguette with goat cheese and fig jam.' He stomps down the companionway to pursue his craving. Seconds later, a sharp cry comes from down below. 'Ahhhh!'

I stick my head through the companionway and find Ivan crotch-deep in bilge. He's at floor level, looking like an amputee with one leg buried in the belly of the boat.

'What are you doing down there?' I ask.

'I forgot. Walked. Straight. In hole,' he stammers, struggling to speak through his agony.

'Of course you did,' I say.

'So. Stupid.'

'Are you badly hurt?'

'Yes. Hurting. Shin. Ow.'

Ivan works slowly to pull his body out of the bilge. One leg looks like a dipstick, covered in black, farty goop. 'Here,' he says pointing to mid-shin. 'I hit it on the way down.'

I take a close look and see that he's gone and ripped himself a new orifice. The coin-sized gash in his leg is so deep that it disappears into darkness like a belly button. It's bloody and flecked in filthy splats of bilge funk. I locate our well-used medical kit and get to work.

LATER, WE GO TO SHORE to rinse our laundry under a tap. There we run into Lisbeth and Lasse and they immediately notice Ivan's bandaged leg. 'What happened *this* time?' Lisbeth asks, swallowing a giggle.

Ivan tells the story and we all laugh – once again – at his knack for provoking slapstick moments.

'Torre, you should always carry a first-aid backpack,' Lisbeth jokes. 'Then you can follow behind Ivan everywhere he goes and you'll be ready for when he hurts himself next.'

We all laugh, but then I wonder if Lisbeth is actually making a joke. A medical backpack? That's not a bad idea. Somebody has to nurse this Olympic klutz.

When the laundry is rinsed, we look for a place among the coconut palms to string a clothesline. I hear a nearby *thud* and wonder if hanging clothes beneath these trees is a bad idea.

A voice calls from nearby, 'Eh!'

I look around and spot a man beckoning us over. He's yelling out to us from his humble house in the palms, overlooking the water where *Amazing Grace* is anchored. Pots bubble over on his outdoor stovetop.

'Eh, come!' he says, gesturing more aggressively. He's an elderly man with dark island skin that's etched with lines. The man jabbers in French and Polynesian and we tell him we don't understand. He gestures to his clothesline. 'Eh.' He wants us to hang our clothes there.

'*Merci beaucoup*,' I say, and Ivan and I work together to string up our wet clothes.

'Eh,' he says again, getting our attention. He holds up a plate of food served up from the bubbling pots and then makes an eating gesture. 'Eh?'

We don't want to be rude in the face of a generous invitation. Okay, we say, accepting the offer of free feed. We thank the man profusely in the only way we know how: by repeating '*merci beaucoup*' several times over.

He dishes up generous piles of chicken curry and taro root and invites us to sit in his dining room, which consists of a few plastic chairs in the open air with a panorama of the bay. While we enjoy his cooking, the old man talks away to us like we're dear friends. The only problem is, we can't understand a word. He doesn't attempt to bridge the comprehension gap with hand gestures or half-paced French. He rambles in the short, sharp song of the Tahitian language. '*Eh-hi-ah-aoh-la-na. Ha, ha, ha.*'

I nod and smile and take cue to laugh when he laughs. Clearly, the man just enjoys having company.

When we finish off our plates, he brings out a pipe and stacks it full of weed from a tiny baggie. He lights the mound in the cone and sucks on the mouthpiece. It catches fire and smoke fills the glass bulb, lingering for a moment before disappearing with another mighty suck. He holds his breath while we watch silently, waiting, holding our breaths too. He lets go and exhales a smoky sigh that seems like it will never end, but when it does he looks up at us with bloodshot eyes, giggles, and then continues jabbering. '*La-na-aorna-eh-hi-na. Ha, ha, ha.*' He stuffs another cone and compacts it with his pinky finger.

'Eh,' he says, pushing the pipe toward us. 'Eh?'

Once again, we don't want to be rude in the face of a generous invitation. Ivan takes the pipe first and holds a struck match to the cone. He takes a small suck, almost a hiccup, and then breaks into a dramatic coughing fit. He squints his eyes and has a few more tokes, and then he passes the pipe to me.

I follow suit and hand the pipe back to the old man.

'Eh?' he says. '*Très bon, non?*'

We each give him a thumbs-up, '*Oui. C'est bon. Merci.*'

My body is buzzing, happy, fed and warm. All three of us relax back into our plastic chairs, facing the water. I'm in the moment, wide awake and hyperaware of the dancing breeze, the white noise of the lapping shore, the tussle of the palm fronds overhead. The sky is coloured with the fiery tones of a setting sun. *Amazing Grace* sits in the centre of the scene, bobbing proudly at anchor not far off the beach, waiting patiently for us to return. Our sweet Gracie.

Then I see something unexpected: an explosion of water, a texture like a raked Zen garden, a slick, knotty head, long fins extended, tail flukes poised, a gigantic beast airborne for an impossible length of time.

A humpback whale!

The whale drops, creating a huge splash. Its great tail holds its pose right in front of our boat, and I get a sense of proportion alongside *Amazing Grace*. This beast is *huge*. It slips below the surface, gone as fast as a shooting star.

I look at Ivan, whose eyes are bloodshot and wide open. His jaw is dangling. He's a mirror of my own expression.

'Holy shit. Did that just happen?'

'Yes. It did.'

'So you saw—'

'Yes, I saw it.'

The palm fronds keep tussling, the water keeps lapping the shore, the breeze tickles across my skin and the sky's saturation intensifies, burning with the colours of sunset.

I look over at the elderly man to see how he's reacting to all of this. A serene expression has been permanently etched onto his face by deep wrinkles. This is just a regular day in his dining room.

'This is the best trip ever,' I say to Ivan.

MY LEGS ARE DANGLING over the smooth teak railing of Gracie and I'm gazing into Moorea's lagoon. The sun illuminates the water all the way to the bottom, and I'm watching a small spotted eagle ray gliding just above the sea floor, its elegant black-and-white wings flapping like those of a bird.

Ivan is lounged beside me in the cockpit, lost in a novel, which is marked with greasy sunscreen fingerprints. We've been in this deep state of relaxation for days.

Without taking his eyes from his novel, Ivan hands me a maté. I fill the wooden cup with hot water and suck the tea through the straw, no longer offended by the smoky taste. I've grown to enjoy the mild caffeine high as well as the ritual of sharing this tradition with Ivan.

'What time is it?' I ask.

'Not sure. Ten, maybe? Eleven?'

'What day of the week is it?'

'Umm... Monday? Oh, no, Wednesday I think. Why?'

'And what date is it?'

He goes quiet for a long time, and I assume he hasn't heard because he's taking too long to answer. Then finally: 'September something. Why?'

'Just curious. Don't you think it's weird that we don't know the time or date any more?'

'It's totally awesome.'

I peer back down at the polka-dotted ray. I think about how I don't check a watch any more: I read the sky and the water. The approximate time of day can be detected by the shade of the water and the direction of the boat's shadow cast on the sea floor. I'm intimate with the moods of my environment, how approaching rain can be anticipated by the smell of a breeze, or how a sunny day to come can be forecast in the palette of a sunset.

I don't know the date, but I always know what phase of the moon we're in. A full moon illuminates everything under its neon glow so that, even at night, our anchor is visible on the sea floor twenty feet below. Everything slips into black when there's no moon, but stars decorate the sky like glitter sprinkled by an excited child. Sometimes the child's hand slips and glitter is spilled in the ocean, creating phosphorescence – bursts of light from hundreds of tiny bioluminescent organisms that flash when the water is disturbed. We spend hours playing with these lights in the water, dipping and swishing an oar to stimulate the sparkling pins of blue light.

Sometimes we make love up on the deck. These nights are so dark that we're hidden by a sheet of black satin. I've never been much of a sex-outdoors type, but the magic of a glitter-sprinkled world inspires impulsive acts.

'You know we only have two more months to travel,' Ivan says, bringing me back into the present moment. 'The sailing season is almost over, so that means *this* is almost over.'

'Oh, yeah,' I say. Sadness yanks me from my reverie.

Over. What a sad word. There are days when missing home dominates my every thought. It's taken me a while to realise that these moods coincide with grey skies. Aligned with our environment, we adopt the weather's temperament: foul when it's foul, fine when it's fine. Rain clouds shield the sun from our solar panels, so that not only are we confined inside the cabin, we also collect very little electricity for watching movies, writing on the laptop or listening to music. Frustration brews and we bicker. But then when the clouds part and blue sky is revealed, my mood and obsessions are cleared too, riding off on the passing gale. I'm present, content, relaxed... like now.

Three spotted rays drift below the boat, flying through water that looks like air. I want to dive in and swim with them.

'Baby?' Ivan says. 'Doesn't it feel like we're rushing to get back to Australia by the end of October this year? There's not much time and we'll have to skip many islands.'

'Yes, it feels like we're rushing. You spent all that money getting the boat ready, plus all those years planning. It's a big investment and it seems like a waste to finish already.'

'Yes, it does,' he says, putting his novel down and sitting upright. 'We still have so many beautiful places to see,' he says.

My gaze drifts and lingers on Moorea's craggy pinnacles.

Ivan clears his throat. 'What if... what if we leave the boat somewhere safe nearby for hurricane season? We could fly to Australia for Christmas and—'

'I can see my family and they can meet you.'

'Yes. Then we can come back for another year and—'

'Take our time and—'

'See more islands and—'

'Make new friends.'

'Yes! Yes! You don't know *how much* I've been hoping you'd want to keep going with me.' He wraps his arms around me.

'And we don't have to finish in Australia, you know,' he continues. 'Maybe we can keep going and live at anchor in different countries around the world. We can earn money in different ports and keep going for... well, forever, really. We can head to Indonesia next. That's the next stop beyond the Pacific, north of Australia. That's where most sailors head if they're doing a circumnavigation, because it's the easiest route, rather than heading south towards Melbourne where the seas gets rough. In Indonesia, you can…'

His voice trails off as I become intoxicated by the smell of his neck. 'Maybe we'll be just like Steve and Carol?' I say.

He kisses my forehead, my cheek, my lips. 'Yes, yes, yes.'

I lap it up, indulging the fantasy, while ignoring my heart's doubts. Sailing the ocean as a permanent, full-time nomad was never something I wanted. Even though Steve and Carol are inspiring beyond words, being permanently married to the sea, to danger and to isolation, is not the sojourn I planned for. When I left my family in Australia, all I wanted was a new experience but now…

'*Te quiero,*' he says. 'I love you so much. You're so beautiful. You're so perfect. You're my princess. *El amor de mi vida.*'

My better judgement is silenced as he swathes me with adoring love. I melt into his affection, breathing in the smell of him.

A SMALL TRACTOR LUGS *Amazing Grace* out of the water and up onto dry land. Strapped into a cradle, she emerges like an amphibian. Salty tears drip from her underside into the dry dirt. Tiny gatherings of barnacles, which have found a home on her belly, begin to fry in the hot sun. The tractor drives Gracie through the yard, parking her in a row alongside other dry-stored yachts.

The island of Raiatea is a place for business, not pleasure. It's here on this island, just over a hundred miles from Tahiti, that we'll need to prepare the boat for storage during hurricane season.

This place is an epicentre of boats in disrepair. Some have gaping holes in their fibreglass hulls, others have been abandoned to rust and crumble. Every boat looks strange out of its natural environment and I feel weird looking at their undersides, as though I'm seeing something that I'm not supposed to. '*Ooh, that one has a big keel. Look at the rudder on that guy.*'

We use a tall ladder to climb into our home and, twelve feet from the ground, we have a whole new reason to keep ourselves from falling overboard: concrete isn't as forgiving as water.

Now the preparations begin. Keeping the boat safely stored is a serious task. We've heard horror stories of people returning to find grave problems after five months away. The tropical heat inside an unventilated boat can melt rubber, but the worst rumour involves rats crawling in through open seacocks and chewing through electronics. I want to make sure this doesn't happen to us. Sailing is hard enough without broken electronics and a party of rodent stowaways.

I go into action mode, compiling a list of tasks gathered from books and the internet, skipping no corners:

Fill diesel tanks to the top.

Check folding prop.

Grease seacocks.

I giggle at the last point while writing Ivan's initials beside it. My list tallies up to thirty individual tasks and involves a vocabulary of words that are lost on me, but I don't want to skip anything, especially the items I don't understand.

I present my long list to Ivan with a proud smile.

He glances at the piece of paper, rolls his eyes and rubs at his forehead, dirtying it up with grease. 'We don't even have a folding prop, baby. There are all sorts of things on this list that don't make any sense. Like, we don't need to put antifreeze in the engine because we're in the tropics, we're not winterizing the boat. You're obsessing over too many small details.'

I take my list and walk off, determined to do it my way.

While Ivan tinkers, I scrub the boat down with a toothbrush, launder all our clothes and bedding, remove rust from the stainless steel and coat the wood with linseed oil. I stuff *Amazing Grace*'s seacocks with copper wool to fend off a rodent invasion and grease moving parts aboard to prevent corrosion. I teach myself to service the dinghy engine, learning about spark plugs, prop lubrication and – tee-hee! – nipple greasing.

I go to the marina shop and buy oils for the service.

'What are you doing?' Ivan says when he sees me returning with a bag of supplies.

'Servicing the outboard engine. I'm following the manual.'

He rolls his eyes and huffs a breath out. 'The engine is brand new, it's not necessary.'

'Which is why I want to do this, to *keep* it brand new.'

'You're wasting time,' he declares, turning his back.

Maybe he's right – I'm a perfectionist prone to agonising over all the small details, but his condescending tone is rubbing me the wrong way.

I bite back. 'Why do you think I'm wasting time? Just because I don't do everything half-arsed like you?'

He turns to face me and goes quiet for a second while his lips turn white with anger. 'Did you just call me half-arsed?'

'Well, okay, sorry, but it's just that you're just not always thorough.'

He stares me down for a while. 'It takes eighty percent of the effort to achieve the last twenty percent of any task,' he says.

'But if you've done eighty percent of the hard work, why not bring it home with the last twenty?'

'Whatever.' He throws down a dirty rag and walks off.

Later that day, he approaches me with a rueful expression. I can practically see his tail tucked between his legs.

'What happened?' I ask in monotone.

'I just broke our watermaker,' he confesses.

'And how did that happen, Ivan?'

'I put the wrong liquid in it and now it won't work.'

'And *why* do you think that happened?'

His lips stay shut.

'Hmm?' I say.

'I didn't follow the instructions in the manual. Okay, okay, you were right.' He pushes out his chest and closes his eyes, inviting a free punch.

I sock it to him in the form of a smug grin.

'And there's something else,' he says.

'Oh, no… what?'

'I stood on the hatch above our bed while it was open and it snapped off. The wood split and the window won't close. I confess: I'm a big idiot and I am sorry for that.'

I tussle his hair. '*So is it,*' I say in Swedish singsong.

AFTER TWO WEEKS of hard work, the time comes for us to leave. Satisfied with our work, we lock up *Amazing Grace*, leaving her in immaculate order. It's October now and we won't be seeing her again until next February.

As I climb down the ladder, I pat her tenderly. 'Take care of yourself,' I say. 'Be good.' There's a sting of sadness to leaving her behind. She's looking so fine – it seems a pity to go. Then, with our luggage, we head home.

PART THREE
AIR

'If one does not know to which port one is sailing,
no wind is favourable.'
Lucius Annaeus Seneca

SIXTEEN

THE PLANE'S TYRES SQUEAL along Tahiti's short runway. It's dark outside and I can't see much beyond the tarmac. We exit through the rear doors and I'm punched with humidity. Wet smells of Tahiti's vegetation stir memories from last year: the breaching whale in Moorea, the long ocean passages, Ivan's many injuries.

How could a new year have rolled over so quickly?

If the air were any more humid, we'd be swimming. I don't recall it being this hot and sticky last year. The weather in Australia was so dry that my nose scabbed up for weeks when we returned home and my skin adopted a scaly white film. Our deep tans washed away after a few hot showers, as did our celebrity status as new arrivals with exciting stories to tell. Our crowd of captivated listeners slowly dissipated and then we found ourselves as displaced hermits without a shell.

In October, I felt naked without our protective husk named *Amazing Grace*. I longed to scurry back into her safe space. But a lot of things changed over the five months.

By February of the New Year, the South Pacific had become a well-worn story that seemed to belong to someone else. Returning here feels like a bizarre déjà vu.

In Tahiti's small airport, we collect our bags from the carousel and find a quiet corner of the airport to set up our bed for the night. We have an overnight layover before we can catch a small plane to Raiatea and back to the boat. I throw a sarong over the dirty floor and Ivan and I huddle together among a crowd of locals doing the same thing.

Within moments, Ivan is snoring, but my mind is too anxious to sleep, sparking with thoughts and memories. *'Hi, everyone, meet the man who sailed me halfway across the Pacific!'* I smile as I remember this moment. My family and friends seemed to adore him, which was a relief. We spent time touring Australia by car. We camped in the blistering hot desert, kept company by kangaroos and deadly snakes – an activity I used to regard as too adventurous for a city girl like me. But sleeping in the dirt was a cakewalk compared to the ocean. Throughout the road trip, I found myself at peace with nature, in love with its solitude and changing beauty. *No two sunsets are ever the same,* I thought, as I sat in my camping chair, using chalk pastels to capture dusk in the Flinders Ranges. For the first time in my life, I felt at ease in wild places, and I learned then how much I'd changed.

In the context of my childhood home, I saw myself morphed into somebody new: an empowered woman who believed in herself. I was equipped with a powerful mantra that cracked open a world of possibilities: *I can do anything. I've faced my fears. I've journeyed half the Pacific Ocean in a sailboat. I can service dinghy engines!*

'There's something different about you,' my mum kept observing, with her hand on her hip and her head cocked, trying to work it out. I'd laugh and tell her it was my hair, no longer the styled, dark brown cut from her memory, but long, centre-parted and woven with strands of sun-bleached gold.

In those five months, my feet began to sprout roots on Aussie soil. I got excited about beginning life anew in Melbourne. With anything possible, life on land looked very enticing. I could start my own graphic design business and get an office dog to keep me company. Or Ivan and I could start a business together – a wine bar and *fromagerie,* so we could have an excuse to eat cheese and drink wine all day. If we got sick of life in the city, we could plan and save for another adventure. A road trip, perhaps? The world, I discovered, was limitless because *we had sailed half the Pacific Ocean.*

When I brought up my plans for Melbourne, Ivan would change the subject to talk of Gracie: where we'd take her next, or modifications that could make her a more comfortable home. 'We can add a fridge next year,' he said with uncontained excitement, 'and a new wind generator! I know you'll be happy if we have a fridge and more power. We can drink cold beers and icy water, and we'll be able to store plenty of fresh food. That means we can cook gourmet meals.'

Sensing my diminishing energy, I knew he was brainstorming ways to pump me full of enthusiasm, to charm me over to his side once again.

Throughout the hot Aussie summer, we'd lunched with friends and enjoyed long, lazy barbecues with family.

'Australia's best-kept secret,' Ivan said with irritation at one such barbecue, swatting tenacious flies off his face. The flies didn't appear to annoy anyone else quite so much.

In a quiet corner of the garden, we sat alone in the shade, sipping on cold beers to cool our sweltering insides.

'Your family is really nice,' Ivan said. 'I half expected your dad would want to, like, slug me in the face for taking his daughter sailing. He's cool, though. Your whole family is. They're good people.'

I beamed at him. 'So you like it here in Australia? Apart from the flies, of course.' I laughed.

He kept his unamused eyes downcast. 'It's… yeah… nice.'

'And?' I sensed it was a mistake to broach this subject while he was hot and bothered, but I was impatient to know.

'It's fine.'

'Fine? Really? Wow – settle down over there!' I said sarcastically. 'You might break a rib with that unbridled enthusiasm.' I, too, was hot and bothered.

He let out a flat laugh. 'Sorry. It's just… It reminds me of Argentina a bit.'

I didn't understand his reference, but from what he'd told me about his home country, I knew it wasn't good. 'In what way?' I ventured.

'It's behind the times. And it feels isolated from the rest of the world.'

His words cut, but I couldn't dispute his observation after having lived in the US, where neon signs buzz 24/7, traffic flows nonstop and the stores are always open. Australia doesn't have all the conveniences of the US, but to me, that's its charm. We know how to relax with a beer in hand. 'No worries, mate' is our clichéd motto, but it's one that I've experienced to be true.

'But isn't that what you like about the islands?' I rebutted. 'That they're remote? That life is more relaxed there?'

'This place is *not* like the islands,' he said with a laugh. 'Where do I start with the comparison? Let's see… it must be forty degrees Celsius in Melbourne today and I just swatted the seven hundredth fly from my face. It's dry as hell. My lips are cracked. You've got about twelve bushfires on the go here at any given time. All the grass is brown and—'

'It's summertime, Ivan.' My tone had turned chilly. 'And we're right in the middle of a drought. It's not *always* summertime. It's called a heat wave, and—'

'Why are you being so defensive?'

'Because you're being a jerk.'

'It's not like I insulted *you* or anything.'

'But, Ivan, this is my home. This is where I come from. This country is a part of me, so it feels like you're criticising *me*.'

'Yeah, well, my only allegiance is for nature, not for any civilisation. People should go to war when a new strip mall is getting built. We should protect the planet from gigantic parking lots. At least that would make some sense.'

'Ivan, I don't disagree with you, but—'

'I moved to the States because I thought I'd be free there. I wasn't. It's the same crap in a different package. You ask me what I think of Australia? Well, I think it's more or less the same as every other civilisation.'

'But...' I trailed off. The dry heat prevented my tears from overflowing. I opened my mouth to ask something, but the question couldn't find its way past the lump in my throat. 'Ivan?' My voice shook.

He looked up and noticed my distress, suddenly realising his callousness. He pulled me into a sweaty hug and covered the top of my head in kisses. 'Oh, baby, I'm sorry,' he said. 'This is your home. I know you love it here. I'm being an arsehole. I'm so sorry. *Te quiero.* I love you so much.'

I pulled back and looked him in the eyes. 'We'll return here when the voyage is over next year, won't we?'

He grew quiet and shrugged, revealing nothing but uncertainty in his eyes.

Flies gravitated toward the fountain of salty drink in the corners of my eyes and I shooed at them with furious swats. *Fuck you, flies! You're ruining everything!*

After Australia, we flew back to the States for Ivan's US citizenship ceremony. He dropped his tongue-twister surname, simplifying his title to Ivan Alexis. 'I can go anywhere in the world with this,' he said afterward, clutching his brand-new US passport. 'Nobody can ever make me go back to Argentina.'

IN THE TAHITI AIRPORT, families lie in corners sleeping. The whole building is resting, except for me. Instead, I look at Ivan. He's curled up on his side, facing me, his skin moist with humidity. I want to press my mouth to his plump lips and be soothed by his affection, but he's sleeping. His eyes are gently rolling behind closed lids – dreaming of what? Gracie, most likely.

I tuck into his spoon, facing the wall, and bury my head in my hands so that my quiet sobs go unheard. I'm just tired, I tell myself. A bad mood, that's all. I'll snap out of this funk after some decent sleep.

I wake up to the tickle of sweat dripping from my hairline. After a quick flight to Raiatea, we reach the boatyard, and the humidity is turned up tenfold. It's oppressive, like being crushed into a kennel with ten feverish dogs panting out the tangy stink of decaying barnacles. We roll our luggage over the muddy terrain of Raiatea's marina, weaving around hulls as we look for *Amazing Grace*.

The yard is eerily still. I step over boat parts and avoid muddy puddles with my new shoes. Red rust seeps down neglected hulls and soaks the earth below. Piles of unwanted equipment, splotchy with mould, collect in corners. Everything is breaking down. The elements in the tropics eat through man-made materials like worms on a carcass. All these rusting, failing boats make me think of death.

We pass by rows of yachts lined up like dominoes. I spot a hull being painted with enormous fish. A woman stands under the hull, brush in hand, perfecting gills and fins with vibrant swishes and dots. When the boat goes back into the water, this artwork will end up below the surface – a travelling exhibition that only the dolphins and whales can see. It makes me smile.

'Hello there,' the woman sings in an American accent.

'Your artwork is beautiful,' I tell her, before skipping to catch up with Ivan, who is singularly focused in his search for Gracie.

'There she is,' Ivan says, pointing to a white hull with forest-green trimmings that looks vaguely familiar. Was our boat really *that* old? The tarp we strung over the boom to provide shade has been shredded to ribbons by gale-force winds. *Amazing Grace* looks tired and aged, far different from the shiny, immaculate boat we left behind last year.

We lug our suitcases up the ladder and onto the deck. Ivan removes the padlock and pulls off the door slats one by one. Hot, stagnant air pours out, the odor of wet socks forgotten in a zipped gym bag.

'We just need to open up all the windows,' Ivan says, spotting me holding my nose. 'We just need to get some air happening.'

Right now I'm thinking that, even if we aired her, sprayed her with freshener and hung little pine trees from every corner, *Amazing Grace* would still smell of fermented foot jam. Ivan removes the last slat from the companionway and we peer down into our home for the first time in 150 days.

'Oh. My. God,' I say, covering my shocked mouth.

'It's okay!' Ivan's voice is all cheer. 'We'll just wipe her down and she'll be good as new. It's only a little mildew!'

'A little mildew' is a powdery layer of mould mottling the teak walls, the vinyl seats, the kitchen cupboards and even the jars of herbs in our spice rack. No wonder it smells in here – we've discovered her in an advanced state of decomposition.

Ivan goes into action, filling buckets with water and vinegar to kill the mould. He rubs the powdery walls down and now our home reeks of hot Gorgonzola cheese.

I gulp down my shock and take a sponge in hand, knowing we need to get her cleaned before we can sleep. When this is done,

I tell myself, I can get some rest and wake up in a happy mood, eager and excited to spend another year living inside this boat.

It takes us two hours to clean the visible mould, but the problem is deeper than that. We discover that mildew has infected every single item on the boat. Our clothes (kept in airtight bags), unopened food, books, foul-weather gear, even our bedding is covered in a layer of spotty green and white. Nothing has escaped the wrath of this wretched funk factory. Our home is the stomach of a dead whale.

Water has leaked in from more than one source, soiling entire cupboards. The bathroom is ankle-deep with black, stagnant fluid. The leak in the ceiling below the mast has mature mushrooms growing on it: large, pancake fungi that are each the size of two hands combined. I peel the crispy white skins off the roof and line them up in a row, estimating that the quantity would make a hearty meal for four. I wonder what the Iron Chef could do with these: '*Today's theme ingredient is... boat mushrooms!* Allez cuisine!'

But that's not the worst of our problems: the maggots steal that prize. Cans of food have burst in the harsh conditions and fat maggots writhe in the mess. The intact cans are bloated, ready to explode, riddled with botulism parasites. I close the food cupboard shut, not yet ready to deal with that problem.

Instead, I pull everything out of the boat for airing, covering the deck with pillows, settees, blankets and mattresses. I can hear the mildew getting zapped by the sun, squeaking as it shrinks and melts (*Oh, what a world!*). I wield a bottle of vinegar solution from my hip pocket and shoot at the mildew. *Pow! Pow! Take that!* My energy is coming back.

I find Ivan with his hands in a bucket of water, whistling a merry tune and working his hands through a foamy mix containing our best set of sheets. They were a splurge, a little piece of thousand-thread-count luxury. But now, any hope of simulated luxury is gone because the chocolate-brown sheets are covered in patches of bright orange. My energy takes another nosedive. 'You're bleaching our sheets, Ivan,' I say.

He wears the face of an innocent mutt: cocked head, doe eyes. 'Was I not supposed to use bleach?'

'Not with colours. Bleach *bleaches* things.'

'Oh… right. Well, how was I supposed to know that?'

I shove down my frustration and take over the washing. I fill buckets with water, add scoops of powder and softener, then stomp on the clothes with bare feet until the water overflows. After the soapy water has warmed in the sunlight, I churn them again, rinse, wring and hang them to dry. When I pull the clothes off the line an hour later, I go in for the odor test and find that… *everything still stinks.*

I suppress the urge to toss it all in the mud and unleash a tantrum. Instead, I calmly fill more buckets and scoop more powder and repeat. I cram my emotions deeper. I ignore the tightness that's gripping at my throat.

Next, I glove up and attack the worst job: wiping up piles of maggoty mush. I hold my breath and scoop up the chunky stew, tossing it in garbage bags. All of our food gets flung into the dumpster; over a thousand dollars' worth of canned goods, flour, sugar, grains, pastas, dried potatoes, cereals, olives, yeast, long-life dairy – all spoiled. Despite our triple-airtight bagging system, everything's contaminated with boaty odor.

The deeper we dig, the greater the damage.

Our wooden tiller has split in half, the fans are broken, the lights aren't working, the stove won't ignite, the water pump doesn't pump and the stereo is dead.

'This is unbelievable,' I say when we discover that our battery bank is not charging.

'Don't stress out, it's just a few electronic issues. We can get a mechanic to fix them.' Ivan's trying to keep both of our spirits high, but not only is my glass half empty, it's cracked.

I begin to unpack the luggage, pulling Ivan's clean clothes out of his suitcase and storing them away in our smelly sweatbox. When I get to my bag, I discover a bottle of hair product – my one beauty indulgence brought from the US – has burst through its bag on the flight over and permeated my clean clothes with de-frizzing serum. Not a drop of serum is left. Not an item of clothing is unsoiled. My throat tightens. *Don't stress out*, I tell myself, *breathe... just breathe!*

But the cracks in my half-empty glass shatter. I'm broken. I fall to the floor and begin to weep.

'Don't worry, I'll get you some more.' Ivan says.

I can't believe I'm crying over spilled serum. But now that I've opened the floodgates, all the pressure is erupting, and I can't stop it. 'My... *hih-hih*... hair gets so knotty... *hih*... *with the* humidity and... *hih*... this was my one special hair product... *hih-hih*.'

'Don't worry, it's okay. I'll order another bottle. We can get some FedEx'ed over.'

A sweet gesture, but somehow I don't think a new bottle of de-frizzing serum will make this better. It isn't the product or the soiled clothes. It's the accumulation of grievances. It's the mould-infested boat. It's our splotchy orange-and-brown sheets. It's the isolation of a place where you can't replace anything. It's the shock of changing worlds. It's missing Australia. It's the fear that Ivan will never want to return to land. And it's the knowledge that, if he doesn't, the only way to keep him involves getting permanently cozy inside this dead whale.

I fill the bilge with pathetic tears until I'm ready to collect myself up off the floor to resume cleaning, to keep myself distracted.

When our backs are aching and our nails are split and dirt-filled, we crawl into bed under bleached sheets that now smell only a little bit mouldy. Without working fans, we sweat ourselves to sleep.

SEVENTEEN

'HEY, THAT BOAT looks like *Tamata,*' Ivan says, as we're eating baguettes smothered in pâté for breakfast in the cockpit. He points to the boat stored alongside *Amazing Grace* and jumps up for a closer look.

'Huh?' I ask, twirling my hair with the pen I'm using to write our latest to-do list.

'*Tamata.* You know, Moitessier's boat.'

'Ha! Wouldn't that be funny: your hero's boat rubbing shoulders with *Amazing Grace*. How cute would that be?'

Ivan continues inspecting the nameless boat, which sits, like ours, propped in a cradle on top of the marina's muddy soil. 'That's weird,' he says. 'It has the same acrylic dome that Moitessier's boat had so he could keep watch without going outside in a storm.' Ivan strokes at his rough chin stubble. 'Three cleats in the cockpit for tying up halyards – just like *Tamata*. Two seats on the stern. This is really bizarre. I would *swear* that's Moitessier's boat.'

'But isn't he dead?'

'Yeah, he died more than ten years ago. I don't know why his boat would be here. But he does talk about Raiatea in his books, so maybe... I mean, this boat is so "Moitessier". Basic, practical design with no frills, just purely functional. I'm going to go ask someone.' He climbs down the ladder and disappears into the boatyard.

Moments later, he comes back with a huge grin. 'I knew it,' he yells up to me. 'It's his boat! That's Moitessier's boat!'

'Are you kidding me? What's it doing here?' I say.

He shrugs. 'The guy at the hardware shop told me Moitessier's wife, Françoise, pays the annual fees to keep the boat stored on Raiatea.'

Ivan circles around *Tamata*, staring up at her with saucer eyes. I can only imagine what he feels seeing his own boat beside this famous sailor's boat – the very icon whose words inspired the birth of Ivan's dream.

He joins me in the cockpit again, finishing his breakfast while marveling at our neighbouring boat.

'It's strange, don't you think?' I say. 'I mean, it's weird that his wife still pays the fees to keep Moitessier's boat here, even though he left her all those years ago. It's very loyal, she must've adored him.'

'I suppose she did,' Ivan says.

'It still doesn't make sense to me why he left her.'

Ivan shrugs. 'He said he felt happy at sea. He loved the ocean. He felt free.'

'But… didn't he miss having a companion?'

'Not sure. All I know is that after he abandoned the race and turned back out to sea, he wrote his wife a letter saying he didn't have the courage to return, but maybe someday he would.'

'And did he?' My words come out strangled and desperate. 'Did he ever return to her?'

'No.'

'But why not?' I say, a little too loudly. 'She sailed the world for him. Why couldn't he find courage for her?'

'Dunno,' he says indifferently, ripping off a piece of his baguette.

I stare at Ivan, urging him to read between the lines, silently pleading with him to give me the answer I want to hear. 'Didn't he love her?' I hold my stare on him, waiting for him to look at me. *Tell me you're not like him, Ivan. Tell me I'm being paranoid.* But his gaze is a million miles away, fixed on *Tamata*. 'I guess he loved the ocean more.'

I take a deep breath and return to my to-do list to tally the growing number of hazards involved in this slow journey home. The boat's hardware isn't the only thing at great risk of breaking.

THE MARINA IS BUZZING with reports of sailors returning to mould, equipment failures, broken engines and dead batteries – it's not just our boat. In fact, I decide we got off easy when I hear of a couple who returned to hamster-sized rats who'd chewed through electronics, pooped in food cupboards and made sweet love on all the soft furnishings.

According to the cruisers who stayed here during hurricane season, the rainfall was twice its average – an incredible quantity of water, given that torrential rain is abundant on these lush islands. This has meant more mould and corrosion. The rain has also brought an outbreak of dengue fever in the area and we've heard several reports of sailors being knocked flat in agonising pain for weeks. A few people went to the hospital and one sailor passed out in unbearable pain midway through a five-day ocean passage, leaving his wife in charge of solo sailing the boat to safety.

Out of the water, without a breeze, we're even more vulnerable to mosquitoes. Puddles floating with larvae surround *Amazing Grace*. I light up some citronella coils and cross my fingers – contracting dengue fever would really be the icing on my multitiered cake of self-pity.

Then there's the other bad news. This year is set to bring a *La Niña* – a weather phenomenon that occurs once every three to five years. Like its bratty brother, *El Niño*, 'the girl' brings unpredictable weather. While *El Niño* warms the seas, *La Niña* does the opposite, cooling the ocean's surface, triggering increased winds, heavy rains and moody skies to match. Our perfect trade-wind weather is in a glitch year.

We arrange for *Amazing Grace* to be put back in the water, hoping the ocean's breeze will help us sleep. But floating on the water, we discover a new assortment of problems: the toilet won't pump, the depth sounder won't read, and when Ivan tries to twist the engine's throttle lever, it snaps off clean in his hand.

The worst of our problems is the engine. It won't start because an important item on last year's list remains unchecked – 'Fill diesel tanks.'

'It'll be fine,' Ivan had said last year when I asked him about filling the fuel tanks. I'd marked it up on our to-do list, having read that it was necessary before storing the boat for a long time. 'They're *almost* full,' Ivan said. 'Eighty percent. That should be enough.'

But 'almost' is not enough, as it turns out. During our hiatus, water has condensed in the empty part of the tanks, which has now mingled with the fuel, contaminating it.

The haunting words of the greasy mad mechanic from Los Angeles flash to mind. *'If your engine fails, you will die!'*

Not only has our engine failed, our electronics aren't working and important levers are snapping off. I don't know if I can trust *Amazing Grace* with my life any more. If our boat were a dog, now would be the time to get her put down. She's into the soiling-herself stage, the blind-and-running-into-furniture stage. It's time to put her out of her misery. I don't admit it out loud, but deep down, I'm hoping that the boat will be too sick to continue on. In this fantasy, a compassionate boat mechanic tells us: 'I'm sorry, there is nothing more we can do, we have to let her go.' Ivan and

I hug, weep a little (cue: crocodile tears) and get the bloody great burden put to sleep. No more Gracie. One happy Torre.

I think of the incredible coincidence of seeing Moitessier's boat alongside *Amazing Grace* in the yard and wonder if it's a message to me from the sailing legend himself. Tamata, *Torre*. *You must try.*

I TICK THE FINAL ITEM off our list and Ivan and I clank our frosted bottles of beer – a well-deserved treat after three busy weeks in the marina. The chilled liquid cools my insides. Refrigerated by our newest addition to the boat, I'm choked up with excitement that we can store fish, meats, vegetables and dairy, and – most importantly – watch sunsets with a cold beer in hand.

To power our new fridge and provide sufficient energy to all our electronics, Ivan arranged for a wind generator to be installed behind the cockpit, alongside Wendy, our autopilot. The generator zips around, day and night, buzzing like it's trying to lift us into flight. We also had an awning made from forest-green fabric to shade the cockpit. It serves as a water-catcher too, so we don't need to repair the complicated, power-hungry watermaker that Ivan broke at the end of last year. And since the humidity fried all our batteries, we had a new bank of cells installed.

All of this has cost a pretty sum, but we're much more self-sufficient now and our home has been restored to good health.

We're delighted to find that our Swedish friends, Lisbeth and Lasse, are docked alongside us in *Hilda*, so close that we can step to and from each other's boats. Lasse, a carpenter by trade, helps us to restore *Amazing Grace* into a seaworthy vessel. He shows me how to repair our split tiller with epoxy, clamps, a sander and several fresh coats of varnish, while Ivan and Lasse work to mend the broken hatch above our bed. With time and hard work, we get everything back in order, including my morale.

The marina's mechanic comes by and changes the engine's filters. He bleeds the lines to clear out the contamination from the water condensation and for the first time in six months our old engine fires up.

On top of all this, my dad has decided to come and visit us when we reach Tonga. A few months from now, I'll get to show Dad my nautical world.

I'm infused with energy. I've mustered the excitement to explore new places and I'm recovering confidence in our old lady, *Amazing Grace*. She's going to make it. I'm going to make it. There is lots of promise on our horizon.

'Guess what?' Ivan says, lounging back with his beer in hand. 'We have the whole world waiting for us. Are you ready?'

'Yes,' I say. 'I'm ready.'

IVAN PUSHES THE STARTER BUTTON and the engine roars to life. Our great, ancient beast has been bled, transfused and pumped back to good health. We begin motoring through the lagoon toward Raiatea's main town, where we'll provision with food and fuel for our next destination: the Cook Islands. It feels wonderful to have the wind in my face. I wave to the marina, happy to put that place behind us. The last three weeks have been stressful, with us trying to wrangle up booked-out mechanics to fix boat problems and install new equipment.

The lagoon is a transparent cyan, reflecting glittering sun rays off its surface. The breeze is a gentle tickle across my skin. Ivan stands at the helm, steering us through a forty-foot-deep passageway that cuts through shallow coral reef.

As we enter a particularly slim pathway, I imagine that I hear a hiccup coming from the engine, a momentary pause like a skipped heartbeat. I find myself pondering what we'd do if the engine failed. I love to visualise worst-case scenarios; it's brain food for the paranoid. In my head, I run through a full emergency plan, detail by detail, stewing over each step just to exercise my brain. Then –

Brub... Brub... Brub... Brub... Br... ub... b.

The engine cuts out and, this time, it isn't my imagination.

I look at Ivan; he looks back. He's frozen to the spot, caught off guard. He frantically thumbs the ignition button, trying to get us going again, but I know it's not going to work. Our engine is dead. We're adrift, with coral walls to our immediate left and right. If we don't do something now, we're going to hit the reef.

I take over as captain – having already catastrophised this exact scenario, I've worked out what to do.

'We need to get back to the marina and pick up a mooring,' I say. 'Roll out the jib, I'll steer the boat.' I take the tiller and manoeuvre our ship within the tight space between the coral shelves. With the remaining momentum from the engine, I swing the boat back in the direction we came from.

Ivan catches on and unfurls the jib sail. It fluffs out, collecting the light breeze. We glide back toward the marina and I look for a vacant buoy to pick up and tie to. We can't throw our anchor here: the water is too deep. We need to find a mooring but, in this crowded place, there are only two available.

'Okay,' I say to Ivan, 'you take the tiller and steer us towards that buoy there. I'll go forward and catch the mooring. If we miss the first one, we'll aim for that other one right there.'

There's little room for error. If we miss both buoys, we'll struggle to weave through all the moored boats with our clumsy, engineless Gracie.

I go to the bow and position myself over the railing with the mooring stick stretched out, waiting to catch the buoy's eyelet. The boat closes in fast – we're too far away! I miss it. 'Okay, head to the second buoy,' I say to Ivan. 'Get as close as you can.'

The wind pushes us up to the second buoy – we're going too fast! – but I stick out the hook and catch the eyelet. 'Got it.'

Ivan drops the sail, but the boat is trying to run forward with the wind and I'm losing my grip on the stick. It's sliding out of my sweaty hand.

'Help!' I yell.

Ivan runs forward, grabs the stick, pulls it up, grips the buoy rope and wraps it around the cleat. The rope creaks under the weight of *Amazing Grace* tugging to a stop. We're moored, unscathed.

Ivan turns to me, shocked. 'You're a sailor!'

I'm surprised to learn this myself. I could have sworn, until now, that I didn't fully understand how wind and sails worked together.

WE SPEND ANOTHER TWO WEEKS on the mooring, waiting for the yard's mechanic to fix our engine.

News of a shipwreck reaches us. It was Wayne's boat – the G-string-wearing gigolo of the sea. His boat went down off an island near Fiji. Word is, he was caught in a storm and was pushed to shore. There were four people aboard: Wayne, his 'client' and two backpackers taken on as crew. They ended up in raging water in the middle of the night, but when the boat went down, they all managed to swim to a rock and pull themselves out of the water. They were lacerated by barnacles and very traumatised, but nobody was badly injured.

And then comes news of *another* shipwreck: a boat we saw when we arrived back to Raiatea, the distinctive yacht with its underside painted with colourful fish. We're told from a friend of theirs that the couple was on passage when the boat started taking on water. Unable to source the leak, the boat filled faster than they were able to bail it. They sent out a Mayday and a ship in the area rescued them. The boat sank.

I think of that vibrant artwork three miles below on the sea floor, colourless in the black depths. Danger lurks uncomfortably close to home and it haunts me. Not one but *two* captains we've met have sunk their boats. And don't bad things happen in threes?

While I'm fretting about who is next, Ivan's urgency to get going is like a fierce itch in his underwear. He can't sit still.

After several missed appointments, the mechanic finally arrives. Once again, he bleeds our water-contaminated fuel until all traces of sediment are gone, and then changes the filter. I can't help but wonder why *this* cleanse will be any more effective than the last one, but lacking the skill to do anything about it, I tell myself that it'll be fine. The mechanic knows better than me anyway.

The engine roars back to life, vibrating dread through my body.

EIGHTEEN

I GULP DOWN THE metallic taste of worry as Raiatea's green mountains disappear over the horizon. We have five days ahead of us on the open ocean and I'm wondering how I can surrender trust over to our old Gracie. I've learned a horrible reality about boats: Shit breaks. Especially when your boat is from the disco era.

On land, when breakages happen, we hire a mechanic to fix them. Mechanics don't make mid-ocean call-outs, so what happens if something breaks out here? I don't ask Ivan this question because I'm scared there's no answer.

I've just finished this thought when Ivan announces the GPS isn't switching on. I feel personally responsible, as though my paranoid thoughts have shorted the device.

'So we're turning around?' I say.

Ivan grows irritated. 'No. Why would we turn back?'

I stare at him, confused as to why he's making me explain. 'Um… so we can get the GPS fixed.'

'We have a handheld GPS. We'll use that.'

'The handheld? It chews through AA batteries and we don't have a stocked supply of spares. What if we run out of batteries?'

'You're just being a perfectionist. The handheld is fine.'

'Ivan—' I give up trying to argue with him. There's only one way to settle this, the way my mother taught me: 'If you want it done right, do it yourself.' I get behind the unit and wiggle some cords. It works. The system boots up and the GPS is back in business.

If only I could wiggle some cords in my own system.

WE'RE TWO DAYS AWAY from Raiatea and the engine has died again. Ivan scratches his head while thumbing the pages of a book: *Troubleshooting Tips for Diesel Engines*. It's a thin, forty-page book with large type and cute illustrations. We haven't an ant's fart of wind to push us along. We're adrift. Becalmed. At the mercy of the sea. Our one-and-only fix-it guide looks like a bedtime storybook. My anxiety decides it's a good time to break into hysterical laughter.

'What's so funny?' Ivan asks.

'You're reading a storybook. On how to fix the engine!' I try to control myself but laughter keeps busting out.

'And?'

'And we're bobbing about in the middle of the ocean! And we have no wind! And our engine... it's broken!' The laughing is now hurting my abdominal muscles.

'Yeah, I know. And that's funny because...?'

'Because we don't know anything about engines! You're reading a how-to guide! Remember that guy at the marina? *If your engine fails, you will die!* Oh, man, that's hilarious.'

'But *why* is that hilarious?'

'I... don't really know,' I say, my smile evaporating.

Ivan goes back to studying the illustrations, then tinkers some more with the greasy engine. He pumps out little cups full of pink fuel, trying to filter out impurities. He mumbles to himself. 'Dammit! Why? Why didn't I just top up the fuel? Ah! Such an idiot.' He tries the ignition again. Nothing. He goes back to the diagrams, annotated with Comic Sans. 'Ahh, idiot. I'm such a massive idiot!'

I bury my head in a pillow to continue my crazy cackling.

IT'S OFTEN SAID that you can achieve anything if you put your mind to it, that you can conquer things you didn't even know you could do, such as fixing a complicated diesel engine when your life possibly depends on it.

Bullshit.

After two focused hours, Ivan throws in the oily rag and gives his diagnosis: The diesel is infected with too much water and sediment. Eighty gallons of fuel in our tanks has turned bad.

Our voyage to the Cook Islands has become indefinitely long. We're going nowhere at all without wind or an engine. Getting to our destination is now a waiting game with the weather.

'Becalmed' is a pleasant word that implies quiet time, perhaps a cup of tea, a pair of slippers and some Jack Johnson acoustics in the background. But there's no calm in our becalmed. Even without wind, there's still the ever-present ocean swell that rolls beneath, causing a sickening stagger that makes hardware jangle in a discordant ensemble of drumming ropes and metal-on-metal percussion. It's like being stuck in a moving elevator with a Hare Krishna mob.

There is no calm in our weather, either. Despite the absence of wind, the horizon is lined with creeping, bulbous clouds that appear as though they're nine months pregnant with something very ugly. The clouds are backlit by flashes of rumbling white. Lightning clouds. They've been on our trail for three days.

Becalmed?

No.

Befucked?

Yes.

SWOOSH... SWOOSH... SWOOSH.

I open my eyes in the early morning to an unfamiliar noise. It's the sound of a gently lapping shore. I relax into a stretch, enjoying the tranquil sound of the trickle of water.

I snap upright. *A watery noise? Coming from inside the boat?*

I crawl out of bed to investigate, following my ears to the floor. I pull the cover off the bilge and peer down into a sight that would make even the most stoic sailor scream in high pitch. There must be over a hundred gallons of water filling the hollow of space below my feet. The water is ten minutes shy of spilling into the cabin.

Holy shit, we're sinking!

'Ivan?' He doesn't reply. He's preoccupied outside. 'IVAN!'

'Hmm?'

'Water is coming in the boat!'

'Huh?'

'The boat is leaking! Quick – come see!'

'Um. Yeah. Okay.' He continues pulling ropes. He's been sleep-deprived for days and can no longer be referred to as just plain tired: he's now in the intellectually challenged phase of exhaustion.

'Ivan. Seriously. This is bad. *Our boat is leaking and the bilge is almost full!*'

'Okay.' He continues to tug ropes with a lost expression.

I can't waste any more time trying to wake a dead man. I flick the bilge pump on, then I go outside and see water gushing overboard from a thru-hull. Back down below, I check the bilge and see it's emptying out. *Good.* The boat is draining much faster than she's leaking. We won't be sinking just yet.

The bilge gurgles as it sucks the last of the water out. I flick the pump off.

'Ivan? I emptied the bilge. I'll keep checking it to make sure we're not sinking.'

'Okay,' he says, still distracted. Either he hasn't listened to anything I've said, or he thinks I'm crying wolf. I must have lost all credibility coming down the coast of Mexico when I insisted thrice hourly that we were going to die.

Ivan has his own crisis to worry about. He's busy trying to set the sails to capture a meagre breeze. It's not much to sail by, but it's all we have. He puts the weight of his body into raising the stubborn mainsail.

'You should sleep,' I tell him. 'I worry about you when you're this tired. You might zombie-walk overboard or something.'

'Nah.'

'Well, you should at least eat. Let me get you some food?'

'Yep.'

I go below into the kitchen and juggle some cereal and powdered milk into a bowl while dancing a boot-scoot to keep balanced. I bring the bowl of cereal to him in the cockpit, but he's now too busy to eat. His hands are in a frenzy, pulling in the sails he's worked so hard to raise.

'Squall,' he says.

I put his bowl of cereal in the sink. I pull on my Gore-Tex jacket and sit with Ivan in the cockpit.

A telltale line of black clouds is approaching. As it nears, I see a ripple of disturbed water coming straight for us. We're hit head-on with a punch of wind. It screams through the rigging and sends us sloshing around in agitated water. It roars to a climax and then departs behind us like a passing train.

Rain arrives late to the party, falling in heavy splats that hit surfaces with the sound of rock confetti. Once satisfied with its handiwork, it too passes, and we're left drifting with only a tiny breeze for company. *Hello, La Niña.*

Ivan begins to crank winches again, grunting with exertion as he raises the tenacious mainsail for the twentieth or thirtieth time in three days. His movements are robotic, as though he's a piece of heavy-duty boating hardware that can be switched on and off. *Sails in. Sails out.* He doesn't complain or grow impatient. He just gets it done.

More wind and rain attacks. *Sails in.*

Amazing Grace creaks as she's pushed over into a heel. The sky opens and spews. The wind picks up and makes the generator whistle, the blades spinning fast. *Whomp, whomp, whomp.* They seem like they can't spin any faster, but then they do. The generator gives a voice to the wind: a discordant, spine-chilling shrill – the soundtrack of death.

A jagged fork shoots down from the clouds and hits a space of water a few miles ahead. We're playing chicken with great daggers of electricity. I get scared for a moment and then realise that fear is an indulgence; it's a luxury afforded only when there's room for escape. We can't escape this. The boat is leaking. The engine is dead. The clouds are stabbing electric daggers all around us. I can only surrender.

I'm not scared any more, but I've decided how I want to go down if something should happen to the boat. I don't want to be alone.

I take Ivan's hand and we sit together, watching the clouds overhead. 'Ivan? If we end up in the water—'

'We won't.'

'But if we do, can you hold me?'

'Of course I'll hold you.'

'Don't let go of me, okay?'

'I will never let go of you, baby.'

The wind and rain stop dead. It's eerie – where is it hiding?

The sky still looks like doom and I know this isn't over yet. Then wind blasts from a whole new direction. We sit under the dodger, sheltering ourselves from the driving rain and flickering sky. We turn on the radar, which can detect cloud mass to tell us how big the system is. A scribbled mass of black takes up the entire LCD screen, and it's at least eight miles in diameter.

FOR TEN HOURS, we're stuck in the middle of the foul belly of a giant psychotic squall.

When the wind and rain finally pass, Ivan lets the sails out, and we slice through the water. *Amazing Grace* heels over in her sprinting position. Ivan has been manning the deck, while – unbeknownst to him – I've been draining the bilge regularly, keeping us afloat.

Ivan comes down below to get something to eat. He opens a box of crackers, rubs them down with butter and jam and stuffs them into his mouth without once breaking his gaze into thin air.

'Ivan? I *really* need to show you something now.'

He stares directly ahead, not blinking. 'Hmm?'

'Brace yourself. We have a problem.' I take his arm and lead him over to the bilge. I lift the cover. No words are required: the bilge is almost full again and we have our very own cruise-ship-style swimming pool inside the boat.

Ivan's eyes focus, then widen. He snaps awake. '*Oh, SHIT.*'

'I know. The good news is it's only a slow leak. I emptied it this morning and—'

'Oh, *shit*, baby!'

'Stop saying that, you're freaking me out. Where do you think it's coming from?'

'Ahh… usually leaks come from seacocks or thru-hulls,' he says, blubbering words as he thinks fast. 'So a hole.'

'Yeah, no kidding, a hole. Any idea where the hole is?'

'We're heeling to the port side, so it's gotta be— *oh, shit.*'

'What? What?'

'The watermaker – I never reinstalled it!' He throws open the watermaker's cupboard behind the nav station to reveal a coin-sized hole that's pumping out a thick arch of seawater. The hole used to be connected to a hose that drained residue overboard. Now it's draining the ocean into our boat.

We both stare at the leak, slack-jawed, for several long moments.

Then everything speeds up into fast motion.

'Oh, shit! I forgot about that.' Ivan dances on the spot.

'There's a hole in our boat!' I yell.

Ivan paces frantically up and down the boat, with his hands clapped over his ears. 'What-da-we-do? What-da-we-do?'

'We should do something!'

'I know. We should!'

'Well? What?'

'Fuck!'

An idea comes to me. I poke my finger into the hole, plugging the squirting artery. 'Okay, now what?'

'Oh, yeah. Of course,' he says, relaxing his shoulders now that the situation is no longer critical.

'Thanks, but now what?'

'Um…'

'Please, think of something quick. I can't stand here forever.'

'Would you like me to put *my* finger in there?' Ivan offers.

'But that's not a solution, is it? We're in the middle of the Pacific Ocean! We can't just keep fingering the hole until we reach land.'

'Good point.'

'So?'

'Duct tape?' Ivan fumbles with the toolbox and finds a wheel of silver tape. He tears off a piece and I move my finger while he covers the hole. It works. He winds extra tape over the hole to add strength – a perfect amateur fix. We both breathe again.

'Oops,' Ivan says with a nervous laugh. 'Forgot about that.'

I eye the patched hole. I'm trapped in a remote location of the Pacific Ocean on a tiny boat with a gaping hole covered in… tape? Could this really be happening?

I STARTLE AWAKE in the middle of the night with a worry in the back of my head. *I have to drain the bilge!*

Then I remember that we fixed that problem. I lie in bed, unsettled with the adrenaline that woke me. I decide the only way I can relax back to sleep is if I carry out my routine and check the bilge, just to make sure.

I open the cover and my hair stands on end. *It's half full!*

The tape must have come off. I throw open the cupboard and check the patch job. It's still intact with no leaks. That can only mean one thing: *there's a second leak.*

I rush outside to tell Ivan, only to find him steering the boat by hand. He never steers by hand, especially not in the middle of the night. 'Why are you hand-steering?'

'The autopilot is broken,' he says in a defeated monotone.

'What do you mean?'

'Wendy. She won't steer on course. She's broken.'

With no engine, it seems fitting that Wendy decided to join the workers' strike too.

'I've been out here for twelve hours,' Ivan says. 'Twelve fucking hours trying to get her working. I thought I was doing something wrong but I've tried everything. I thought if I kept tweaking, I'd get her to hold course. But I get it now – it's not me: Wendy's broken. There's no choice, I have to hand-steer the rest of the way there. I'm really sorry, baby.'

'Sorry? Why are you sorry? It's not your fault. We'll get through this. I'll help you steer. We'll do shifts, and—'

'Yeah, but... sorry. I want to keep you comfortable and happy more than anything and... I'm just... really sorry this has happened.'

He's grim. Ivan doesn't do grim. This is bad.

'Don't worry, I'm okay. We'll get through this. It could be worse, we could be—' I think hard for something to say. *We could be sinking? We are sinking!* 'The boat is still taking on water,' I tell him.

He replies with a prolonged sigh, like he's been holding a breath full of hope and he's exhaling it all out, every last vapor.

'Don't worry, I'll keep on emptying it,' I say in a perky tone. 'It can be my job, don't you worry. It's okay. We'll be okay.' I'm trying to save the day with a squeaky, forced cheer. I know if I let myself fall into a pit of despair, I'll never get out again.

On our electronics panel, I find the switch that reads *Bilge Pump*. I flick it. Nothing happens. I should be hearing the low rumble of a pump in action. *Flick. Flick. Nothing.* I go outside to see if anything is happening. Water from the bilge should be gushing overboard through an opening in the side of the boat right now, but I see only a string of dirty drool.

I compile a mental checklist of our situation: No engine. No autopilot. Boat leaking from at least two locations, one patched with duct tape. Bilge full of water. Bilge pump broken. Several hundred miles from land.

This is beyond grim, but I don't want to die out here. I'll suck that bilge dry with a drinking straw if I have to.

I reluctantly deliver the bad news about the pump to Ivan.

'It may be blocked,' he says. 'Can you steer while I check?'

I adopt the driver's stance: headlamp on head, hand on tiller, eyes on compass. If I take my eyes off the compass for a moment, then the boat will fall off course and the sails will start banging in protest of losing their wind. Momentum is lost and our journey is delayed. I find a sweet spot with the wind, leaning Gracie's weight into the quadrant that catches her sails and makes her take off. She may be old and falling apart, but she still loves to ride the wind.

Ivan goes belowdecks, gears up in yellow rubber gloves several sizes too small, and goes into The Dark Zone with all but his mask and snorkel. The water reaches beyond his elbow, rendering the gloves useless.

'Nothing is blocking it,' he says, peeling off the gloves. 'It must be the batteries.'

'We just bought brand-new batteries, though.'

'I replaced three of four batteries at the boatyard.' Ivan pauses. 'Oh, shit. I didn't replace the emergency battery, the one the pump is hooked up to.'

'Why not? It's the emergency battery. *This is an emergency.*'

'Yeah, I know. I guess I didn't expect we'd need it with all the power from the wind generator and our new batteries. I just… man, I'm an idiot.' He drops his head into his hands. 'I just forgot that the bilge pump was hooked up to it.'

'What do we do now? Send out a Mayday? Get in the life raft? I'll get the ditch kit!'

'No, we're not at that stage yet. There's a manual pump.'

He shows me the secondary pumping system. I'm grateful that the boat designers thought of this. It's much better than my idea of sucking out that putrid black water with a straw.

I crank a handle in the cockpit and water starts to spurt overboard. I pump and pump until my arm aches but I can't stop until it's empty. When the water finally turns to a dribble, I know the bilge is empty… for now.

If we lived within the normal structure of land life in a house in the city, perhaps I'd be mad with Ivan over the mess we're in. Maybe I'd go into attack mode, throwing around accusations, like, 'Why didn't you top up the fuel?' or, 'You should've remembered to patch that hole, dammit!' But blame is useless here. Anger is nothing but weighty baggage.

On land, with separate jobs, responsibilities and friends, there's a clear distinction between 'you' and 'me,' and 'your fault' and 'my fault,' but those divisions become unclear when we pull up anchor and head toward an empty horizon together on little more than a floating bathtub. Each time before we set out to sea, before we tie our lives to each other's in a precarious way, we must make a sacred, unspoken commitment: *I trust you. You trust me. I'll protect you. You'll protect me.* Our lives become inseparably married and there's a fusing of 'me' and 'you' and 'Gracie' so that there is only 'us'. We are one single floating entity, trying to survive.

After all, if we can't resolve this mess that we've created, then Gracie will not be sinking, and Ivan will not be sinking – we will all be sinking.

WE'RE BECALMED AGAIN.

Ivan calls his mother on the satellite phone to see if she can look up the weather for us online. Monica reports back with bad news: no wind is forecast in the region for a while. For *two weeks*, in fact.

Ivan's speech becomes laboured. Then he chokes up. Then he's crying on the phone. Ivan is crying. My rock. My optimist. My *everything-will-be-fine* man has crumbled into a pool of misery and lost hope.

I begin to cry too.

He hangs up the call and I hug him and rub his back. I feel protruding bones that weren't there before – he's lost weight from not eating for days. His eyes are buried somewhere inside dark sockets. He's disappearing. The ocean is taking his soul.

'Don't worry,' I say. 'You just need sleep. You've been working too hard for too long. Leave the boat. She'll be fine. I'll keep watch to make sure everything is safe. I'll wake you if there's wind. Relax, *please*. You need sleep.'

Ivan crashes into bed like an axed tree and he snores before he's even hit the pillow.

I check the bilge. Half full again. It's filling just as fast as it was before we applied the tape. That means the leak is much bigger than the coin-sized hole we patched.

I pump. I check for ships. The night is very black, but there are no lights on the horizon. A small mercy, as, since we're broken down, we can't move out of the way of an oncoming ship anyway.

I lie down on our bed on top of a large wet patch from our roof that still leaks. It's the one reliable feature of this boat, that *drip, drip, drip* above my bed. I reset the egg timer to buzz in ten minutes so I can check for ships and for wind.

If the wind picks up and the sails become something more than useless piles of flabby canvas, we'll have to carefully time our arrival in Aitutaki with high tide at 10 a.m. tomorrow. The island's pass is notoriously shallow and it's only possible to make it into the anchorage at high tide. According to our calculations, the pass is only just wide and deep enough to accommodate the proportions of *Amazing Grace*.

At least, I hope it is.

If estimations are correct, we have eight inches of play room between the deepest part of our boat – the keel – and the sandbank in the pass.

We've heard stories of sailors with six-foot keels getting wedged by the sand on the way in. Those yachts needed to be towed back out to sea by a local boat, where they were forced to carry on to a new destination. The nearest island, Rarotonga, is an additional twenty-hour sail away. That's two or three days for us. Or weeks. Or forever. It depends on the wind and if our boat decides to stay afloat.

After hours of keeping watch, finally, by the light of the moon and stars, I see the wind generator spinning a few half-hearted rotations. *Yes, yes, c'mon, spin,* I cheer quietly. *Baby needs a new pair of shoes.*

It responds to my encouragement and starts turning at a steady pace. Ripples disturb the ocean's surface. Our old friend, Wind, has returned.

It's time to wake Ivan. I'd rather let him get some much-needed sleep, but we have to get this sinking ship to safety.

'Ivan.' I shake him until he lurches upright and gasps like he's woken from a nightmare. In fact, he's woken *into* a nightmare.

'Sorry to wake you. There's wind to sail now.'

'Okay, thank you, baby.'

The breeze keeps a steady pace and we're whisked through the night at six speedy knots. I silently whisper sweet nothings to the wind to keep it going. *Oh yeah, that's right. Keep that good stuff coming. Don't stop. That's right.*

It holds. Miraculously, thanks to Ivan's careful navigation, we're delivered to Aitutaki Island at 10 a.m. on the dot, right on high tide. A five-day distance took us seven. Only two extra days, but it's a monumental stretch of time when you're aboard a sinking boat.

Ivan calls the harbourmaster on the radio to ask for a tow. The voice over our radio says they've been expecting us. 'Your mother, Monica, called me,' the harbourmaster says to Ivan. 'She said you have no engine.'

A blue towboat called *Mary J* beelines toward us. The men aboard toss a coiled rope, which I grab from the air in my outstretched hand. I run forward and tie it to the cleats. *Mary J* revs and our boat is jerked in her direction.

As we approach the reef, I can't make out a pass, only waves breaking on the shallows. I make a conscious effort to relax, reminding myself that these men know what they're doing. This is their home – of course they know where the pass is. Plus, we couldn't have more bad luck… could we?

Snap. The towrope breaks. *Of course it did!* We're adrift, right next to the break. This is a voyage that seems destined for doom.

The men on *Mary J* act fast and we're tossed a frayed line of rope, which I catch and work quickly into a bowline. All those hours of bored fingers fiddling with a length of rope come in handy. I loop the bowline onto the cleat and we're back in the command of *Mary J*.

Just off the reef's edge, *Mary J* veers ninety degrees into a tucked-away pass that makes all the other passes we've been through seem like freeways compared to this tiny bike trail. We swing side to side behind *Mary J* along the narrow passageway. Dead coral heads protrude above the water to either side of us, looking like a watery graveyard. There's a sandbank in the pass ahead, which looks alarmingly similar in colour to the pale aqua of an inflatable wading pool.

'Please, please, please,' I murmur to Ivan, to *Mary J,* to *Amazing Grace,* to the powers that be, 'please let us clear this pass. Please don't reject us and send us back out there. *Please!*'

The depth sounder reads 10 feet, 6 feet, 5 feet, 4.5...

'How shallow can we go?' I ask Ivan.

'Not sure. Guess we'll see.'

The reading drops to 3.8... then 4, 6, 8, 10...

The boat slips through with a keel-tickling.

We pick up a mooring inside Aitutaki's one and only anchorage, which is not much more than a pond. There's just one other sailboat here.

The island is a green Eden. I want to flee the boat, wrap myself around the nearest tree and never let go.

We didn't die, I think, shocked. *We actually made it.* I turn to Ivan and break into nervous giggles. 'We're here.'

He hugs me with his sweaty, weakened body. 'I'm so proud of you,' he whispers. 'So very proud.'

NINETEEN

EVEN IF THIS place were the ugliest eyesore on the planet, I'd still be euphoric to be here, but Aitutaki happens to be drop-dead gorgeous.

Ivan ties the dinghy to a palm trunk and we make our way up the boat ramp to a flat, grassy landscape that would make a perfect golf course.

A man dressed in flowery board shorts and an oversized T-shirt approaches, looking like he's ready to pull us into a bear hug. He offers his meaty handshake and introduces himself as the immigration officer. After welcoming us, he invites us to follow him. I'm guessing we'll be led to a standard dreary government office to pay fees and fill out forms with identity details and boat specifics – an activity we've done so many times that I can quote all of Gracie's stats by rote:

Draft: five feet two inches

Beam: eleven feet

Tonnage: six

Hull number: N01091758

But we're not directed to a government office. We're guided over to a rock. The immigration man sits himself down on the smooth surface and looks into our eyes, pausing to give emphasis to what he's about to say. 'This rock is sacred. It represents our island and our people. I would like to invite you to, please, sit on this rock.'

We oblige.

'You have come here by sailboat,' he continues. 'So you have worked very hard to arrive at our island and it is a great honour for us to welcome you. This rock is symbolic. Once you sit on it, the people of Aitutaki consider you one of us. We will look upon you and treat you as one of our own people. As long as you are here on our island, you are one of us.'

His words give me goosebumps. What a welcome.

The island's officer chats to us like we're guests in his house. Sitting on the rock, we discuss sailing, our journey, rugby, more rugby. I tell him I'm Australian and he attempts to speak cricket to me until I go cross-eyed trying to pretend I have a clue. All over the world, 'I'm Australian' somehow translates to 'I love cricket!'

We laugh together. We tell stories. We shoot the breeze like good friends at a weekend barbecue. It's the most bizarre and delightful customs and immigration experience I've ever had. 'Come, please, there is more.' He beckons for us to follow.

Where now? I wonder with excitement. *A spiritual induction? A dancing ceremony? Kava drinking?*

A dreary grey government office.

'Please fill these forms out,' he says, pushing a stack of paperwork toward us. 'Your visa is valid for strictly thirty days.'

He pulls out an oversized calculator and begins tapping his finger. 'Visa fees times two, plus customs fee, plus anchorage fees, plus agricultural fee, plus health fee, plus *Mary J*'s towing fee. Okay, that comes to three hundred New Zealand dollars minus the five-dollar fee for anchoring per night, which you can settle upon exit.'

That's more like it – a customs and immigration experience that makes me feel at home.

WE'RE CHECKED into the country. We've slept twelve hours, we've eaten, we're safe inside a womblike anchorage in an enchanting place with charming people who speak a language we can understand. I must be the happiest person in the world.

It's drizzly, so we're giving ourselves a day of rest inside. The boat has been put back in order and everything is organised except for the bilge, which still needs to be pumped twice a day. Today, we're giving ourselves the gift of not having to think about the state our boat is in, but soon we'll have to find the island's mechanic to get our problems repaired, which I'm not in a hurry to do. As long as the engine is broken, we don't have to go back to sea.

I'm slipping off into a nap when a squall hits. It body-slams us from nowhere. *Amazing Grace* is pushed into a lean and my coffee mug slides along the table and sloshes to a stop, saved by the table's lip. My body springs into defence and I fling myself out of bed.

'Holy crap, it's really blowing,' I say. 'Do you think the boat is going to hold? Maybe we should put an extra anchor out for insurance?' We don't have any spare room to drag in this tiny anchorage.

Ivan huffs and goes out the companionway. I'm not sure if he's agreeing with me or trying to escape my nagging. After a few moments, he comes back down, soaking wet and shaken. 'The wind is really strong. The rain is so violent, it hurts my skin. I'll put that other anchor out.'

There isn't enough time to close all the hatches before rain is pummeling inside, driven almost horizontally into the companionway. Half the boat's interior is hosed before we secure all the open windows and hatches.

We go outside into the stinging rain. The palm fronds are trying to wrestle themselves off their trunks. You could call this type of wind forty knots... or you could call it palm-beheading wind. It's blowing onshore, straight from the open ocean, and our only wall of protection is the shallow coral reef that surrounds the island.

The boat is straining on her anchor and we seem to be getting closer to shore. Putting another anchor out has become urgent. Ivan fumbles around in a cockpit locker and finds the second anchor. He cleats it on and throws it out, but it's too late – we're swinging now, closing in on the shore.

Ivan runs up and down the deck, trying to figure out what to do. I stand with my hand pressed to my forehead, watching the rocky outcrop on the beach become close enough to jump to. One big leap and I could be off this boat. We're going to shipwreck. Maybe we've already run aground.

'I'll try the harbourmaster,' Ivan yells. 'Maybe they can tow us with *Mary J*.'

But the radio is thick with weather static. Nobody hears him.

Ivan tries to work the anchors, but we're helpless under the pinning weight of the wind. It will take us where it pleases and all we can do is watch.

I notice a crowd has gathered. Nearby shop owners and passing school kids endure the driving rain to watch the spectacle. They're probably wondering if they're going to end up with a new piece of play equipment on their beach: a climbing fort called *Amazing Grace*.

This isn't how I want to see her go. What a sad way to end this after so much time and money put into her repair, after battling with squalls and lightning and no wind or engine. Moitessier wrecked his boat, *Joshua*, when he was struck by bad weather in Cabo San Lucas. He'd sailed the boat around the world two times without major incident. Land is a dangerous place for boats.

A man is swimming over to us: an old salt from the only other sailboat in the anchorage.

'I will help you,' he yells through the wind in a thick French accent. 'I will move your ropes for you.'

He climbs into our dinghy and begins shuffling our anchoring ropes. The mooring we're tied to must be a toaster on the sea floor – hardly enough to secure a heavy yacht. The Frenchman moves the line from the small mooring and takes it to a larger mooring a distance from shore. He loops the line through the mooring's eyelet and brings the rope back to us.

'Pull this in very tight,' he instructs.

Ivan works fast, turning the winch to tighten the rope and, in doing so, draws us away from the shore.

The man takes our stern anchor and resets that too. Then he secures an extra rope from *Amazing Grace* to a palm tree. 'I think this should now hold you,' he says.

'Thank you!' Ivan yells through the wind.

'Goodbye.' He dives into the water and freestyles back toward his aluminum boat, leaving us held tight by a triangle of tethers.

Ivan turns to me, soaked with rain. 'That was extremely close.'

'Very,' I say.

'That's the first squall we've ever had from the west. Totally caught me off guard.'

I look off into the horizon, feeling betrayed by the psychotic weather episode. Winds are supposed to come from the east at this time of year. All the anchorages are chosen for their protection from the easterly trade winds, but with *La Niña*, these normal rules do not seem to apply. Anything can happen.

IT SEEMS that Cook Islanders trim their gardens with nail-clippers and magnifying glasses. The plants look as though they've been cut using rulers and tidied with Dustbusters. Each lawn resembles a military flattop.

'Hello,' a woman says, sitting on her scooter with a child between herself and the handlebars.

'Hello,' I reply.

'You're from that sailboat, right?'

'Yes, we're from *Amazing Grace*.'

'Oh, I love the name of your boat. We sing that song in church. Where did you sail from?'

'From California,' Ivan says.

'Wow, you've come from so far away to visit our island. I hope you enjoy Aitutaki.'

'Thank you, we love it here.'

She revs her scooter, waves goodbye and takes off.

Everyone we pass greets us with the same warmth. Not a single stranger fails to acknowledge us. Gardeners pause mid-trim to offer an enthusiastic wave. Kids in groups giggle and each offers a coy 'Hello'. An old woman stops us to let us know we're welcome to take star fruit from her tree whenever we like. Even the town drunkard is a kindly fellow, taking time between swigs of his papered liquor to politely inquire where we've travelled from. True to the words of the immigration man, we really are being welcomed as locals.

After a few hours of exploring the island on foot, my left arm is sore from waving to every single passing car, scooter, bike and pedestrian.

At an internet café, I get an e-mail from Dad saying he's booked flights to Tonga and has arranged ten days off to spend sailing with us, in six weeks' time. This means that, as much as I'd like to, we can't hang around and become permanent residents of the friendly Cook Islands. We have to get the boat repaired and keep moving west.

We manage to find the island's mechanic, who stops by and gets our engine working again. All our contaminated diesel is transfused with clean fuel. The leak is fixed up too: it was coming from the boat's propeller – the packing gland – that he tightened. Wendy, our wind pilot, is diagnosed with a bent screw, so the mechanic hammers it straight in his workshop.

The boat is ready to go to sea again, but I'm not.

I SQUEEZE LIME over a cut papaya and tuck in to my breakfast. Every morning we venture to the local market for ripe papayas, eggplants, tomatoes and lettuce. Here in the Cooks, I can eat fresh food to my heart's content.

I sit in the salon eating my breakfast, while Ivan writes in his journal, focused and serious.

'What are you writing?' I ask.

'I'm writing about why this anchorage is so good,' he says.

'Oh, yeah?'

'No cruise ships. They can't get in. It's all ours.'

It's true. The pass is so narrow and shallow that in almost three weeks we've seen only one other boat here: the Frenchman, who left weeks ago.

I'm just having this thought, when I hear: *MOHHHHHHHH*. It's a trumpeting ship horn blaring from outside.

Ivan jerks his head up. 'What was that noise?'

'It sounded like—'

'It did, didn't it?'

I look out the porthole. 'Unbelievable!'

A towering ocean-going Vegas hotel has arrived. The ship has anchored a mile away and is sending the troops in through the pass on orange water taxis.

Ivan and I look at each other in pure shock.

The cruise passengers unload onto the shore right by our boat. It's customary to wave at passing boat traffic, which we do, but nobody notices our foolish flapping hands. They're fixated on the hula dancers and svelte men in palm-leaf underwear who are strumming ukuleles on shore. Today it appears the locals are getting around in grass skirts and coconut bras – a dramatic costume change from the board shorts and T-shirts they usually wear.

A roped barricade has been set up at the top of the boat ramp where the taxis deliver the passengers. It's a cattle drive, directing the crowd into a warehouse that, today, is a craft market. Bum bags zip open, cash registers ding and coins clink together. Afterward, the crowd is ushered out the other end, wearing shell jewelry, Aitutaki T-shirts and sarongs.

When the crowd of new arrivals diminishes, we leave the boat to get our daily staples. We're so close to land that we can get in the dinghy, push off *Amazing Grace* and drift to shore without the engine. We head to the boat ramp that leads from the water to the shore, but an islander who's working as a security guard today holds a big hand in front of us. 'Stop,' he says. 'Cruise-ship passengers only.' I'm sure this same guy was waving to us only yesterday.

I look around for an alternative route. The cattle drive blocks the entire boat ramp. It's the only reasonable way to get from the water to the land.

'But—'

'No,' he says, making it clear that he won't negotiate. We're being cold-shouldered by our Aitutakian compatriots.

Defiant, we look for a new route to shore. We've earned our right to be here. We've paid fees. We sat on The Rock, dammit!

We climb the muddy embankment alongside the boat ramp and scramble to the outside of the roped barricade where the security guard stands. He looks annoyed but we're not inside his cordoned-off zone, so he's powerless. They may have locked their front door, but they can't stop us from jumping the back fence and squishing in through the doggy door.

There's a different vibe on the island today. It's alive with business as the islanders seize their monthly opportunity to cash up. Tourism is a large source of income for many Pacific islands, so they have to make the most of cruise-ship arrivals.

The regular bustle is absent – the kids kicking soccer balls, the fishermen relaxing at the dock, the families cooling off in the water, the people waving on scooters. The friendly town drunkard is absent too. Apart for the costumed performers and the retailers, the town has come to an eerie standstill. The cruise-ship passengers wander around taking pictures of a ghost island.

ARMED WITH A DRILL, I attempt to fix the leak in the roof, once and for all. I'm hoping that if I remove the screws around the mast, caulk the holes with waterproof sealant, wrap the screws in plumber's tape and then reinsert them, the leak will stop. But in truth, I'm just finding excuses to stall our departure.

Ivan sits beside me, handing over screws or caulk when I call for them. He's cataclysmic with a drill in hand, but he makes a great assistant and he's humble enough to hand these tasks over to me.

I look up from my drilling to watch the long lines of cruise passengers waiting for their taxis back to the floating hotel. Just before they step aboard, they each receive a squirt of sanitiser in their hands.

'What's that for?' Ivan asks.

I shrug. 'Germ phobia?'

They board the taxis with loaded bags of souvenirs and head back to the cruise ship, which is signaling its impending departure with a deafening *MOHHHHHHHHHHHHHHHHH*.

I put down the drill, scoot toward Ivan and hold him in a hug, nestling my head into his neck. 'I love you,' I tell him. 'Thank you.'

'For what?' he says.
'For showing me the islands this way, aboard Gracie.'
He smiles. 'Thank you for coming.'
'I'm ready to head back out to sea now.'

TWENTY

When I start vomiting, the palm trees of Aitutaki are still in view, turning golden from the last light of the day. The small ocean waves are striking at an angle that my stomach doesn't enjoy. I scorn my body for its defiance. *Are we not over this yet?*

My sore abs are still squeezing out fluid by sunrise. *Just four more days,* I tell myself as I crawl into my bed after swallowing two seasickness tablets. I enjoy the side effect: the drowsy feeling that seeps through my body like warm honey.

I fall back onto my pillow, ready to melt into non-existence. As the seasickness medicine courses through me, I'm flooded with serenity. The bed sinks away and layers of marshmallow clouds catch my fall. I surrender to the rhythm of the boat, and I become liquid like the ocean.

Just before I drift off, I see Ivan in the cockpit with his maté, scribbling thoughts into his journal, a little happy smile on his lips. We're two worlds apart out on the open sea.

'Baby?' Ivan shakes me firmly and I startle awake.

Emerging from a deep sleep, I take a while to work out where we are. I listen to the lick of the ocean on the hull, the gentle knock of ropes. *We're on the ocean.* I sit up abruptly and my heart starts thumping. 'What happened? Something's wrong? The bilge!'

'No, everything's fine. I didn't mean to startle you.'

'Did you check the bilge?'

'It's dry; the leak is fixed.'

'Where are we?'

'We're getting close to Tonga.'

I rub my eyes. 'Really?'

'You've slept most of the way,' he says. 'I was worried.'

Thanks to the seasickness pills, our five-day journey has been compressed into a concertina of vague but pleasant memories.

As we approach land, the seas grow calm and I sit up on deck with Ivan. Tonga looks unlike any other place we've seen. It's a gathering of rocky, vegetation-covered pinnacles with waterways running between them. Some islands are tiny humps, while others are habitable landmasses. We glide through the maze of islands that lead into the main town and we come to the mirrored expanse of Vava'u Bay. It's dotted with sea gypsies who have left convention behind to sail the South Pacific, like us. We haven't seen so many boats in one place since we left Los Angeles.

I pull up the mooring and fix it to the bow. A sense of relief washes over me as my stomach finally settles. *We're here. We made it.*

'So then,' I say, pausing to build up to a climax, 'I opened the bilge cover and discovered our boat was still taking on water!'

I have an audience of two with whom I'm recalling our awful trip between Raiatea and Aitutaki. We've met a couple, Debbie and Jim, who have stopped by in their dinghy for a sailor's chat. This often involves whipping out horror stories to compare, sizing them up like metaphorical penises. The two are a weatherworn, bohemian duo with permanent horizon-gazing expressions. They've been sailing for years. Debbie does the talking, while Jim nods and adds a casual 'Yup' to everything she says.

'Oh, geez, well that would have been rough,' Debbie says in her expressionless Canadian accent. 'Actually, we shipwrecked our boat last year.'

My penis retreats into gathered flesh. 'Wait, hold up, you were in a shipwreck?'

'Oh, yah, that's right. We hit the island of Niue. Couldn't see it in the middle of the night, eh?' Debbie blinks absently.

'Yup,' Jim says, validating that they did indeed hit a rock two times the size of San Francisco like it was a parked car... a very big parked car.

'So I guess the boat sank?' I ask, enthralled.

'Oh, no. The boat didn't sink, eh? Just gone and pierced itself on the coral in the night. Didn't even see the darned thing coming. Just ran sheer straight on into it, eh?'

'Yup,' says Jim.

'How did you just... run into it?' I ask.

'Oh, geez, well our GPS position was wrong. Thought we were a mile off, but we just ran right into the east side, eh?'

'Bloody hell,' I mutter. Ivan shakes his head. Jim just nods and says, 'Yup.'

'Uh-huh, yah. Scratched ourselves up good on the coral just before we scaled the cliff,' Debbie says.

'Wait. You climbed up a cliff?' The details of this story just keep getting better. My penis has sheer dropped off now and is no longer a competition participator.

'Oh, yah. The rocks were awful sharp, like razors, eh? Couldn't see nothing either because it was in the middle of the night. Didn't even know where we were, thought maybe a deserted island or some uncharted rock.'

'So you scaled up the cliff in the night?'

'Oh, yah, that was real tricky. Got all cut up, eh? We had to bushwhack through the forest for a few hours. Didn't think we'd ever find our way out. Then we came to the road, so it was all good. The locals were real kind, eh?'

'So you salvaged your boat?' I point to their small sloop that looks like it's seen a few good years, maybe a shipwreck or two.

'No, no. Our first boat, she was pierced on the rocks. Had to take what we could, which wasn't much, and just leave it there for good. We needed to buy another boat, so we went to New Zealand and bought this boat for cheap, eh? Pretty much just came from New Zealand, and here we are.'

'So, let me get this straight,' I say. 'You're planning to… continue sailing?'

She tips her head to the side with a look of *Why the hell wouldn't we?*

'Oh, yah.'

Ivan and I stand there, shaking our heads. Talk about getting back in the saddle. Judging by these old salts, in order to be a true nomad of the seas, you need to be endowed with the kind of fearlessness that toes the edge of sanity.

This isn't the only accident we've heard about and until recently I'd assumed that our injuries and breakages were the result of inexperience and Ivan's clumsy nature, but, as it turns out, everyone makes ghastly judgement errors. It comes with the lifestyle. Battling to remain uninjured and afloat is just part of every cruiser's daily itinerary.

MY KNEE IS JIGGLING in the taxi to the airport. I've been anticipating Dad's arrival for months, thrilled to show him my new world. Excitement has morphed into anxiety, anxiety into nerves, and I'm jittering on the backseat, watching the scenery pass. Why am I so nervous?

I look out at the passing scenery and daze off into a memory of Dad.

Dad gave me a push off the shore and the kayak beneath me slipped over the seaweed-soup water. I lifted the paddle above my head and scooped water left, then right, pointing the kayak toward the break where boys in their early twenties floated on surfboards, waiting for the perfect ride.

I was ten years old. My four older sisters lounged on towels, heads in novels, skin shiny with oil to tan their womanly bodies endowed with curves I didn't yet have. My little sister played alone at the shoreline, picking up shells and drawing in the sand. As the tomboy among six girls, I was the perfect fit for surrogate 'son'. The relationship between Dad and me became symbiotic: father-needs-son, fifth-daughter-needs-attention.

I was petrified in the water, but I gulped down my nerves and wore a mask of bravado. It was time to overcome my fear and make Dad proud. I was born with his blue eyes and his long paddles for hands and feet. He called me 'Puddleduck' and I felt an obligation to live up to this nickname, even though I wasn't an ocean lover like him. Growing up as a California surfer, Dad never lost his passion for the sea.

An opportunity to shine had presented itself.

I headed to the reef and angled the kayak perpendicular to a wave, watching over my shoulder to get the timing exactly right. Dad had run through the steps with me; I knew what to do.

The swell was approaching behind and I set off paddling ahead of it. The roll of a wave picked me up and I charged forward with the swell. For a moment, I forgot my fears and I experienced the exhilaration of skiing across the surface of the water, like a true puddle duck.

I looked to Dad onshore. He was too far away to be within earshot, so I simply imagined his reaction. 'Whoa!' he'd always say when he was impressed. Being a man of few spoken words – despite being a writer – that one single word of his approval had the power to fill my heart up for months.

Distracted by Dad on the shore, I was caught in the barrel of the next oncoming wave. The foamy crest rolled me from the kayak in a tangle of limbs and I was cartwheeled through briny seaweed soup by the power of the water. Foam went up my nose, burning my sinuses, and I started to grow desperate for air. The mayhem dissipated and I broke the surface, gasping. My feet were hovering over the reef, kicking frantically as I imagined all the sea life down there trying to lunge for a taste of my flesh. My heavy breathing turned to whimpering.

I looked over to the shore and saw Dad watching from the beach. He sent a thumbs-up my way. I got a jolt of electricity and I knew it wasn't the time to give up.

I retrieved the kayak with a tug on the leg rope and hoisted my body back into the saddle. Through the blur of teary eyes, I headed back into the swell, looking for the right wave. I set off paddling once again, but felt no excitement this time, only dread. I caught another wave, but I lost control and tumbled under the surface.

For a long time, I couldn't work out which way was up. My feet found momentary purchase on the reef but the wave dragged the soles of my feet over sharp rock, tearing skin. Finally finding a rocky outcrop, I pushed off, breaking the surface for air just in time for my forehead to greet the pointy end of my kayak. Drawn to me by the leash on my ankle, the red kayak slipped through the water and charged into my forehead with the determination of a personal attack.

I was thoroughly defeated. I paddled back to shore, face lowered, attempting to conceal the warm tears that dripped onto the sand. Two waves, two wipeouts, and I'd thrown in the towel like a wimp. I didn't even like the stupid sport of surf kayaking, I just wanted to seem brave for Dad.

I rode the kayak up the beach and dragged it along the sand by its tether.

'Giving up?' Dad said with his palms upturned in disbelief.

'Yeah,' I said, wiping my snotty nose.

'Ahh… jee-zus!' he hissed.

Next time, I told myself, *you need to try harder. You need to make Dad proud.*

But I never got another chance to prove myself because by the following summer, I was a teenager and too old to be hanging out with my dad.

OUR TAXI PULLS into the Vava'u airport just as a tiny plane is landing. The airport's doors open and Dad comes walking through, pale-skinned from the insidiously cold Melbourne winter.

I hug Dad and breathe in the familiar smell of him: clean laundry, pack-a-day tobacco and spearmint gum. When it comes to drinking, smoking and sun exposure, Dad does it the old-school way, before doctors and scientists spoiled all the fun with their research. Self-preservation is secondary to life experience in my childhood home, and Mum and Dad live by the mantra, 'You're here for a good time, not for a long time.' I've tried to remind myself of this more than once out on the ocean.

Dad shakes Ivan's hand and pulls him into a man hug.

We taxi to the dock and load into *Little Gracie II*. I step into the dinghy with learned confidence, stomping directly into the centre, arms poised for balance, riding out the water displacement like I'm on a surfboard. I may even be showing off.

Ivan starts the engine and we dinghy out to our anchored boat. I'm aware that I'm introducing my father to someone he's never met: *me* – in this life as a sailor. I'm not the girl he hugged goodbye when I left for San Francisco on my own almost three years ago.

'So this is Gracie,' I say as we climb aboard.

I look at her afresh. Black diesel soot dirties the hull from days of motoring through stretches of flat water. Barnacles cling to the waterline, transported here as stowaways from a far-off place. Her teak trimming lost its last flake of varnish miles back and her bare wood has turned grey from the salt and sun. Her name is peeling up at the edges; any day now her lettering is going to fly away on a breeze and she'll be renamed '*mazi ace*' or '*mag race*'.

I start the home tour, moving through the interior of the boat quickly. Dad catches up with cautious manoeuvring and a grabbing of handrails I'd forgotten were there.

'*Le grand salon.*' I sweep my hand elaborately. 'Kitchen, nav station, our bedroom. You'll be sleeping here,' I say, pointing to the cracked orange vinyl settee.

The entire tour takes place within the single room that makes up our entire living space. The only room that requires a door to be opened is the head. 'Bathroom, toilet and shower here,' I say. 'Cold-water showers only, though.'

'Beauty!' Dad says, and I can tell that he is genuinely thrilled.

I knew he'd like her. I inherited my taste for all things aged and rustic from him. Dad built his hexagonal office in the backyard of the family home from pine and cedar shingles and not a lick of paint covers the gnarls in the untreated wood. Nature loves it – huge spiders, creeping ivy and nesting birds are constantly trying to move in and take over. He's forged his career from that office, which he made, right down to the stained-glass windows that filter light through multicoloured panes. Movie props decorate the interior and each eclectic item is blanketed in cobwebs.

With cigarette smoke wafting from an open window, he has spent a lifetime inside that bungalow, tapping away on his keyboard, swerving between debt and wealth (as many writers do), but always prolific with his output of scripts, which kept us safe from any serious financial woes.

Despite his successes as a writer, he's the most humble man I know, always opting for bare feet, battered Levis and T-shirts, instead of shoes, slacks and tidy pressed shirts. So our humble boat is just his style.

Dad has two pieces of luggage: a large duffel and a small overnight bag. 'This is for you guys,' he says, heaving the big bag our way.

I open it to find gifts from my mum. Clothes, shoes, DVDs, Vegemite and canvas covers to replace the worn vinyl on all the interior furnishings. I sent Mum the measurements back before the trouble began and she had them made up for us in expensive, waterproof fabric. I fit the covers to our sofa and Gracie looks like she's had a facelift. The boat is now shaded a mint green – a colour much more soothing and modern than retro-spew orange.

In the bag, I also find a small pile of handwritten letters from home. Among them are messages written by two of my nephews. Their careful handwriting and mature grasp of language have transformed since I left three years ago. I read through their playful letters with tears in my eyes. One letter contains a poem about two sailors and the sea, written by my nephew, who was about to turn five when I first left. Now, aged seven and a half, Zephyr is sharply observant and sarcastic as hell. For no explainable reason, the poem ends mid-stanza. I turn the paper over, looking for the rest, but there are no more words. It leaves me yearning.

'Cold beer, Everett?' Ivan asks, wasting no time making an offering of our finest luxury, even though it's only ten o'clock in the morning.

'Sure,' Dad says.

DAD BLENDS INTO THE BOAT as though he's also sewn from mint-green fabric. I anticipated that the hot, tiny boat would become crowded with three people, but, somehow, we barely notice him until he clears his throat or turns the page of his book, and then I remember: *Oh, yeah – my dad's here!* It only works because we're three introverted personalities, coexisting in our own little worlds with plenty of comfortable silences.

We take the boat to a tucked-away anchorage that showcases everything tropical paradise has to offer. We swim, chat, eat good food and drink Steinlager beers. We move to another anchorage and do the same thing all over again.

Dad and I spend a lot of time together sitting on the foredeck, discussing everything that's happened over the years I've been away. We bond over the topic of sailing and I hear myself talking fluently in the language of boats. '*Oh yes, I love the lines on the Hallberg-Rassy. I'd love a boat with a centre cockpit, a bimini, furling sails and an electric windlass.*' I've learned a lot in a year and a half.

Tonga's landform is a unique labyrinth of islands and inlets, which can be navigated without having to go onto the open ocean. The wind is serene, creating ideal conditions for the kind of sailing where the boat – set on autopilot – can captain itself while the crew retire as passengers. The only hazards within the wide inlets are other sailboats, also manned by lazy crew sipping beer, enjoying the ride. The journey is the destination in these calm, protected coves.

En route to one of Tonga's most secluded inlets, the three of us stare out into the indigo expanse. I sit at the bow, carefully scanning the surface for ripples. Humpback whales migrate to mate and give birth in the warm waters of Vava'u at this time of year and I'm desperate to spot one for Dad.

The ocean has been our entire world for almost two years and the animals have become our soul mates – the mid-ocean birds, the dolphins, the pilot whales. These animals are gifts from the sea and each visitation feels personal, as though the creature has travelled out of its way just to salute us for taking on the ocean.

Right on cue, from the corner of my eye, I spot a spray of water far off to my right. I fix my eyes to that spot, but there's only flat sea. Seconds pass, then a black shape appears, sending up another eruption of water.

'Whale!'

Ivan dashes back into the cockpit and steers *Amazing Grace* within a few hundred feet of the whale. He shuts off the rattling engine and we drift in absolute silence.

With quivering breaths, we wait for a repeat appearance. The rings where the whale broke the surface have dissipated and the water is an empty reflection of blue sky.

I scratch my head. 'Maybe we should turn around and—'

But I don't finish my sentence because a great black tail breaks through the glassy surface, silencing me. Her tail slaps at the water in a dance, waving her flukes in what seems like a greeting, over and over.

I glance between the whale and my dad. *See, Dad? Look at our whale! Look at what we accomplished.*

'Whoa!' Dad says, and that one word fills my heart up for months.

The whale gets closer, coming within a hundred feet of Gracie, and continues to perform just for us. There are no tour groups, no commotions, no engine noise. Just us, the gentle sound of water lapping, our giant wild beast and our rapid breaths.

This is why we're here. The whale's spectacular dance is our reward for battling against fear, seasickness, wind, waves, boat leaks and engine failures. And it's worth it.

The whale dances for forty minutes.

'Whoa!' Dad says again and again, and my heart is filled to capacity for a lifetime.

THE TIME HAS COME for Dad to leave and I'm trying to ignore the lumpy feeling in my throat. Seeing whales breach won't be the same without him. Ivan takes Dad to shore in the dinghy and we say goodbye at the dock.

'See you in a few months for Christmas?' Dad says.

I nod.

'Have a safe trip, Puddleduck,' he says, as he loads his things into a taxi and heads to the airport for his early-morning flight.

Back on the boat, Ivan returns to bed, and he's sleeping beside me when I hear Dad's plane go overhead. I think of Dad up there, speeding back to Australia. No waves, no lightning, no leaking boat – just seven hours of squishy seating, bland food, bad blockbusters and family waiting to receive him at the other end. How easy it really is to get home.

A thought sparks in my mind: *I can get on a plane too.*

I try to shove the thought back, jamming it into the overstuffed cupboard of my mind, but instead, all of my apprehension comes pouring out: the disconnection, the deteriorating boat, the Russian roulette of going to sea and the constant fear of the elements.

Thunderstorms viewed from my bedroom window used to excite me, but on the boat, storms are not so thrilling. Without shelter, the elements are an omnipresent force, ready to either push you along on a merry breeze, or annihilate you without warning.

This challenge would be bearable if this were a temporary adventure from which to come home, but Ivan wants to live this way indefinitely. To him, this is not an adventure. This is a permanent lifestyle.

I have a sudden urge to shake Ivan awake and ask him: *Do you really want to leave civilisation forever? If we have nobody left to tell stories to, then what is the point of this?*

But I don't wake him. I don't want his answer. Besides, if I confront him, I may have to make a hard decision, and I can't leave now. We just spent money improving the boat with a fridge and a wind generator. And what about the beautiful mint-green covers Mum just gave us? Our boat looks so pretty now. The thought of Mum's covers makes the tears come. I don't want to rouse Ivan, so I weep silently.

We've only got one-third of the Pacific left to cross until we're in Australia; a few more months and we'll be home, reunited with family. We'll have a flushing toilet, a big bed, nice clothes and enough electricity to power the laptop more than once a day. We'll have e-mail and vegetables and cocktails with friends. Everything will be okay.

Tamata. I need to try.

TWENTY-ONE

'THIS LOOKS BAD,' Ivan says, staring down at a weather chart printout. We've been checking the forecast for seven days since Dad left and we've yet to find a fair-weather window to make the five-day jump from here to Fiji. The chart is an incoherent mass of squiggles indicating isobars, pressure systems, cold fronts, highs and lows. I'm not a meteorologist but it doesn't require an expert to see that the weather is seriously confused.

Bad weather is good: it means we don't have to go back out to sea yet and I can live another day without losing my lunch. I relax into my chair and stare out toward the view of the anchored boats from the internet café.

'We could go anyway,' Ivan suggests. 'We have to leave sometime soon. Gracie can handle it. She can handle anything.'

Sure, but what about your other girl? I think. 'Do you really want to head into bad weather?'

He shrugs. 'You can't always expect the weather to be perfect.'

'I know,' I say, hurt by his condescending tone. 'But can't we just wait another week and see if it clears up?'

He crosses his arms over his chest. 'We've been in Tonga for ages. We have to keep making progress and we can't just keep stalling because of a little rough weather.'

'I know, but can we wait a bit to see if the weather clears?'

'Fine,' he says, releasing an irritated sigh.

After days of waiting for the forecast to improve, Ivan decides to enroll in a PADI diving course. I stay aboard the boat, writing and sending out e-mails.

After a few hours, my laptop runs out of battery and, since it's an overcast day, there isn't enough solar power to recharge it. I locate our second laptop – the one Ivan uses for charting and navigation.

I open it up to find a map glaring back. Odd – it's showing landmasses with names I don't recognise. The map has been marked up with plot points where Ivan has routed a course that bypasses Australia. My eyes focus on the map's shapes, and my heart thumps.

Kupang, Indonesia?

Indonesia is north of Australia and certainly not a quick detour. Ivan told me it's usually the next destination for sailors who are attempting a circumnavigation.

I'm overwhelmed with dizziness as I realise that everything I've feared is true.

He's not planning to return to land.

I clap the computer closed, hoping to shut out what I just saw, but I can't ignore the voice echoing in my head: '*You have to choose between your life and a woman and it's got to be your own life, hasn't it?*' Ivan quoted these words the first time he took me to see *Amazing Grace,* words spoken by his greatest inspiration, Moitessier, a man who circumnavigated the globe and, in the end, abandoned love for the freedom he found at sea.

I return the laptop to its cubby and then I crawl into bed while an ice pick drives into the tender yolk of my left eye. Thoughts writhe in my head until they're all twisted up around one another in a big tangle of stress.

Ivan wants to sail forever. The ocean is his asylum. And I'm just a fool in love with a man who's in love with the ocean.

I LIE IN BED, sleeping the days away. When Ivan completes his diving course, we sail to a tucked-away anchorage.

I stare out into the water, transparent down to the sandy floor. Maybe a swim will wash this all away? I want this sadness to crumble off like caked mud and leave my heart sparkling clean. I want to emerge, beautiful and shiny, alluring enough to be the one he chooses over the ocean, over the amazing Gracie.

I dive from the boat and slip through the cool, salty liquid. My strength on this voyage has been found in my vast capacity for endurance. But what am I enduring for, exactly?

With languid strokes, I swim down deep, looping below the keel to pop up on the other side of the boat.

Ivan dives in with the camera around his neck, nested into its waterproof case. He wants to take pictures of me swimming, he says. 'You look like a mermaid.'

At the surface, he fumbles with the camera's switches. 'It's not turning on,' he says.

I swim over to have a look. Water rolls around in the case. A strap has jammed in the seal and water has flooded in. The camera has been drowned. Our tool for documenting our travels, for capturing this alternate universe, is gone.

'It's dead,' I say. I pull myself up the ladder and back onto *Amazing Grace*.

'Oh, shit,' says Ivan. 'We can buy another camera on the next island.'

'Don't worry. Forget it,' I say bleakly.

Ivan pulls himself out of the water, confused by my mood, waiting for me to say something.

Try, Torre, try! I yell in my mind. *Maybe everything will work out? Maybe Ivan will choose me over Gracie?*

We've been together for two years of constant, uninterrupted companionship. In 'land time', that's almost ten years now. The rest of my life with Ivan is bound to be a *ménage à trois* with his true significant other: *Amazing Grace*. No terra firma. No Australia. No lasting friendships. No end in sight, because Ivan is too scared to return to land.

Then my mouth is talking and I can't stop it. 'I think I'm going to… I mean, I'm sorry but I think…'

I look away and hold back the sting in my eyes. No, don't say it. You don't mean it. Keep trying. He's the love of your life. You need to stay to keep him safe. Bandage his wounds. See the world with him. Keep collecting stories to tell your grandchildren. Sail into the sunset until our hair turns grey. Just like Steve and Carol. 'I'm going to… go home now, Ivan.'

His silence pierces the space beneath my ribs and I fight the urge to buckle in two from the grief.

I watch his face contort through a range of expressions, beginning with anger, cycling through hope, then desperation and finally despair.

For a very long time there are no words. His silence goes on and on, and a sense of disappointment swallows me whole. All I can think is: *I've failed him.* Tears come and a hole of guilt opens up inside me. I try to stuff the hole full of words. 'I'm so sorry, I can't do it. I'm not enjoying this any more. I've tried so hard for such a long time and… Please, don't hate me for this. I'm so sorry. The ocean is beautiful; it's just not the life I want forever. Ivan—' I speak into his eyes. '*Please* say it's okay for me to fly home. *Please* tell me you're not angry. I don't want to lose you. I'm so in love with you. I've been trying so hard, but I can't keep trying like this forever.'

'Whatever you want,' he says in an exhausted voice. 'I'm just really sad that I couldn't make you happy out here. Sorry.'

'It's not your fault. Please don't say "sorry".'

But it is pointless saying anything at all, because I can see in his muted eyes that his heart has already broken.

PART FOUR
EARTH

'A sure cure for seasickness is to sit under a tree.'
Spike Milligan

TWENTY-TWO

I TAKE IN MY surroundings: brown scrub; thirsty eucalyptus trees; bushfire-blackened forests; animals on the side of the road like wax statues that have been pushed over on their sides. It's an exhibition of dead Australiana on the Newell Highway. You can measure distances in roadkill and, out here, an animal corpse marks every ten kilometers or so. Right now, on my solo road trip, I'm approximately two fallen wombats, one sleeping emu, one mashed echidna and around ninety-two tipped kangaroos north of Melbourne.

Oh, wait... make that ninety-three.

I could challenge a truck driver – high on stimulants – to a competition of endurance across this big country. I'm halfway between Melbourne and Bundaberg in one day: thirteen hours of pedal to metal and my right knee is wishing my little black Honda had cruise control.

Empty cans of Red Bull ride shotgun on my passenger seat. I've never been on a road trip of this scale, much less on my own, but I can do anything now because *I sailed the Pacific.*

The young girl I used to be was shed among the trade winds and seawater, and I've returned home as a woman who, it seems, has lived an entire lifetime. I'm strong, self-assured and deeply connected to the earth by feet that have widened into solid, grounded supports from years without shoes. Life now feels like a game without rules, one I can design to my liking within this enormous playground called Earth. Nothing is unobtainable, and this knowledge brings a deep sense of contentment, even if I'm only half of my whole without the one I love by my side.

The sky is tinged with the dirty purple of dusk. I know I should stop driving: it's dangerous to be on the road during this time of day when kangaroo collisions are common, and I don't really enjoy playing chicken with heavy mammals, knowing my car won't take well to a hefty impact at high speed. But every time I pass a motel vacancy sign, I challenge myself to drive a little farther, to the next hotel. A few more kilometres closer to my destination.

I pass my last dead roo for the evening, a fresh-looking carcass that was probably put there by the truck that just barrelled past, displacing the air around my car. Poor little roo.

It's time I found a place to stop for the night. I pull into a motel driveway with a neon sign advertising suspiciously cheap rooms. I've got no need for luxury – I'll be back on the road by sunrise.

'Drivin' at this time a day?' the motel manager says as he hands me the keys to my room. 'Suit yerself, mate, but I'd watch out for the roos if I were you. Lot of 'em around these parts.'

'Yeah, I've seen them around,' I say. Ninety-nine percent of them belly up.

'You wouldn't wanna hit one in that city car you're drivin'. Yer got no bull bar, mate, not even a bonnet on that tiny thing. Roo will go straight into the windscreen of that bloody poor excuse for a car.'

'Oh, really?' I say, playing stupid, as though this is the first time I've heard of this danger. I'm too ashamed to admit that I know better, but kept driving on through dusk anyway.

'Well, obviously yer in a hurry to get somewhere. Where ya headed, darl?'

'Bundaberg marina.'

'Well, take it easy, mate.'

My room is clean, but bleak. It doesn't matter, though, because after a day of nonstop driving, sleep hits like a road train.

FIRST LIGHT WAKES ME. I shower, dress and throw the room keys into the early-check-out box. I'm back on the road before the sun has broken the horizon. I guzzle a Red Bull for breakfast, turn Missy Higgins up loud on the stereo and enjoy having the empty stretch of outback road all to myself.

An hour later, my phone buzzes on the passenger seat, showing a distinctive mix of numbers. I pick up. 'Hello?'

There's a long delay, followed by the sound of wind whipping into the earpiece.

Just above the bluster, I hear his voice. 'I just saw a pair of turtles. Two enormous turtles locked together – *hugging each other*. It made me so excited to see you.'

I laugh and tear up.

'I can see Australia on the horizon. I'm used to seeing small islands from a distance, but your island takes up the entire horizon.'

We say goodbye and I hang up the call, then I push my Honda a little harder into the hazy northern distance.

We agreed that Queensland was the best place to meet up, since sailing the rough southern latitudes toward Melbourne would've been challenging, and Bundaberg offers warm weather, cheap docking and ample services for sailors.

Ivan has kept regular contact over the satellite phone. 'I miss you so much,' he said on a call just after I left. 'I'm sailing straight to Australia. It'll take me two weeks.'

Meanwhile, I completed Ivan's immigration papers, compiling a mound of paperwork with statutory declarations, photos and stories of our trip and a range of other evidence to prove our relationship to the Department of Immigration. The visa would give Ivan permanent residency as my de facto spouse – a bond considered similar to marriage by Australian law. There's only one key item missing from the visa application: my spouse.

Two weeks ago, Ivan called from Vanuatu with a raspy voice. 'I've been yelling at Wendy. She broke again and I had to hand-steer for eighteen hours straight. And my jib sail broke, because I went through a gale and I didn't shorten the sails in time. If you were here, you would've told me to slow the boat down. You're always my voice of reason.'

I giggled at this.

'I had to stop in Vanuatu to fix it. Lisbeth and Lasse are here and they're helping me with the repairs. We've been eating together a lot. We're having a great time.'

In Vanuatu, as the boat was being fixed and while he waited for weather to go back out to sea, he hiked to the top of an active volcano and feasted with natives. 'It's incredible here,' he said. 'Truly incredible.'

His estimated arrival date became three weeks, then one month.

And now, as I make my way to the Bundaberg marina, excited beyond measure to see Ivan, there's one haunting image I can't push out of my mind. It's Moitessier's wife, Françoise, waiting hopelessly on the dock for Bernard after he changed his mind about returning home to her.

THE BUNDABERG MARINA looks like any other marina, except it's the first time I've seen grazing kangaroos alongside palm trees.

After nine hours of driving, I get out of the car and stumble a few steps, stiff from so many hours of sitting. A resident roo family startles into a stare when my door slams. They lose interest and return to their grass-munching, hands curled up like furry grey arthritis sufferers.

I lock my car and head out toward the marina, searching the rows of masts for a familiar canoe-stern Valiant – the one I made a small, cozy nest inside of for almost two years. Among the masts, I recognise *Red Sky* and *Hilda* and I'm overwhelmed with joy that I get to see my dear friends in my home country.

I shield my eyes from glare and search the docks, looking for Gracie. The noon sun warms my face, which isn't nearly as tanned as it was a month ago.

The marina is full of boats but none of them has the distinctive forest-green trim, diesel-smudged hull and scrapes and dings from conquering the world's biggest ocean. My heart sinks. Gracie is not here.

A strong northeasterly wind blows in, disturbing the marina's silence with banging ropes and halyards. It travels in a Mexican wave along the row of docks until it reaches out to fondle the curls of my sun-bleached hair. From upwind, I hear a faint sound being carried my way on the breeze, but I'm not sure if it's only my imagination. '*Wheee-wooooo!*'

I strain to hear it again, but I'm distracted from my search by someone who, from the corner of my eye, I notice is marching in my direction. A marina employee, most likely, probably getting ready to kick me off the premises for trespassing. '*You'll have to leave immediately,*' he'll no doubt say. '*This marina is for yacht owners only.*'

I give him the cold shoulder, refusing to make eye contact, willing him away until he's right in front of me. I look up, ready to argue, and stare into the face of somebody who's faintly familiar. Ivan.

He pulls me into his arms and I breathe in the smell of him.

'It's you!' I squeal into the nape of his neck. 'You're here!'

'Of course,' he says, clinging on and rocking me back and forth.

I pull back to inspect him. After only a month, he's lost so much weight that I hardly recognise him. He's sinewy and strong, but his now-oversized pants have been cinched at the waist with one of my scarves to make up for the loss of body fat. Even with the makeshift belt, the pants fall down well below his hips to reveal a flash of bushy hair that is far too low to be classified as a snail-trail.

'Ivan, your pants! They're obscene!' I attempt to censor him with my outstretched palms, until I look around and see we're in the company of only seagulls.

'I couldn't find a belt,' he says, gasping for breath among his giddy laughs. 'My pants don't fit any more.'

'Did you check into customs like that?'

'Yes, I did. They detained me for seven hours before they finally let me ashore. But look – I shaved.' He pats his smooth cheeks. 'I didn't want them to think I was an ocean bum.' I take note of his hairless face, unable to remember the last time I saw him with a clean shave.

'You could have trimmed a little more,' I say, pointing south. 'No wonder they detained you.'

More giddy laughs. He hikes up his pants, which settle back down to where they started. 'I had a close call with customs and immigration,' he says. 'After the officials boarded the boat, checked everything and left, I did a big clean-up. I found the stash that guy gave us in Nuku Hiva, buried in a cupboard! Shit, imagine if they'd found it? They might have permanently banned me from entering the country.'

I cover my mouth. 'I probably should have remembered that.'

He takes my hand and we walk over to the lush grass overlooking the marina to find a spot to sit.

'So how is it out there on your own?' I ask.

'Good. It's great to sail solo, to know I can do it. And guess what? I caught a three-foot dorado!'

'Nice. Maybe you broke your bad luck with fishing?'

'Nope. The arsehole jumped the line – I lost him. My reputation as worst fisherman of the South Pacific lives on. But, oh well, *so is it*.'

I laugh. 'How's the weather?'

'Good, good,' he says. 'I've had some really rough conditions and I'm glad you weren't there – you would've been really seasick. I don't mind it, though. I enjoy pushing Gracie to her limits to see what she's made of. Under full canvas, she can really fly.'

'That's great.'

'You won't believe what else happened,' he says. 'I spoke to my parents on the satellite phone today. Mum said she's been bragging to her yoga students about my trip and some of them asked if they could pay to come sailing with me.' He laughs. 'Dad suggested I visit New Caledonia. Can you believe that? My parents finally supporting my sailing?'

'That's so great,' I say, trying to conceal the lump in my throat that I've been holding back for a month now.

Ivan catches my shaking chin and he turns his whole body to face mine. 'What's wrong? You're crying?'

'I'm so sorry.' Tears spill out.

'Why? Sorry for what?'

'I left you out there alone. I knew you'd be okay; you're a little clumsy when it comes to hardware,' I say with a laugh, 'but I've always known you're a skilled sailor. An artist of the wind and waves. I just… I tried my best. We had the most incredible experience. I had an unbelievable time with you and the ocean is beautiful. I just couldn't live it as a lifestyle like Steve and Carol do, like Moitessier did. I needed to come home.'

'I get it. I understand, okay? Everyone has a summit. You reached yours. You got to the top. You did amazing. You made it *all that way* with me. And you did that even though you were scared and seasick. Do you know what that means? It means you've got a hell of a lot of courage.'

I giggle through tears.

'Two-thirds of the way from America to Australia with a fear of the ocean. You did that. I bet you never thought you could do that. I bet, when you left Australia three years ago, you didn't think you'd sail two-thirds of the way home on a leaky boat.' He wipes tears from my cheeks. 'I bet your family never guessed you'd do that either.'

I'm laughing hard now, or crying hard – I'm not quite sure which.

'They're proud of you. Your dad's so proud of you. I'm proud of you.' He gathers my windswept hair off my sticky cheeks. 'Thank you for coming with me. When I decided to do this trip, never in my imagination did I think it would've been that amazing. I thought I'd be out there alone.'

'Thank you for taking me.'

'We're going to have a land adventure now. We have so many more adventures ahead of us, so many possibilities.'

'So you're staying here with me then?' I ask. 'You're not going to take off without me and leave me behind, like Moitessier?'

He looks out at the boats bobbing in their slips as the breeze picks up. Finally, Gracie comes into my view, bouncing on her dock lines, restless to feel the full force of the wind against her perfectly trimmed sails. 'When I spoke to my mum,' Ivan says, 'she suggested I keep the boat and not sell it – she thinks I'll miss it too much. But I don't want to keep the boat. After you left, I couldn't eat. That's why I'm so skinny. Just outside of Tonga, after I dropped you off at the dock with your suitcase, I saw a mother and her calf in the water. It gutted me that you weren't there. It hurt so much that I couldn't eat any more. Or sleep. Life's most beautiful things are empty without somebody to share them with. That's why I want to sell the boat.'

I give up my effort to control my river of tears. 'But what if we keep her in Melbourne? We can sail her on the bay. It's calm, so I won't get seasick.'

'Nah. I wouldn't do that to her. Gracie is an offshore boat, designed to cross oceans. It'd be a waste to keep her in a slip on a bay. Besides, we can use the money to get a new life started in Melbourne.'

'Are you sure?'

'You know how I'm sure? I once read about how, when Moitessier was in hospital, Françoise came to see him. When she arrived, she said Bernard was "shivering under a sad blanket of grey cotton, his face drawn, skin and bones, white, white hair." It was the first time she'd seen him in twenty years. He had late-stage cancer.'

He pauses to gather his trembling voice. 'At sea, when I was sailing alone, I had a lot of time to think and I realised that I don't want to waste all those years of life without somebody to share it with. When I met you at the bar, I felt like I'd won the lottery. Why would I let that go? I want to spend my life with you, Torre. I want to grow old beside you. I had no sense of home on land before we met and I had nothing to lose by going to sea. But now I know. My home is wherever you are.'

He wraps me up in his arms and I give in to his chest. The racket of impatient boats in the marina becomes distant. I don't want to let go… and I don't have to. He's here to stay.

We drive into town and find a nice hotel. After long hot showers, we wrap ourselves in luxurious white sheets.

Then we hug like turtles.

TWO YEARS LATER

'And forget not that the earth delights to feel your bare feet and the winds long to play with your hair.'
Kahlil Gibran

TWENTY-THREE

THE LANDING GEAR touches down and I wince, fretting that the plane is going too fast to stop until brakes are applied and the small aircraft slows to a crawl.

I breathe again.

My clammy hands are relaxing themselves out of the tight balls they've been scrunched in for an hour. This has become a regular exercise in finding my inner calm, standing here on the grass, watching that plane take off and land, wondering if it'll burst into flames or fall from the sky with its precious cargo inside.

I watch the little Jabiru taxi toward me, bouncing over grass and dirt. This is only a small airport, forty minutes from Melbourne, and it's not your typical tarmac terrain. The landing strip is a bumpy dirt road that adds a four-wheel-driving element to flying a plane, in case it wasn't exciting enough already.

The small door swings open and Ivan steps out of the pilot's seat. He sends me a wave and he can't hide his beaming grin, the one that exposes nothing but top gums. I wave back, airing my sweaty palm in the process.

He walks toward me in a swagger that you only ever see on pilots and pushes his aviator sunglasses up onto his forehead. His eyes are full of exhilaration.

'Did you see me?' he says.

'Yes, I saw you.'

'Well? What do ya think?' He's acquired a slight Aussie lilt to his mixed accent.

'I was nervous,' I say. 'The plane wobbles a lot up there. It looks like a gust of wind could send it spinning. And did you see that massive dirt devil trailing you when you were trying to take off? It looked like a mini hurricane. Are those wings big enough to hold that plane up in a mini hurricane?'

'But didn't you see how perfect my take-off was?'

'It was good,' I say.

'And did you see my landing?'

'Yes, it was impressive.' I avoid pumping him up too much because I'm afraid of how far Ivan likes to take his hobbies. And in a light aircraft, if the engine fails – you *will* die.

We walk back toward the Jeep and I notice a skip in his step.

'What's with you?' I ask.

'I've been thinking... pretty soon I'll get my pilot's licence.'

I gulp hard, knowing exactly where this is going.

'And, well, what if once I get my licence, we take off on an adventure in our own small plane?'

I stare at him with wide eyes. It's not that I'm opposed to adventure – since sailing the Pacific I've come to love it. The flexibility of Ivan's contract work in project management, as well as my home-based graphic design business (complete with a mini fox-terrier office dog), gives us the freedom to slot in three to six months of adventure per year.

'Think about it,' he says, eyes wide. 'We can go to so many beautiful places. We can fly to remote islands off the Australian coast and shuck fresh oysters collected off the rocks. We can tour the outback and watch kangaroos bouncing across deserts. From the air, we can watch pods of whales migrating along the coast, then land in a flat field and camp under the wing of the plane.'

I go silent and bite my bottom lip.

'That's okay,' he says with a cheeky smile, 'I'm just trying my luck.' He wraps his arms around me and I look into his green eyes. 'What if you just come up with me one day? We don't have to go anywhere, we can just do circuits of the valley. I want to show you the view. You can see the wineries and the bush and way off into the mountain ranges. It's stunning up there.'

My body surges with a familiar blend of terror and exhilaration, a feeling I've come to know well since I met Ivan. 'It sounds incredible,' I say. 'I'll pack the ditch kit.'

Amazing Grace leaving Marina del Rey, California

To see photos of the voyage of *Amazing Grace*, visit
www.fearfuladventurer.com.

ACKNOWLEDGEMENTS

I've been touched by the generosity of so many people who have been willing to give their time and energy by offering advice, critiques and reviews: Stephanie Lee, Toby Lawson, Pia Blair, Stefanie Kechayas, Karin and David Leonard, Alwyn Gidley, Karen Charlton, Emma Stewart, David Toyne, Nancy McKeowen, Bianca Fusca, Lauren de Lange, Moira Henrich, Phil Thompson, my parents – Chris and Everett DeRoche – and my sisters – Monique, Tassy, Bree, Abra and Summer. Your honesty and insight helped my book grow. I'm especially indebted to my sister, Bree DeRoche, a talented professional editor who not only read my manuscript enough times to make anyone crazy, but who also acted as a sounding board for my daily neuroses, offering constant positive energy and praise to keep me going.

Thanks to Elizabeth Evans, Jessica Regel and the team at Jean V. Naggar Literary Agency for believing in my book. Your graceful choreography of auctions and book deals were a pleasure and a thrill to behold.

Thanks to Robert Schwartz from Seismic Pictures, who discovered this book when it was originally self-published. We were united by your random clicking on Twitter and my mouth is still agape over this chance encounter. Your offer to buy the film options set off a snowball of success for me, which has taken this book to new heights. Likewise, thanks to Jennifer Barclay from Summersdale Publishers, who also discovered my story on Twitter.

Thanks to Christine Pride, Ellen Archer, Kiki Koroshetz and the team at Hyperion for your enthusiasm for my story. It's been a true honour to polish my book with a publisher that celebrates people's life stories. I feel incredibly privileged to have your precious insight and expertise.

To Kirsten Abbott from Penguin for believing in my book, in part because of our shared *Jaws*-induced aquaphobia. Which makes me think I should probably give a big thanks to Peter Benchley and Steven Spielberg for my post-traumatic stress disorder, and all the PTSDs you gave to the masses. (Yes, I'm being sarcastic, Pete and Steve, but therapists everywhere are genuinely thankful.)

Thanks to my social media community for your encouragement. Many bloggers, whom I've never met in person, reviewed and promoted my book and blog out of the kindness of their own hearts. I'm lucky to be a part of this digital community of innovators and entrepreneurs. Jade Craven's genius and generosity is especially noteworthy.

Thanks to Daniel Ostroff and Euan Mitchell for your wealth of industry knowledge, and to Dad and Summer for imparting insight and tips from your filmmaking experience.

I owe a thanks to Tania Aebi, who taught me that inexperience is no reason to shy away from an immense challenge.

Apologies go out to my parents, as well as Ivan's parents – Monica and Jorge Nepomnaschy – for putting them through two years of stress while their romantically reckless children were at large on the high seas. You each inspire me with your courage, generosity, chutzpah, talents and *milanesas*.

To my dear little Frida – you kept me from loneliness, you licked me when I was sad and you kept my lap warm in winter.

I'm not sure I could've done this without you. A dog is a writer's best friend.

There's one person who persistently believed in me no matter how much I tried to talk him out of it – once to sail an ocean, and again to write this book. With patience for my many anxieties and with endless encouragement, he taught me that great feats are accomplished mile by mile and word by word, and I'm forever changed by the wisdom and experiences he has given me. He's been my creative partner and my producer. He's been my punching bag, my cook, my masseur, my fetcher of wine and my therapist. At times, he's used all of his strength to hoist me up from a dark pit of self-doubt. I found him in a cocktail bar. Ivan, my love, my best friend and my inspiration, thank you for showing me the world.

ABOUT THE AUTHOR

Torre DeRoche is an Australian native and self-proclaimed fearful adventurer. She is a writer and creator of the blog, fearfuladventurer.com, which chronicles refreshingly honest travel and adventure stories from the perspective of an alarmist who likes to arm-wrestle her fears. When she's not at home in Melbourne, Australia, DeRoche is large in the world, writing, snapping photos, painting pictures, pursing adventures and facing her fears one terrified step at a time.

Follow Torre's adventures on Twitter at @FearfulGirl and on Facebook at Fearful Adventurer.

A NEW YORK TIMES BEST-SELLER

a delicious love story, with recipes

LUNCH
in
PARIS

ELIZABETH BARD

LUNCH IN PARIS
A Delicious Love Story, with Recipes

Elizabeth Bard

ISBN: 978 1 84953 154 2   Paperback   £8.99

Has a meal ever changed your life?

Part love story, part wine-splattered cookbook, *Lunch in Paris* is a deliciously tart, forthright and funny story of falling in love with a Frenchman and moving to the world's most romantic city – not the Hollywood version, but the real Paris, a heady mix of blood sausage, pains aux chocolats and irregular verbs.

From gutting her first fish (with a little help from Jane Austen) to discovering the French version of Death by Chocolate, Elizabeth Bard finds that learning to cook and building a new life have a lot in common. Peppered with recipes, this mouth-watering love story is the perfect treat for anyone who has ever suspected that lunch in Paris could change their life.

'Whether you're a hopeless romantic, a domestic goddess or somewhat lacking in the culinary skills department then Lunch in Paris *is sure to provide food for thought for all tastes'*   French Property News

'Escapism doesn't come much more delicious than this… If you enjoy French cuisine and are a sucker for a well-written romance, Lunch in Paris *will go down a treat'*   France magazine

'A truly delicious love story… this delectable delight is the perfect way to enjoy lunch in Paris if you can't be there yourself'

Living France *magazine*

TOUT SWEET
Hanging Up my High Heels for a New Life in France

Karen Wheeler

ISBN: 978 1 84024 761 9   Paperback   £8.99

In her mid-thirties, fashion editor Karen has it all: a handsome boyfriend, a fab flat in west London and an array of gorgeous shoes. But when Eric leaves, she hangs up her Manolos and waves goodbye to her glamorous city lifestyle to go it alone in a run-down house in rural Poitou-Charentes, central western France.

Acquiring a host of new friends and unsuitable suitors, she learns that true happiness can be found in the simplest of things – a bike ride through the countryside on a summer evening, or a kir or three in a neighbour's courtyard.

Perfect summer reading for anyone who dreams of chucking away their BlackBerry in favour of real blackberrying and downshifting to France.

Featured in *The Daily Mail*, *The Sunday Times*, *Living Abroad* magazine, Thomas Cook Travel magazine and *French Property News*.

'an hilarious account of a fashion guru who swaps Prada for paintbrushes and Pineau in rural France'   *Mail on Sunday* Travel

'Perfect summer reading for anyone who dreams of chucking away their Blackberry and downshifting to France'   *French Property News*

David Mercy

"Berserk"

BERSERK IN
THE ANTARCTIC

sailing to the world's most unihabitable continent

BERSERK IN THE ANTARCTIC
Sailing to the World's Most Uninhabitable Continent

David Mercy

ISBN: 978 1 84024 479 3   Paperback   £7.99

'This is suicide!' Manuel screamed frantically.

So begins an amazing true story of a journey to Antarctica in a 27-foot sailing boat. After travelling through South America to Tierra del Fuego, the only continent David had never visited beckoned to him across treacherous waters. Ships booked for scientific expeditions wouldn't take him, and tourist cruises didn't appeal. Then he saw a little boat in the harbour, its name hand-painted in red on the hull: *Berserk*.

Together with a 'crazy Viking' and a down-on-his-luck Argentinian, the author set sail to follow Shackleton's voyage with little idea of the tumultuous storms, mishaps and emergencies that loomed on the journey to the world's coldest and most inaccessible continent. He brilliantly recounts their experience of the huge waves, the bleak darkness and the delicate balance of personalities where a mutiny was always in the air.

'Some extreme adventure books strike you as so off-the-wall outrageous that you can't believe anybody would take that kind of risk, and you just can't stop turning the pages. David Mercy's Berserk *falls into this category with a vengeance... it should probably come with a consumer warning: Don't try this at home'*   **Offshore** magazine

Have you enjoyed this book?
If so, why not write a review on your favourite website?

If you're interested in finding out more about our books, find us on Facebook at **Summersdale Publishers** and follow us on Twitter at **@Summersdale**.

Thanks very much for buying this Summersdale book.

www.summersdale.com